D1094456

Bohemians and Critics

American Theatre Criticism in the Nineteenth Century

TICE L. MILLER

 The Scarecrow Press, Inc.
Metuchen, N.J., & London
1981

Library of Congress Cataloging in Publication Data

Miller, Tice L
   Bohemians & critics.

   Bibliography: p.
   Includes index.
   1. Theater--United States--History. 2. Theater
critics--United States--Biography. 3. Dramatic
criticism--United States. I. Title.
PN2248.M5   792'.01'50973   80-24430
ISBN 0-8108-1377-7

To Carren

TABLE OF CONTENTS

"In New York ... are gathered together a number of men--literary persons and others--who have a strong desire to favor anything which shall extricate us from the entangled and by no means creditable position we already hold of play-ing second fiddle to Europe. These persons--most of them young men, enthusiastic, democratic, and liberal in their feel-ings--are daily acquiring a greater and greater power. And after all, anything appealing to the honest heart of the peo-ple, as to the peculiar and favored children of freedom--as to a new race and with a character separate from the king-doms of other countries--would meet with a ready response, and strike at once the sympathies of all true men who love America, their native or chosen land."

Walt Whitman "Why Do Theatres
Languish? And How Shall the
American Stage Be Resuscitated?"
Brooklyn Daily Eagle, Feb. 12,
1847.

"We want no more French Fashions, no more under-ground carousals and all night dissipations; we want the Amer-ican home, with the domestic attractions and ties that God and nature provide for those who obey physical law; we want no more smoke-dried beer sodden brains to dribble commonplace trash, and call it criticism; we want ... the fresh, vigorous thoughts of clear intellects, impelled from hearts that are not withered in their youth by wild indulgence."

The Round Table, February 6, 1864.

INTRODUCTION

An important area of the American theatre which has been neglected in historical studies is the critic and theatrical criticism. Unlike acting or drama, there are no books which treat the subject with perspective and insight. A recent work, Lehman Engel's The Critics (1976), discusses major contemporary critics, noting their tastes and biases. For information on the past, the historian must turn to anthologies of reviews, biographies, an occasional article in a scholarly journal, a paragraph in theatre textbooks, and doctoral dissertations.

Why have American theatre historians neglected this subject? Several reasons seem valid. A major problem until recently has been the inaccessibility of research materials. Now, the availability of periodicals and newspapers on microfilm has provided the researcher with a wealth of materials, including nineteenth century weekly papers: Wilkes' Spirit of the Times, Albion, Saturday Press, New York Clipper, New York Leader, and the New York Dramatic Mirror.

The ephemeral nature of journalism also has discouraged historians from pursuing such an arduous task. Theatre reviews are quickly forgotten, especially when written in a little known paper by a dramatic journalist. They do not seem as worthwhile to the scholar as lengthy essays in literary periodicals or books written by well known men of letters. In addition, the questionable reputation of the theatre critic has contributed to the neglect of this subject. During the nineteenth century, it was not uncommon for a newspaper to send a reporter to "write up" the opening night of a play instead of hiring trained critics. Nor was it uncommon for a critic to review only those productions which bought advertising in his newspaper. As a result, his opinions were suspect. If he praised, he was "a puffer"; if he damned, he was a "jackal of the trade." His comments often prompted libel suits and violence. The actor Thomas Hamblin's mauling of the New York Herald editor and Abe Erlanger's fist fight with Dramatic

<u>Mirror</u> editor Harrison Grey Fiske were but two such inci-
dents reported in the past century.[1] Yet despite such adverse
publicity, the critic was considered a necessary evil. As one
early nineteenth-century writer observed: "The office of a
reviewer is in a republic of letters, as beneficial and necessary, though odious and unpleasant, as that of an executioner
in a civil state."[2] This attitude prevailed throughout much of
the century.

While we may have had reasons for not studying critics
and criticism of the nineteenth century, we know less about
the American stage because of this neglect. Theatre criticism provides the sound, smell, and taste of contemporary
stage activities. The critic observes theatre being created,
works close to the event, and over a period of time gains
some perspective. He also gains an audience for his column
from theatregoers who share his tastes. To learn about a
specific New York production today we turn to a review by
one of our major critics: Walter Kerr, Clive Barnes, John
Simon. We want to know what he thought about this production. Over the years we have come to understand his critical philosophy and appreciate his insights. Yet when we turn
to criticism of the past century, we hardly know the names of
the critics, much less their backgrounds. Were they untrained
reporters writing their first reviews or educated, well traveled
men who had attended the theatre in London and Paris? What
did they know about the professional stage? Where did they
gain their ideas? Did they have any influence upon the American theatre? This study aims to answer some of these questions.

This book focuses on five journalistic critics who established their careers in the mid Victorian period, in the
1850s and 1860s, at a time when French critical and cultural
ideas were very popular in New York. Their criticism reflects this influence. While we usually consider the roots of
our culture to be Anglo-Saxon, in the mid-nineteenth century
the influx of French social customs, fashions, music, literature, art, and drama played a large role in the development
of our native culture. In 1845, Mrs. Mowatt ridiculed our
worship of French social customs in her popular comedy,
<u>Fashion.</u> French plays which were successful include: <u>The</u>
<u>Corsican Brothers</u>, <u>Don Caesar de Bazan</u>, <u>Camille</u>, <u>Frou-</u>
<u>Frou</u>, <u>Pink Dominoes</u>, <u>La Marquise</u>, <u>Denise</u>, <u>Odette</u>, <u>The</u>
<u>Count of Monte Cristo</u>, and many others. It is not surpris-
ing, then, that American theatre critics turned to the French
for ideas and methods. What is surprising is that little has
been written on the subject.

The organization of this book should be helpful in placing these critics, historically and critically. The first chapter provides the background necessary to understand the American Theatre and its criticism during the middle decades of the nineteenth century. An epilogue summarizes the state of criticism in the 1880s and 1890s and draws some conclusions. A second book--now in preparation--will present critics who established their careers in the late Victorian period. If this study has a bias, it is that each critic deserves a balanced evaluation. It will serve no purpose to castigate the Victorians once more for their beliefs.

The terms "theatre critic," "dramatic critic," "theatre journalist," and "reviewer" have all been used in the past to designate a writer who offers critiques of plays in production. It is not the purpose of this study to become embroiled in arguments about which term is correct or when a "theatre journalist" is "only a reviewer" and not a critic. "Theatre critic" will normally be the term used in this study.

I am indebted to librarians at the University of Nebraska-Lincoln for providing me with microfilms of contemporary newspapers and periodicals. Many were purchased and now are part of the library's holdings. This study also could not have been completed without the cooperation of numerous librarians, including those at the Harvard Theatre Collection and Houghton Library; Yale School of Drama Library and Beinecke Rare Book and Manuscript Library; Folger Shakespeare Library; Pierpont Morgan Library; Columbia Rare Book and Manuscript Library, Columbia University; Humanities Research Center, University of Texas, Austin; Boston Public Library; and the Theatre Collection of the New York Public Library. In particular, I am grateful for the help and courtesy extended me by Dorothy Swerdlove, First Assistant at the Theatre Collection of the New York Public Library.

I owe a special debt to several colleagues who shared information with me from their research in nineteenth-century theatre: Daniel Watermeier, Thomas K. Wright, and William Morris. Alan Woods, Julia Curtis, Daniel Watermeier, and Virginia Faulkner read portions of the manuscript and offered suggestions about revision. Robert Young, Jr., great-grandson of William Winter, unselfishly shared his research and his unpublished biography of Winter. I am grateful for all advice and assistance.

A Maude Hammond Fling Faculty Fellowship from the University of Nebraska-Lincoln supported my early research into this subject. A Junior Faculty Summer Research Fellowship enabled me to complete the research and begin the writing.

My deepest gratitude belongs to my wife, Carren, to whom this book is dedicated. Her understanding and encouragement throughout this project enabled me to complete it.

Tice L. Miller
Lincoln, Nebraska

CHAPTER ONE

THE BACKGROUND

In the 1850's, a lively school of theatre journalism
made its appearance in the New York press--a school noted
for its gaiety, aggressiveness, and subjectivity. While critics
differed in the degree of their iconoclasm, they united in their
opposition to traditional standards and values. They opposed
New England puritanism, the worship of Anglo-Saxon critical
dogma, and especially the conservative literary and artistic
circles of Boston. They ridiculed the pomposity and extreme
prudery of the cultured elite, and rejected the worship of high
art which dominated the middle and latter decades of the nineteenth century. Instead of writing in the elevated scholarly
style of the period, they offered personal opinion in an im-
pressionistic manner. Clever, witty, and aggressive, they
introduced into New York journalism the French dramatic
feuilleton. Pseudonyms--Mercutio, Trinculo, Personne, Figaro, Ariel, Dodo, Pierrot, Nym Crinkle--thinly disguised
their identities while adding to their mystique. For about a
decade--from 1855 to 1865--they dominated the field of theatre
criticism in New York, and they remained influential for the
remainder of the century. The conservative Round Table magazine of January 2, 1864 acknowledged their power, calling
them a "Bacchanalian Mutual Admiration Society" which hangs
"like a millstone around the neck of the drama." The writer
of this comment also noted: "Managers despise them, yet
dare not resist their suction. Actors despise them, yet dread
their waspy stings in case they ignore them." Underlying
such verbal abuse was a tacit admission that journalistic as
well as aesthetic standards were undergoing subtle but significant changes.

Development of Early Theatre Criticism

It is not surprising that the Round Table opposed this

brash new school. During the first half of the nineteenth
century, theatre criticism (where it supplanted paid puffs)
was written by educated men of the professional classes who
assumed the role of both reviewer and censor. Considered
a powerful influence for good and evil in the lives of men,
the theatre as a public institution was thought prone to frequent violations of social and moral laws. The editor of the
Theatrical Censor wrote in 1806, "The stage must refine our
manners, enlarge our minds and ennoble our hearts, or, it
must degrade, contrast and debase."[1] Ministers declared it
"The Synagogue of Satan." Lyman Beecher, for example,
preached that the theatre was "the centre of the valley of pol-
lution."[2] Opponents of the theatre advanced arguments which
labeled the playhouse as wicked, listing as evidence the attendance of prostitutes, the use of profanity in plays, and the
scanty dress of actresses.

It is no surprise, then, that theatre criticism in the
early years of the nineteenth century was highly judicial in
tone. Stephen Cullen Carpenter, writing in 1810, expressed
a widely held belief that "Since it is the young, the idle, the
thoughtless, and the ignorant, on whom the drama can be supposed to operate as a lesson for conduct, an aid to experience
and a guide through life ... it becomes a matter of great importance to the commonwealth that this very powerful engine
[the theatre] ... should be kept under the control of a syste-
matic, a vigilant and a severe, but a just criticism."[3] In
the absence of professional critics, the task of maintaining
control of "this very powerful engine" fell to the professional
men--journalists, men of letters, lawyers, doctors, and businessmen. They served as the voice of the "enlightened public" in an attempt to weigh each play, each actor, by a "permanent standard of taste." While they seldom agreed on a
definition of this phrase, they were concerned with art which
presented an idealized view of life and upheld conventional
morality.

These part-time critics drew their critical principles
from Europe, from the essays of neo-classical scholars as
well as from such English romantics as Samuel Johnson, William Hazlitt, Charles Lamb and Samuel Coleridge. They inherited a literary tradition which taught that drama should
portray the ideal in human behavior. The stage must show
life elevated and made more meaningful, evil punished and
virtue rewarded. They lauded Shakespeare but did not seem
to understand that his plays hardly mirrored the rigidity of
their standards.

For a model, they turned to the English periodical essay as developed in the eighteenth century by Sir Richard Steele and Joseph Addison. The periodical essay included theatrical news, reviews, letters to the editor (real and fictitious) as well as leading articles. Pseudonyms were common. Since few daily papers published theatre criticism on a regular basis until around mid-century, the critic depended on the weekly and monthly publications. Many of these were short-lived: Theatrical Censor (1806-07); Rambler's Magazine and New York Theatrical Register (1809-1810); and Mirror of Taste and Dramatic Censor (1810-1811).

Since few signatures were attached to dramatic columns before the end of the nineteenth century, we know little about our first theatre critics. According to Arthur Hobson Quinn, the earliest extant example of printed dramatic criticism appeared anonymously in the Maryland Gazette in early 1760. It evaluated Orphan and Lethe in Annapolis, Maryland, performed by Douglass's American Company. [4] George C. D. Odell has suggested that the 1802-1803 season was an important milestone in the development of criticism in American periodicals. During this season a large amount of criticism on the theatre began to appear. William Dunlap devoted a chapter to the subject in his A History of the American Theatre (1832). Dunlap explained that in 1796, a group of men-- John Wells, Elias Hicks, Samuel Jones, William Cutting, Peter Irving, and Charles Adams--organized themselves into a "band of scalpers and tomahawkers" to review the current productions in New York. They were "gentlemen," Dunlap reported, "regular frequenters of the New York theatre ... men of education and lovers of literature," who "wished to correct the abuses existing in the costume, demeanour, and general conduct of the actors on the stage." [5] They desired to remain anonymous. One of their group reviewed a performance; then, on the following evening, the entire band critiqued the review. Following this procedure, they signed the review with the initials of their names, "the last letter being the actual writer." Dunlap denied any connection with the group himself.

This "company of critics" were all distinguished men of their day. Charles Adams, for instance, was the son of John Adams and the brother of John Quincy Adams--the second and sixth presidents of the United States. More important to our purpose, however, was Peter Irving, the older brother of Washington Irving and the proprietor of The Morning Chronicle. In 1802-1803 he published Washington Irving's Letters

of Jonathan Oldstyle, Gent., regarded by theatre historians
as a valuable chronicle of early American theatre. [6] Irving's
letters resemble Joseph Addison's essays for the Tatler,
Spectator, and Guardian. He used a persona with an identity
different from the author: Jonathan Oldstyle, an old bachelor
more experienced and worldly wise than the nineteen-year-old
Irving at the time. In the nine extant Oldstyle letters, it is
clear that Washington Irving satirized the pretense and pomposity as well as the crudeness of the native stage.

Irving's career as a theatre critic was not limited to
The Morning Chronicle. He founded another journal in 1807
called The Salmagundi: or, the Whim-whams and Opinions
of Launcelot Langstaff, Esq. and others. Here Irving again
wrote about the theatre in a satirically critical style. He
later called his criticism "Pardonable as a juvenile production."[7] Irving's theatrical criticism can also be found in the
Select Reviews, later the Analectic Magazine, while he was
editor in 1815. Modern historians consider him the best and
most readable American theatre critic of his day. [8]

Irving's humor and eye for detail are not reflected in
other early nineteenth-century criticisms. More typical are
the writings of William Coleman and William Leggett of the
prudish New York Evening Post--men who considered it their
cultural duty to protect public morality. Coleman distinguished himself as a lawyer, state representative, politician,
and journalist. Leggett gained a measure of success as a
man of letters, journalist, and politician. Neo-classical in
taste and highly moralistic, both men thought the theatre
should be an ennobling and powerful influence for good. Ac-
knowledging the prejudices held by Americans towards the theatre, Coleman, in the Evening Post of November 30, 1820,
asked to be excused "for having permitted our attention to be
engrossed by the theatrical department of our paper, as it is
a sort of truantry, we admit, from our more grave and regular
pursuits."[9] Leggett, in the same paper on September 18,
1832, expressed the opinion of much of his audience when he
suggested that it would be better to keep Shakespeare's finest
plays off the stage: "When we see them attempted there, we
think less of them."[10] Such comments reflected not only the
Puritan strain in American culture, but the low regard in
which educated men held the native stage and its drama.

During the middle decades of the century, two academi-
cians provided a measure of trenchant criticism for elitist
tastes. Richard Grant White and J. W. S. Hows wrote re-

spectable if not distinguished reviews and essays, much like
those of their London colleague, Henry Morley. White wrote
the musical and dramatic column for the New York Courier
Enquirer from about 1846 to 1859; Hows served as critic for
the Albion during the mid- and late 1840s. Men of taste,
education, and refinement, they believed in a classical and
moral drama. Between 1857 and 1865, White published in
twelve volumes an edition of Shakespeare which he prepared
from original sources. [11] He was the first American to do
this. As a practicing theatre critic he took aim on the low
state of American acting, advocating a "less robustious"
style than the Forrest school then in vogue. [12] While moralistic and conservative, White wrote serious criticism with the
aim of reforming the American theatre. E. P. Whipple, in
Atlantic Monthly, February, 1882, praised White's "acute-
ness, independence, force, and fertility of thought." Hows
served a distinguished career at Columbia as Professor of
Elocution. He prepared a Shakespearean Reader for schools
and colleges. [13] An authority of elocution, he gave private
lessons to Anna Cora Mowatt, helping her eliminate much
that was declamatory and artificial from her style. [14] He
joined White in denouncing the Forrest school of acting.
White and Hows were men of ability. Like their educated
contemporaries they looked to England rather than to this
country for their critical standards.

Existing side-by-side with serious attempts at criticism were paid puffs--press releases--manufactured by managers or their agents to circumvent criticism and increase attendance. Editors were given season passes for themselves
and their families; they in turn were expected to provide
space for the puffs. Critics were provided with gifts, including refreshments at the theatre. A "cold cut room" at
the Bowery Theatre in 1826 offered beverages, food, and
writing materials for the press. [15] According to Charles
Durang in his History of the Philadelphia Stage, Between the
Years 1749-1855, Charles Gilfert, manager of the Bowery
Theatre, began the practice of hiring a press agent to manu-
facture public opinion about plays and actors during the 1827-
1828 season. [16] P. T. Barnum demonstrated the effectiveness
of such public relations techniques in advertising his "Dramatic Museum" in the 1840s, and in promoting the American
tour of Jenny Lind in 1850. He fed the press stories com-
posed of personal and professional gossip; such stories were
printed as news by uncritical editors. [17]

These practices became commonplace and led to repeated accusations that theatre managers and newspapers traded favors. In 1849 the author of New York in Slices, by an Experienced Carver ridiculed the idea that impartial theatrical criticism existed in that city.

> Who has ever read an honest, faithful account of the theatres of New York--how they are carried on, what they do, and how they do it? ... It is true that we have daily articles in several papers, about the performances of the night previous, with glowing eulogisms upon each of the performers, upon the author, the manager, the property man.... But these articles are either written by a Peter Funk [name to denote a puffer] employed and paid by the managers, and inserted at so much a week, more or less, good, bad, or indifferent, or else for the most part are the sublime emanations of some police reporter enamored of the 'legitimate' and panting for the honors of a free admission. ... As to such a thing as an impartial and independent criticism upon Theatres and theatrical performances, in the present state of the relations between Editors, reporters, managers, actors-- and actresses--the thing is palpably out of the question. [18]

Managers did not deny that such practices existed; they regarded them as normal.

Attacks on the undistinguished quality of American theatre criticism came in the 1830s and 1840s from two of our most promising writers. In 1836, Edgar Allan Poe insisted that American stage criticism be rescued from the control of illiterate mountebanks and placed in the hands of gentlemen and scholars. [19] He set out to do this nine years later when he assumed control of The Broadway Journal. According to N. Bryllion Fagin in his study of Poe's dramatic criticism: "That his standards were high is obvious; they obliged him to be cantankerous and cruel; and they involved him in much unpleasantness and--like his literary criticism-- made bitter enemies for him. "[20] Fagin concludes that Poe expected much from the theatre of his day, and that was "rarely to be found. "

Poe demanded verisimilitude in the theatre. He wanted acting and drama to reflect life, not the conventions of the stage. In his first review of Mrs. Anna Cora Mowatt's

Fashion (March 29, 1845), he objected to the "rectangular crossings and recrossings of the dramatis personae on the stage; the coming forward to the footlights when any thing of interest is to be told; the reading of private letters in a loud rhetorical tone; the preposterous soliloquising; and the even more preposterous 'asides.'"[21] In the American Whig Review for August 1845, he objected to the plays of Sheridan Knowles as "the most preposterous series of imitations of the Elizabethan drama, by which ever mankind were insulted or beguiled."[22] He did not think old models--especially the artificial plays of Knowles--valid for the contemporary theatre. Drama should be based on real life rather than on the dramatic literature of another age. He demanded that contemporary drama be "conceived and constructed with feeling and with taste, but with feeling and taste guided and controlled in every particular by the details of reason--of common sense--in a word, of a natural art." But Poe did not want photographic realism; he wished to combine naturalistic elements with what he called the "general intention of nature." In other words, he wanted nature's ideal pattern--not its everyday happenings. Thus, he demanded more truthfulness to nature than the theatre offered in the 1840s--but without rejecting romanticism.

Poe also advocated that the theatre be evaluated on aesthetic rather than on moral grounds. He wrote in Godey's Lady's Book, March, 1846, that "... the conveying of what is absurdly termed, 'a moral,' ... should be left to the essayist and preacher."[23] He went on to conclude that "the truthfulness, the indispensable truthfulness of drama, has reference only to the fidelity with which it should depict nature...." While he did not deviate too far from his romantic roots, Poe became a prophet for the generation of writers that came to prominence in the 1850s.

Walt Whitman also found the condition of the professional stage and theatrical criticism deplorable. As editor of The Brooklyn Daily Eagle from 1846 until 1848 he kept the critical pot boiling by attacking the vulgarity of New York theatres, excepting the Park which he regarded as a third-rate imitation of London theatres.[24] Whitman encouraged New York managers to cast off their slavish dependence on English managers, actors, plays, and critical dogma. He ruffled some feathers in a September 1, 1846 editorial which claimed that there were plenty of native stock actors-- Charlotte Cushman and Henry Placide for two--who were better than visiting English stars, Charles Kean and his wife

Ellen Tree.[25] Whitman was optimistic about reform in the
New York theatre. "With all our servility, to foreign
fashion," he wrote on February 12, 1847, "there is at the
heart of the intelligent masses there, a lurking propensity
toward what is original, and has a stamped American character of its own."[26] While he attacked the "Miserable State"
of the native stage, he defended the institution of theatre:
"For the drama has been, and still must be, a great element
in the amusement and instructive agencies of civilized life."[27]

Whitman demanded reforms in theatrical reviewing.
He wrote in 1847: "There is hardly anything more contemptible, and indeed unprofitable in the long run, than this same
plan of some paid personage writing laudatory notices of the
establishment which pays him, and then sending them to the
newspaper, to be printed as spontaneous opinions of the editors." He accused all New York theatres of "keeping a
'puffer' who sends daily notices to the newspapers."[28] The
practice of puffing he found so widespread that he claimed
five-sixths of the criticism was written before the performance.[29]

Whitman envisioned the American stage as a school for
democracy, independent from foreign influences. To gain
such an end, he believed impartial and independent criticism
essential. Considering his strong nationalistic bent, sometimes these two objectives were at odds. But he did under-
score the need for newspapers to hire trained critics rather
than depend upon the paid puffs. With the success of Leaves
of Grass in 1855, Whitman attracted a large following among
the young writers and journalists who came to New York in
the 1850s. His anti-establishment views permeated the beer
halls and cellars--salons of New York's intellectual prole-
tariat in the mid-nineteenth century.

Poe and Whitman wanted a quality American stage as
well as objective and knowledgeable criticism. Forces already at work in American culture were destined to have a
significant impact on both.

Changes in the American Theatre

By 1850 the Industrial Revolution had created a new
monied class with resources and leisure to enjoy the arts.
More attention was paid to elegance and refinement, to an
outward show of one's wealth and cultivation. The new rich,

with no social rituals of their own, looked to the old world
for acceptable means to advertise their wealth and position.
In New York this display was mainly French: French
fashions, French books, French plays, French language,
French music, and French actors. This included a visit to
New York in 1855 by the leading French actress--Mlle.
Rachel. Opera bouffe, novels by George Sand, plays by
Emile Augier and Dumas fils--all were imported and sampled
by New Yorkers. At the same time many of this country's
leading artists and writers considered their education and
training incomplete until they had experienced life in Paris.
French culture, perhaps more than English, softened and
mellowed the harsh edges of industrial nineteenth-century
America.

The influx of French acting methods and French melodrama in the 1850s moved the American stage away from its
Anglo-Saxon roots. A few milestones should be noted. The
visit of Mlle. Rachel to this country in September 1855 offered native audiences a style of acting which seemed simple
and unaffected when compared to the heroic style then in
vogue. Playgoers--especially the masses--had become accustomed to the robust declamatory style of Edwin Forrest
or to the masculine forceful style of Charlotte Cushman,
America's leading tragedians for two decades. The upper
classes thought the intellectual, polished acting of English
actor William C. Macready more desirable for refined tastes.
By 1855, however, these actors had passed the peak of their
popularity in America. The Astor Place Riot of May 10,
1849, which pitted the followers of Forrest against those of
Macready, resulted in twenty-two deaths, and in a practical
sense, damaged the professional reputations of both men.
Macready never again acted in this country. Forrest further
squandered his professional standing by a scandalous divorce
suit against his wife in 1852. While the masses continued to
support him, he never regained the respect and applause of
the cultured classes. Charlotte Cushman, considered cold
and mannered by many, spent much of the decade in Europe.
The time was ripe for new ideas, new methods, new actors.

Two young players, at least, were able to benefit
from this artistic vacuum. Edwin Booth served his apprenticeship in the West during the 1850s and at the end of the
decade launched his career in the East with a style of acting
more graceful and dignified than Forrest's, but with more
passion and power than Macready. He correctly judged the
artistic temperament of the age and attracted the attention

and support of the intellectual elite.   Matilda Heron, an
Irish-born actress, became an overnight success in 1857.
She had served her apprenticeship in the West and visited
Paris in 1854 to observe French acting methods.   Here she
saw Mme. Desirée Doche perform Marguerite Gautier in
Dumas' La Dame aux Camélias.   Impressed, she returned
to this country with the role firmly in mind, and in 1855
attempted it unsuccessfully in New Orleans.   Undaunted, she
tried it again two years later in New York, opening at Wallack's Theatre on the night of Jan. 22, 1857.   Successful
beyond her wildest dreams, Heron played forty-six sold-out
performances in seven weeks, establishing both herself and
the play as major forces in the American theatre.   She ex-
hibited a style of emotional acting which seemed real to the
audiences of her day.   Although her fame was short-lived,
this style in various guises would continue to attract playgoers for the next half-century. [30]

It was Rachel's visit in 1855, plus the immense popularity of Camille, which established the new French drama
in America.   An international star, Mlle. Rachel created
widespread publicity and interest.   She performed contemporary French plays--Scribe and Legouve's Adrienne Lecouvreur and Hugo's Angelo--in addition to her classical repertory which included Corneille's Horace and Racine's Phèdre.
Adrienne Lecouvreur became her most popular play in this
country in spite of (or because of) its tale of illicit love.
One historian credits the popularity of this play with prepar-
ing "sophisticated audiences to accept the current Parisian
drama."[31]   By the end of the decade, adaptations of French
romantic melodramas began to displace the standard repertory of American companies: Shakespeare, eighteenth-century
English classics, and nineteenth-century pseudo-Elizabethan
romantic tragedies including James Sheridan Knowles'
Virginius, John Banim's Damon and Pythias, and Bulwer-
Lytton's Richelieu and The Lady of Lyons.

There was a good reason why the new French drama
achieved instant popularity.   It dealt with contemporary events
and discussed subjects formerly considered taboo (adultery for
example).   The nineteenth-century imitations of Shakespeare
seemed old-fashioned and dull beside the bright, charming,
and exciting French fare.   For a time in the late 1850s and
throughout the next two decades, it seemed that any writer
with a knowledge of French was adapting Gallic drama for the
American stage.   The prolific Dion Boucicault recognized
sooner than most of his colleagues the intense interest in the

new drama. At first in London and later in New York, he made a profession out of Anglicizing French plays. In 1857 his The Poor of New York, borrowed from Les Pauvres de Paris by Édouard Brisebarre and Eugene Nus, was very successful and provided a model for other playwrights. Boucicault transferred the setting from Paris to New York, alluded to the financial panic of 1857, showed recognizable scenes from New York, and excited the audience with a burning house. Augustin Daly would follow in his footsteps. Between the Civil War and the end of the century, Daly was responsible in part or whole for forty-four adaptations of French drama.[32] Contributing to their popularity were their vivid theatricality, a logical structure which made translating simple, and the ease with which they could be pirated because of inadequate copyright laws.

Sensational melodramas held the stage for the remainder of the century. Each play, like Boucicault's The Poor of New York, was marked by an obligatory sensational event: a steamship blowing up, a man tied to the railroad tracks facing an approaching train, or a villain threatening to saw a man in two. Suspense and novel disasters provided the main ingredients designed to excite the public. These dramas had broad emotional appeal and played to large popular audiences.

The musical extravaganza also attracted a mass audience and further contributed to the decline of the traditional repertory. Historians seem to agree that The Black Crook, first presented at Niblo's in 1866, started the vogue for elaborate musical spectacle. The production owed much of its success to a Parisian ballet troup which provided one hundred "beautiful girls" in flesh-colored tights. The Black Crook created a sensation and ran for four hundred and seventy-five performances. Its success resulted in a number of imitations.

Another genre of drama which became popular in New York at Wallack's Theatre during the 1860s and 1870s was the "cup and saucer comedy" of T. W. Robertson. Robertson's plays dealt with contemporary English life instead of the romantic fare of Knowles and Bulwer-Lytton. His settings were realistic interiors, his dialogue was credible, and at times his plots seemed true. The London success of Society (1865), Ours (1866), and Caste (1867) established his reputation. Perhaps his major contribution was to prove that drama could be written about ordinary life. He was a forerunner of realism.

The changes in dramatic tastes were matched by changes in the existing theatrical order. Throughout the first half of the nineteenth century, the resident stock company had been the most stable element in the theatre. Each major city possessed at least one company which performed a repertory of old and new plays. The opening of new territory in the South and West, and the improvement in transportation, encouraged major stars to travel from city to city. They at first performed with the local companies. As their number increased, the quality of resident companies decreased. Stars then began traveling with one or two actors for support. Finally, in 1860, Dion Boucicault took the next logical step, organizing an entire company for touring. Although he first introduced this practice in the English theatre, by 1872 it was being copied here. A play would open in New York; it would run until attendance lagged, then be transported in its entirety--actors, sets, properties--from city to city. The number of such "combination companies" steadily increased after completion of the first transcontinental railroad in 1869. The New York Dramatic Mirror reported nearly one hundred combination companies on the road during the season of 1876-1877. [33] Interest in local plays and actors was replaced by interest in touring attractions. Papers including the New York Clipper and Wilkes' Spirit of the Times began offering theatrical news and reviews for a national audience. The combination company destroyed the old theatrical order and replaced it with a system which for a time made the theatre our national pasttime.

Changes in Journalism

By 1850 the democratization of culture in this country had created a large reading public with an appetite for popular literature. Newspapers and magazines met this need. In the early years of the century the newspaper was little more than a political propaganda sheet, but James Gordon Bennett's innovations during the 1830s and 1840s radically changed its function. His New York Herald reported with vivid details the sensational events of the age. He wanted the Herald livelier, saucier, and more independent than its competitors. He shocked the nation with stories of illicit sexual relations and introduced into newspaper journalism the modern gossipy interview. His enemies accused him of vulgarizing the profession by lowering its standards and tone. But he built up a large circulation for the Herald--from 20,000 daily in 1836 to 77,000 in 1860--an increase not overlooked by his rivals. [34]

While newspapers such as William Cullen Bryant's New York Evening Post and Horace Greeley's New York Tribune attracted the educated classes, journalism for mass tastes had become the dominant mode.

There is a certain amount of chaos in any revolution and this was especially true in American journalism at mid-century. Revolutions create vacuums which must be filled before the order stabilizes. Improvements in presses and paper-making machinery led to a rapid proliferation of newspapers and magazines. Lowered postal rates and mass circulation enabled publishers to drop the price of newspapers, thus accelerating the rapid expansion. Newspaper organizations grew not only in size but in complexity. No newspaper could afford to be without a number of aggressive reporters capable of covering a fire, murder, political meeting, opera and theatre opening, or society function--all in the same day, if needed. The revolution in journalism also resulted in the shift of the publishing business from Boston to New York because of location and innovations in news gathering and transmitting. For the aspiring young writer, New York was clearly the city in which to pursue a career.

From Boston, Philadelphia, Charleston, New Orleans, Cleveland--from all parts of the United States--ambitious young writers streamed into New York. Others came from Europe--from Ireland, England, Germany, France--during the depression and famine of the 1850s. "Every editor of that period will remember the swarms of English and Irish writers who filled his sanctum," a Harper's Weekly editorial noted in 1862. "If a man with a notable cockney or Hibernian accent brought in a specially worthless manuscript, he was sure, by his own account, to be a leading writer for the Edinburgh or Blackwood, Fraser or the Dublin University, Punch, the Times, or Household Words--or, quite likely, for all of them; and his articles were eagerly awaited by these publications; but he preferred to publish first in America."[35] Despite their varied backgrounds, the majority of these writers shared two attributes: youthful enthusiasm and poverty.

William Winter, writing fifty years later, remembered literary life in America during the 1950s as difficult: "The number of writers who were obtaining a subsistence from a distinctively literary labor was small."[36] While the number of jobs multiplied by leaps and bounds, the salaries were pitifully low. Even successful literary men such as Bryant, Longfellow, Hawthorne, and Holmes made their living from

sources other than their literary product. "A precarious vocation! there could be no doubt about it," Winter concluded.
The establishment of theatre criticism as a separate and important department of American journalism depended upon
this revolution in the newspaper marketplace.

French Critical Influences

The young writers who swarmed into New York brought
with them not only their poverty and unpublished manuscripts,
but a disdain for established critical standards and practices.
They turned away from New England critical dogma preached
in Boston, the "Athens of America," and looked instead to
France. What met their approval was the style of essay
which the French called "feuilleton." Why? Clearly it was
the wit, liveliness, and lightness of touch. The dramatic
feuilleton had been created during the reign of Napoleon by
Julien-Louis Geoffroy, a leading critic for Paris's first important newspaper, the Journal des Debàts. Formerly a professor of rhetoric and poetic, and an avid theatregoer before
the Revolution, Geoffroy possessed the credentials to domi-
nate his field in the unstable period. Marvin Carlson notes
in his The French Stage in the Nineteenth Century: "In his
columns there was information for everyone: summaries of
the plays, informed comparisons with similar earlier works,
critical judgments, anecdotes of author, play, and actors,
and regular news of happenings backstage."37 Increased circulation of the Debàts insured the feuilleton's success. During the reign of Louis-Philippe (1830-1848), it reflected the
tastes of the bourgeoisie. To attract more and more of the
poorly educated lower and middle classes, journalists offered
stage gossip and clever essays, but little traditional criticism, under the heading of dramatic feuilleton.

In the 1840s and 1850s, Jules Janin, dramatic critic
for the Journal des Debàts, established a vogue for the dramatic feuilleton. No one wrote more brilliantly about trifles.
"He has created a style," one of his contemporaries noted,
"which, in his best days and when the sun shines, is lively,
graceful, captivating, made up of nothings, like those gauze
stuffs that the ancients called l'air tissue; this style, ready,
piquant, and sparkling, produces the effect of a fresh and ef-
fervescing sherbet drank on a summer's day in some leafy
bower."38 Albert Rhodes, in The Galaxy for January 1875,
describes Janin's work as "a sparkling bavardage in which
the writer was often miles away from his subject. It was

light, pleasant reading, which required no effort of the mind,
and left little impression. "[39] Janin did not pretend to write
about significant themes. He wrote pleasant essays which
were gay and frivolous. Considered a literary eunuch by
many of his contemporaries, Janin would have had little influence in America had it not been for his popularity among
the younger journalists of the 1850s. Newspaper and magazine critics followed him not only in style and tone, but in
advocating a closer relationship between art and life than was
normally seen on the American stage, and in being less
prudish than their predecessors. There was less concern
with formal principles of aesthetics than with "hot impressions" based on the critic's common sense and artistic taste.

The Pfaffians

The Round Table had called the French school a "Bacchanalian Mutual Admiration Society." Literary and artistic
clubs were common at that time. Many of the struggling
young newspaper writers and artists met in the evenings at
favorite cafes and beer cellars. John Brougham--actor,
manager, and publisher of a comic paper, The Lantern--gave
a weekly dinner at Edward Windust's Restaurant (near the old
Park Theatre) in 1852-1853 for the staff of his paper. About
the same time, a society of writers and artists began meeting
at a new restaurant on Spring Street. They named both the
restaurant and their society The Ornithorhynchus paradoxus,
the zoological name of the duck-billed platypus. Francis
Henry Temple Bellew, an artist, painted a sign representing
the Ornithorhynchus smoking a pipe while grasping a glass of
beer. [40] While there were undoubtedly many such societies
in the 1850s, most were ephemeral.

A society which formed around Henry Clapp, Jr., at
Pfaff's Restaurant and Bier Saloon, 647 Broadway, in 1855
or 1856 proved to be more enduring. A writer, editor, and
socialist, Clapp had returned from a lengthy stay in Paris
where he lived on the Left Bank among the students and artists. He sought to create a Latin Quarter in lower Manhat-
tan for artists, poets, journalists, critics, magazine litho-
graphers, and engravers. The cellar at Pfaff's proved to
have the right atmosphere. Its low ceilings, walls of stone,
stacks of barrels, buxom waitresses, and eccentric clientele
reminded journalist Charles T. Congdon of Auerbach's Cellar
in Faust. [41] A writer for the Saturday Press of December
3, 1859 described the saloon as the "rallying-place of the

subjects of King Devilmaycare; this is the anvil from which
fly the brightest scintillations of the hour ... the womb of
the best things that society has heard for many-a-day; this
is the trystingplace of the most careless, witty, and jovial
spirits of New York,--journalists, artists, and poets. "
Charlie Pfaff installed a long table with seats for about thirty,
and there Henry Clapp, Jr. held court each night.

The Pfaffian crowd kept late hours, flouted conventions, and clothed their poverty in an "eat, drink, and be
merry for tomorrow we die" attitude.   Most of the group
wrote for Saturday Press and Vanity Fair.   The former,
edited by Clapp, borrowed freely from French periodicals.
The latter, edited by Frank Wood and later Artemus Ward,
tried its hand at humor.   The Leader of April 6, 1861 disapproved of the group's drunkenness, sloth, and philosophy.
The Round Table of January 2, 1864 associated the Pfaffians
with free love and Bohemianism, "the feculent product of
Parisian low life. "   The same paper of February 6, 1864 accused the Pfaffians of gaining notoriety by blackmailing newspapers and by "inordinate laudation" of each other: "With one
or two exceptions, they are young men of the brazen, sharp
sort, who have a certain facility for didactic composition, or,
perhaps, with the aid of Walker's 'Rhyming Dictionary' and
Roget's 'Thesaurus' may set down lines that jingle sweetly. "
Clearly the Pfaffians had aroused and angered the more conservative element of the literary community, who responded
by labeling the group "Bohemians. "

Who were these "brazen" young Bohemians?   According
to the Leader of February 6, 1864, "The real Bohemia includes all the best writers and best artists in the metropolis. "
This author pointed out, however, that "Its members do not
call themselves Bohemians--stupid outsiders do. "   While not
a precise term, the name Bohemian came to mean the young
literary and artistic types who met at Pfaff's.   This included
a brilliant crowd: Fitz-James O'Brien, Edward G. P. Wilkins, Thomas Bailey Aldrich, William Winter, Frank Wood,
George Arnold.   No occasion at Pfaff's would have been complete without Ada Clare--actress, feminist, lecturer, and
writer.   She was the acknowledged leader of the bluestockings
--those daring female literati of the 1850s who sought equality with men in both professional and personal life.   Other
bluestockings joined Ada Clare at Pfaff's including Jenny Dan-
forth, Mary Fox, Adah Isaacs Menken (of Mazeppa fame),
Dora Shaw, and Getty Gay.   Walt Whitman dropped by Pfaff's
occasionally.   Charles B. Seymour and Edward H. House,

theatre critics of the <u>New York Times</u> and <u>New York Tribune</u>, respectively, were regulars. Artemus Ward drank here whenever he was in New York. Stephen Ryder Fiske drifted in on the eve of the Civil War. Andrew C. Wheeler came here in 1864 after serving as a war correspondent. Prudish William Dean Howells even visited the smokey bier saloon. To Howells, Pfaff's crowd represented the new literary life of the city.

The Civil War disrupted this way of life, however. After the war, few of the original Pfaffians returned. Five had died or been killed. Others had attained some degree of success, broke with the group, and embraced respectability. The <u>Round Table</u> of February 6, 1864 called for "no more French dissipations." In the language of a reformist weekly, the paper demanded a return to old values: the American home, domestic attractions, and "ties that God and nature provided for those who obey physical law." Conditions which encouraged the Bohemian life in the 1850s had vanished in the war's aftermath. The industrialization of the North, which had brought victory, changed the face of this nation. Commercialism dominated American life. The chaos caused by a rapidly changing American society prompted writers of similar tastes to seek refuge in tradition, not to attack it. Regulars at Pfaff's, such as William Winter and Thomas Bailey Aldrich turned their backs upon Bohemianism and embraced standards of taste we call "The Genteel Tradition." Others, such as Stephen Ryder Fiske, went to Europe and did not return for several years. Bohemianism, then, as a conscious critical school existed for only about a decade. Yet the liveliness of the French dramatic feuilleton appealed to American tastes, a fact not lost upon a number of young journalists after the war. Many of the practices of the Pfaffians were carried on in the theatre criticism of Andrew C. Wheeler, perhaps the most popular critic in the Victorian era.

CHAPTER TWO

Henry Clapp, Jr.
"figaro"

William Winter described Henry Clapp, Jr. as "brilliant and buoyant in mind; impatient of the commonplace; in-
tolerant of smug, ponderous, empty, obstructive respectability; prone to sarcasm; and ... reckless of public opinion. "[1] By all accounts, Clapp was one of the most colorful
and radical of American journalists during the middle decades
of the nineteenth century.

Born in Nantucket, Massachusetts, November 11,
1814, he grew up in a large family of sailors and merchants,
and went to sea himself at an early age in a brig provided
for the benefit of Nantucket boys by Sir Isaac Coffin of the
British Navy. [2] His father, a bookbinder by trade, had moved
to Nantucket from Hartford, Connecticut in 1809. The following year he married Eliza Stoddard, a local girl, who died
in October 1811, after giving birth to a daughter. Henry,
Sr., then married for the second time in December 1812, to
Rebecca Coffin, daughter of a prominent Nantucket merchant.
To this union was born at least seven children including young
Henry. While information about his early life remains ob-
scured, a few details can be ascertained. Living by the sea
and sailing in Sir Isaac's brig made indelible impressions
upon him. In 1864 he would remember the "seaside where I
studied nothing and learnt everything" as more beneficial than
the "grim old school-house where I studied everything and
learnt nothing. "[3] Clapp loved Nantucket and returned to it
many times in his last years.

As a young man, he engaged in the candle and oil
business in Boston and New Orleans before new forms of
energy made this trade obsolete. He then turned to journalism, first as a writer for The New Bedford Bulletin, edited

18

by Charles T. Congdon. "I found him not without value, "
Congdon recalled in his Reminiscences of a Journalist, published in 1880 (p. 339). "Whatever he could do at all he
could do readily; his conversational powers were uncommon. "
He abandoned this job after he met Nathaniel Peabody
Rogers, editor of the Herald of Freedom and a staunch abo-
litionist. With religious fervor he took up the causes of
temperance and abolition. To Rogers, Clapp is indebted for
his views on religion, slavery, and temperance. [4] Congdon
remembered him as a "radical of the first class. "

The doctrine of French socialist Charles Fourier was
to exert a stronger influence upon his life. In the late
1830s, Fourier's ideas of a new economic order based upon
a system of "passionate attraction" had gained a following in
America, especially among intellectuals. Albert Brisbane,
the most prominent American Fourierist, in 1840 published
a volume discussing the Frenchman's ideas, entitled "Association, or a Concise Exposition of the Practical Part of
Fourier's Social Science. " To Fourier, "Man's desire to
fulfill the totality of his passionate nature was the will of
God. Since nature and nature's God had bestowed passions
upon man, they must be afforded absolute free expression. "[5]
God never resorts to coercion, constraint, or violence in any
form, he reasoned. He employs no other force than attraction. "He impels all beings to fulfill their destiny from the
pleasure, the charm, the delight he connects with it, and not
from fear of pain or punishment. " Consequently, Fourier
rejected all other philosophical theories for unnecessarily re-
pressing the passions.

To solve existing social problems, he proposed developing an ideal community to give man the greatest possi-
bility for expressing his passions. Called a phalanstery,
this community would number about 1600 members, to include
all of the fundamentally different varieties of men and women.
Property would be shared. Labor would be voluntary. The
traditional family unit would be scrapped. All forms of love
relationships--homosexual as well as heterosexual--would be
permitted. Where bourgeois thinking with its moral bent had
isolated people, the gospel of Fourier would allow them to
joyfully live together. Man with his diverse, passionate nature could seek a style of living which suited his own individual tastes.

Due to the work of Brisbane and of Horace Greeley,
editor and proprietor of the New York Tribune, Fourierism

enjoyed a brief period of popularity in America during the economically troubled 1840s. Numerous phalansteries sprang up throughout the Eastern United States. Brook Farm, outside of Boston, and the North American Phalanx in Red Bank, New Jersey, were the best known. Fourier's theories made sense to Henry Clapp and undoubtedly affected his philosophy, his life style, and his critical methods. From this time, he would be regarded as a disciple of Fourier.

Clapp set himself up as a reformer by lecturing upon temperance, slavery, and socialism. Between 1844 and 1848 he edited the Essex County Washingtonian--renamed The Pioneer in 1845--a reformist weekly published in Lynn, Massachusetts. His editorial policy was to be "independent in everything, neutral in nothing." No subject was considered sacred. While he professed faith in Christianity for its system of ethics, he found its churches unsympathetic and unfeeling about social problems, as evidenced by the following editorial:

> The writer sees no beauty in its [the church's] rites, and no comeliness in its temples. They seem to him cold, barbarous, repulsive, and degrading. Seeing its priesthood enlisted against every radical movement for the removal of human misery, and its places of worship closed hermetically against nearly all the advocates of human progress,--he fails to perceive in that Religion any elements of moral beauty or spiritual life. — Its faith is a gloomy, inhuman, sepulchral principle which may, as its partisans contend, do very well 'to die by,' but which is utterly unfit for any intelligent being to live by--either here or hereafter. [6]

Henry Clapp reminded his readers on numerous occasions that the Law of God is Love: "We must love our enemies and feed them. We must return good for evil, blessing for cursing, kisses for blows." He blamed the orthodox church for denying the true spirit of Christianity: "It worships a God with whom hate and revenge appear to be cardinal virtues, and whose alleged intention toward the great mass of the human race are [sic] perfectly devilish." Such statements were intended to create controversy and get his views before the public. They also reflected the thinking of the "Comeouters," a radical group which existed in Lynn in the early 1840s. The "Comeouters" opposed religious organizations and on occasion disturbed public worship, although they

"professed great regard for morality." According to the
History of Lynn (1883), Clapp fraternized with the "Comeouters" although he was guiltless of their extreme behavior
(p. 408).

Clapp's stand on temperance, like that on religion,
was never moderate. In 1840 he accused the following persons of drinking intoxicating liquors: members of the legis-
lature, judges of courts, lawyers, school-masters, clergy-
men, officers of temperance societies, professing Christians,
state and town officers, physicians, lecturers, men of property and standing.[7] The entire group he labeled enemies of
the human race. In 1846 such extreme views were to result
in a 60-day jail term in Salem for libel. Winter recalls in
Old Friends that Clapp was imprisoned "for his audacity and
severity in attacking the traffickers in spirituous liquor."
In reality he libeled a justice of peace named Aaron Lumnus
by "having pronounced a trial before a New England Court,
to be 'a ridiculous farce.'"[8] While serving his sentence,
Clapp wrote to John Pierpont, the ordained minister of the
Lynn Unitarian Society: "I am happy to inform you that
there is not, probably, a man in the town of Lynn, who sup-
poses that I have libelled, or that I or any other man can
libel the character of Aaron Lumnus either as a man or a
magistrate."[9] If Clapp ever regretted his libelous statement,
there is no record of his remorse. He continued to edit his
paper from his jail cell. When released, he was received
as a hero by fellow townsmen and honored by a parade
through Lynn.

And his views on slavery were just as extreme.
"Slave-holding is a sin, and, like all sins should be immediately abolished," he lectured a Mobile, Alabama clergyman
in September, 1844; "... as you love your Bible, [do not] ...
attempt to prove that it sanctions or even 'winks at' chattel
slavery; for if you succeed, I'll trample your Bible beneath
my foot, as I would a reptile; and so will every man in the
land who is not a dastard."[10] As William Winter would
later explain, Clapp held few moderate views and "excited
venomous antagonism" on every subject.

While detained in the Salem jail, Clapp made plans to
attend the World's Temperance Convention to be held that
August in London. "I have a notion to be gone about a
year," he wrote John Pierpont, "and in that time to pour into my intellectual demijohn all the knowledge which I can beg,
buy, or borrow. I propose to extend my travels to France,

Switzerland, and possibly to Italy. "[11] He asked Pierpont for "a few hints" to save "many kicks," admitting "I am a green boy, green as grass and need all the ripening before I go, which such sunny minds as yours can give me." Friends and associates helped raise money for his voyage. He departed for England in May 1846, immediately after being released from jail. Clapp spent a year in England lecturing on Fourierism, slavery, and temperance.

The chronology of his life during the next decade is difficult to determine. In The Pioneer, March 2, 1848, he wrote in an editorial: "It is my intention to spend most of the time for the next two or three years in travelling." He relinquished the editorship to George Bradburn and assumed a new position as "Corresponding Editor." His letters were regular features of the paper until its demise on August 30, 1849. [12]

After resigning as editor of The Pioneer, Clapp sailed immediately for Liverpool. Between this time and 1856, he lived at least three years in London and three in Paris. [13] "I know the dear old fogie metropolis by heart," he wrote in 1858 of the English capital. "The plump dome of St. Paul's, swelling over the proud capital like a plum-pudding over a Christmas dinner, is as familiar to me as the Old South Steeple rising like a ghost over the City of Notions. "[14] While living in England, he traveled to Oxford, Cambridge, Windsor, Brighton, and Coventry. He also visited Ireland and Scotland. Sometime, apparently in 1851, he crossed the English Channel from Dover to arrive in Calais; then took the train to Paris. While he enjoyed London, he was delighted with Paris: "The American traveller spends a week in London and a month in Paris, and returns home thinking of the one and dreaming of the other, resolved all the while to revisit France before he dies, but to go by the way of England. "[15]

To avoid living near Americans, he found lodging in the Latin Quarter among the Bohemians--poverty-stricken artists and writers who idealized their poverty and considered themselves superior to the money-grubbing middle classes. Clapp was among the first Americans to experience the Bohemian life in Paris. While the term "Bohemian" had long meant vagabond or gypsy, in 1840 Balzac had penned it on impoverished writers and artists in his short story "Prince of Bohemia." According to his definition, "Bohemia is made up of young people, all of whom are between twenty and thirty years

of age, all men of genius in their own line, as yet almost
unknown but with the ability to become known one day, when
they will achieve real distinction. "16 Balzac thought the
term self-explanatory: "Bohemia possesses nothing, yet con-
trives to exist on that nothing." But it was Henri Murger,
not Balzac, who made the term a household word. In 1844,
Murger, a poverty-stricken Parisian artist, began a series
of articles in Corsaire Magazine describing in humorous
terms life among the struggling young writers and artists.
Entitled "La Vie de Bohème," his word sketches were published in serial form from 1844 to 1849 and achieved world-
wide popularity. Murger's writings are largely autobiographi-
cal. Born in 1822, he left home at an early age to live
among Parisian would-be painters and artists. These relationships provided him with his characters: Rodolphe, based
loosely upon his own life; Marcel, a painter; Schaunard, a
musician and painter; and Colline, a philosopher. Murger
also drew upon the women he knew for his delightful Mimi
and Musette.

Murger captured the charm and gay melancholy of the
Paris of Louis-Philippe with stories of tempestuous love affairs, all night parties, and youthful camaraderie. He succeeded in making the artist's way of life appealing despite
its unfriendly landlords, empty stomachs, and rejected manuscripts. In 1849 Theodore Barrière, a dramatist, collaborated with him on a stage version of La Vie de Bohème that
opened at the Théâtre des Variétés on November 22, 1849,
to resounding success. Widespread acceptance of the term
"Bohemia" dates from this first performance. Two years
later a collection of Murger's Corsaire stories was published
under the title "Scènes de la Bohème, followed within a few
months by the second, Scenes de la Vie de Jeunesse. Some
forty years later, in 1896, Murger's stories would be trans-
formed by Puccini into the opera La Bohème.

Henri Murger had defined Bohemianism as a stage in
an artist's career: "the preface to the Academy, the Hospital, or the Morgue. "17 Such a definition suggested that the
Latin Quarter might be the place to begin one's artistic
career. Young artists and writers flocked to Paris. The
American artist James Whistler, for one, read Scènes de la
Bohème in 1855 and departed immediately for France. 18
Prior to this time, however, Clapp had managed to survive
three years in the French capital. True to his word, he
poured into his intellect "all the knowledge" which he could
"beg, buy, or borrow." Winter later wrote that he spoke

French fluently, and in temperament, mental constitution, and conduct of life "he was more a Frenchman than an American."[19] It was during his years in Paris that Clapp broke his temperance pledge.

Evidence is not clear as to the means of his financial support while living abroad. According to Congdon, Clapp told him he wrote for one of the London newspapers as a correspondent. And while living in Paris he met Horace Greeley and contracted to write letters to the New York Tribune. Clapp was paid a sum in advance but the letters, if written, were never printed. And in addition to the preceding employment possibilities, it is likely that Clapp wrote the Paris Letter for the New York Herald in 1854-1855 under "Figaro," a pseudonym identified closely with his later writings.[20] Figaro became known as a political satirist for his attacks on the French regime of Napoleon III. Clapp suggests in his "Portrait of Paris," a serialized memoir published in the Saturday Press (1859-1860), that his departure from France may have been involuntary.

After returning to New York either in late 1855 or early 1856, Henry Clapp worked as a secretary to Albert Brisbane. He translated from the French, Fourier's The Social Destiny of Man, or Theory of the Four Movements, which Brisbane published in 1857 with his own "A Treatise on the Functions of the Human Passions" and "An Outline on Fourier's System of Social Science."[21] During this time, Clapp also worked as a free-lance writer, submitting poems and short stories to leading periodicals. In 1857 he published Husband vs. Wife, a humorous booklet about marriage.[22] But such activities took a back-seat to his major vocation--establishing an artists' colony in New York. In 1856 he discovered Charlie Pfaff's Restaurant and Bier Saloon, 647 Broadway, and began to meet there with his circle of friends. Within two years, it had become known as New York's answer to the Left Bank.

At first glance, it may seem surprising that Henry Clapp would attempt such a venture in New York. Boston had been recognized as the "Athens" of American culture. One looked to the New England Brahmins--to Longfellow, Holmes, or Lowell--as the arbiters of taste; one looked to New York for trade and commerce. But the dominance of American literature by the blue-blooded Brahmins was passing by mid-century. New York had become the preeminent American metropolis. Where Boston represented convention, respectability, and academicism in arts and letters, New York represented promise. According to William Dean Howells, Clapp thought it proof of the inferiority of Boston that "if you passed down Washington Street, half a dozen men in the crowd would know you were Holmes, or Lowell, or Longfellow, or Wendell Phillips; but in Broadway no one would know who you were, or care to the measure of his smallest blasphemy."[23]   While this might reflect New York's lack of culture more than its sophistication, Clapp chose to view it differently.

Few today, however, would deny that Herman Melville and Walt Whitman, both New Yorkers, were the outstanding writers of the 1850s. What separates them from the New England Brahmins is what they shared in common with Clapp --a distrust of established traditions in arts and letters. Whitman turned his back on New England in 1855 with Leaves of Grass. An affront to Puritan tastes, Leaves of Grass found a champion in Clapp, who praised and promoted it.   In his later life, Whitman acknowledged his debt to Clapp: "Henry was in our sense a pioneer, breaking ground before the public was ready to settle. . . .   Henry Clapp stepped out from the crowd of hooters--was my friend, a much needed ally at that time. . . .   He did the honorable with me every time.   I have often said . . . that my own history could not be written with Henry left out."[24]

Whitman was not alone in his debt to Clapp. Mark Twain, Artemus Ward, William Dean Howells, Thomas Bailey Aldrich, E. C. Stedman, Richard Henry Stoddard, and William Winter were but a few of the promising young writers he assisted.   And it is not surprising that they would turn to him.   Older, knowledgeable, and well-traveled, he was a socialist in a capitalistic society, attacking the greed of American business and the sham of American politics--favorite subjects among young rebels.   He had experienced the real Bohemia in Paris--certainly a status symbol in the 1850s.   And he ridiculed the Brahmins which the new generation of writers hoped to replace as leaders in American letters.   His satirical thrusts against the sacred cows of brownstone respectability gave him a position of leadership among writers and artists who had not yet "made it."

After establishing his Pfaffian Bohemians, it was obvious to Clapp that a publication was needed to gain a wider audience for his views. Between 1856 and 1858, conversations at Pfaff's focused upon the direction this magazine would

take. During the summer of 1858, Clapp met a young Harvard scholar, Edward Howland, and interested him in joining
the project. Without investing a penny of his own money,
Clapp launched the New York Saturday Press on October 23,
1858, to "speak the truth as to books and the literary profession." An editorial in the first issue noted that the growth
of letters in this country had been repressed for years by
"the withering influence of a ponderous old fogyism and that
many solemn quacks had succeeded--by dint of writing elegant
commonplaces and of strenuously puffing one another." The
staff was small: Howland took charge of the business side;
Clapp edited; Thomas Bailey Aldrich reviewed books; and
Fitz-James O'Brien wrote about the theatre. All were members of the Pfaffian coterie. On December 17, 1858, Aldrich wrote F. H. Underwood, assistant editor of Atlantic,
that "The 'Saturday Press' is on its feet. It is growing. It
will be a paper."[25] The Bohemians knew more about writing,
however, than they did about business. Howells, Winter,
Aldrich, and Stedman all attested to the unbusinesslike
methods of the weekly. Stedman wrote: "The paper was
usually hard up, and Mr. Clapp took in several business
partners, one after the other. When he got what he called
'fresh blood,' he used to divide it up among the boys."[26]
James G. Derby in his Fifty Years Among Authors, Books,
and Publishers recalled that "there was no cash book or other
account books kept, thus avoiding the expense of a book-
keeper. Whatever money was received went into the hands
of which-ever proprietor happened to be in the office at the
time."[27] It is no surprise that the Saturday Press had severe
financial difficulties. It suspended publication after the December 15, 1860 issue for lack of funds, and was revived for
only a few months after the war.

Despite its deficiencies, the Saturday Press had energy
and vitality. "It was clever and full of wit that tries its
teeth upon everything," Howells later recalled. "It attacked
all literary shams but its own, and it made itself felt and
feared."[28] The importance of the Saturday Press to the Bohemians should not be minimized. Howells thought it "very
nearly as well to be accepted by the Press as by the Atlantic." Without the Civil War and with better business practices, the publication might have proved as endurable as Atlantic, its main competition in 1858.

From his editor's desk Clapp set the style and tone of
the publication. He hated and liked with intense passion and
did not hide behind either conventional morality or aesthetic

dogma to defend his verdicts. Editorial policies were out-
lined in the first issue. The weekly would not print lengthy
political articles or deal with squabbles of politicians:
"Most of our newspapers, filled as they are with such trash,
would appear to be edited for the exclusive benefit of hack-
politicians and servant girls. "[29] Two weeks later he added:
"The simple fact is that the party politicians of this country ... are nothing more or less than a vast brotherhood of
thieves, conspiring together to plunder the public purse; and
to pretend that their wretched squabbles, with which most of
our papers are filled, are of the least importance to any human being but themselves and their tools, is utterly absurd. "[30] Before the 1860 Presidential Election he quipped:
"The two great parties are on the eve of another fight, to
determine which shall have the privilege of plundering the
country for the next four years. "[31] His comments about the
repressive regime of Napoleon III led to the French Government banning the Saturday Press from France in 1859. [32]

Despite his skill in political satire, Clapp did not
want a political but a literary paper to compete with Atlantic
and Harper's--magazines which published short stories and
poems together with literary and dramatic criticism. His
three years in Paris were not wasted. Borrowing ideas
freely from French papers and journals, he assembled a
more colorful and lively publication than his hated rivals.
Instead of serious scholarly essays, he preferred the lighter
tone of the French feuilleton. William Dean Howells described the prose of the Saturday Press as "shredded ... into
very fine paragraphs of a sentence each, or of a very few
words, or even of one word. " This method prevailed for
some time, Howells believed, with some of the dramatic
critics who "thought it gave a quality of epigram to the
style. "[33]

The labor of editing and writing for the Saturday Press
between 1858 and 1860 did not deter Clapp from reigning each
night at Pfaff's as the King of Bohemia. Beside him sat Ada
Clare (her real name was Jane McElheney), regarded by the
coterie as their Queen. [34] In the mid-1850s she scandalized
good society by acquiring a son, Aubrey, without benefit of
marriage. Louis Gottschalk, the composer and pianist, was
thought to be the father, although neither party would confirm
or deny his parentage. Like Clapp, she lived for a time in
Paris (1857) and returned to New York determined to establish
a Bohemian society in this country. Finding that Clapp had
anticipated her plans by a year, she joined his efforts and

proved his match at repartee in late night sessions. [35] Her
column in the Saturday Press sparkled with comments on the
latest play, poem, novel, or bit of gossip. She helped to
create the aura of mystique around the Bohemians with statements such as: "The Bohemian is not, like the creature of
society, a victim of rules and customs; he steps over them
all with an easy, graceful, joyous unconsciousness, guided
by the principles of good taste and feeling. "[36]

Clapp admired her beauty, respected her tastes, and
supported her causes. They seldom disagreed on important
issues. A champion of the bluestockings, Ada Clare thought
the success of European actresses Ristori and Rachel proof
of the superiority of women: "[on the stage] ... the highest
honors, the proudest triumphs, the chief part of the world's
worship, and the largest pecuniary profits, belong to wom-
en. "[37] Why? "It is only on the stage that the woman is
taken out of the world's straight-jacket, and left with free
limbs and free soul. " Where in literature and the other
arts the woman has to bow before the calm judgment, the
superior education, and the strong physical health of the man,
on the stage she can rely on her instinct--"the one sublime
gift that nature gives us to cope with men. "

The Saturday Press suspended publication after its December 15, 1860 issue because it lacked the necessary funds
to continue. Henry Clapp's creditors finally had caught up
with him. He had begged for his friends to promote the
weekly in order to increase business. In an October 22,
1859, editorial, he confessed that he had no capital and "a
thousand or two dollars is all we need. " Few persons could
deny that for two years he had produced the most innovative
and exciting literary paper in this country. The Philadelphia
Sunday Mercury of September 2, 1860 had called it "a bold,
free spoken, don't-care-a-snap-ative sort of a journal, ...
It is the sworn foe of elaborate commonplace respectability
and nicely-turned platitudes, in which the 'Mutual Admiration
Society' of Boston delight. Its criticisms are candid and
readable, if not always sound. Its morals, we fear, are very
bad. The editor, we imagine, sits up late o'nights, in the
haunts of Bohemia, discussing art and literature between
drinks and whiffs of the weed. "[38] Apparently, Clapp had intended to suspend publication of the Saturday Press for only
about a month. The New York Leader of December 22, 1860
announced that he would resume the Press about January 8
with an original story by Harriet Prescott, "the most gorgeous
of Yankee blue-stockings. " It would be five years, however,
before the next issue would appear.

The collapse of the Saturday Press left the Bohemians in control of only one weekly paper--Vanity Fair--which they had founded the previous December. Undaunted, they took over the Leader, a weekly paper sponsored by the New York Democratic Party. Edward G. P. Wilkins, dramatic critic of the Saturday Press from February 1859 until June 1860 had anticipated the paper's demise and deserted to the Leader six months before the end. After December 15 he was joined by many of his Pfaffian comrades including Henry Clapp. From December 1860 until the following May, Clapp wrote a literary feuilleton for the Leader under the pen-name of Figaro. After the death of Wilkins on May 5, 1861, he took charge of the dramatic page.

No stranger to the stage, Henry Clapp had acquired a taste for theatrical art as a boy when he was taken to the Old Tremont Theatre in Boston. He soon knew every role which actor/manager W. H. Smith played. Later he became an avid playgoer on both sides of the Atlantic. Clapp then brought impressive credentials to the job: knowledge of theatre and experience as a journalist. He dissected a production with the skill of a surgeon, using wit and satire as his scalpels. Although hard evidence is lacking, he apparently shared the Saturday Press dramatic post with William Winter after Wilkins resigned. Internal evidence such as word choices and phrasing suggest that he wrote several of the dramatic feuilletons which were printed under the name of Quelqu'un (someone, anyone). His reputation as a theatre critic, however, rests on his dramatic feuilletons under the signature of Figaro for the Leader from 1861 to 1869; for the New York Weekly Review in 1865; and for his resurrected Saturday Press in 1865-1866.

Henry Clapp was not a highbrow critic; he thought the theatre chiefly useful as a place of amusement. "When I want to be instructed (which I do occasionally) I go to a library; when I want to be moralized (which I hardly ever do) I go to a lecture; when I want to be converted (which I sometimes have an idea of) I go to a church; but when I want to forget all these things and have a 'good time,' I go to the theatre. And I rather think that in this I am pretty much like other people."[39] He regarded plays that put him to sleep as immoral; consequently, he denounced dullness rather than wickedness.

His eclectic tastes led him to disagree sharply with William Winter in 1866 over the standard by which to judge art. Winter had repudiated his Bohemian ideology by this time and was ensconced as dramatic critic of Greeley's New York Tribune. In Clapp's view, Winter had sold out to the "Procrustean standard of what is called High Art." "Don't do it, my dear fellow," he advised in the Saturday Press of February 3. "'Procrusteanation is the thief of time.' High comedy is doubtless a good thing; but so is low comedy--and farce, and burlesque, and extravaganza, and every other form of the Drama." One should attend Merry Wives of Windsor and Macbeth, but one should also view popular entertainments such as De Walden's The Balloon Wedding and Charles Gayler's The Child-Stealer. One should be delighted as much by the Ravels and Hanlons (pantomimists) as by Edwin Booth and the Wallacks. "When the Hanlons were performing at Wood's Theatre, last week, taking part in what was intended to be a grand carnival scene," Figaro argued, "it no more occurred to me that they were out of place in the Drama, than that a Taglioni or an Ellsler would be out of place in the Opera." Drama is more than an intellectual exercise, he preached. Aesthetic pleasures which appeal to the senses--ballet, pantomime, dance--must not be neglected because they are not "intellectual." Clapp reasoned that if good people want to purify the drama by excluding from it all vulgar accessories such as dancing and pantomime, they should put a pulpit on the stage "and be done with it." But he warned about the consequences: "No effort to phylacterize or dismalize the stage will stand the slightest chance of success, till you discover a means of modifying human nature and enabling it to get along not only without the senses, but without any of the elements which now adapt it to the globe we inhabit."

Henry Clapp did not mourn the decline of interest in the old romantic drama. He regarded worship of tradition as the major reason why American drama at mid-century lacked vitality, and applauded the "realistic" melodramas imported from Europe and dressed up in native feathers. Dion Boucicault captured his interest with his exciting adaptations of French sensational dramas. But Dumas fils' La Dame aux Camélias delighted him more because it offended the moralists. The play was widely produced. Jean M. Davenport (later Mrs. F. W. Lander) introduced Camille to New Yorkers in December 1853, and again in August 1854, in an adaptation which removed all references to sexual improprieties. Laura Keene and Matilda Heron followed closely in their own versions of the controversial play. Highbrow critics were disgusted by a plot that illustrated the life and death of a courtesan. Clapp found the tone and style of the

piece to his tastes, and expressed amusement over the up-
roar: "I notice that some of my brother critics ... are so
shocked by the appearance of any such character on the
stage ... that they seriously think of resigning their posi-
tions and never going hence forth to any worse place than a
barroom or a concert saloon.... "40 He hoped Camille had
weeded out of the theatre the "Pharisees and fanatics." Ada
Clare thought the success of the play a clear indication that
audiences were tired of drama built upon purple robes and
affairs of state. She wrote in her Saturday Press letter of
August 27, 1859, "... the plain, unvarnished tale of a woman
who knew how to love and to grieve, already eagerly embodied into four great languages, had struck one of the key-
notes of the world's heart.... " Like Clapp she believed the
theatre needed fresh characters and plots.

In the April 1, 1865 New York Weekly Review, Figaro
discussed why this country lacked an American drama.
First, he dismissed the notion that Americans were different
from other races:

> Hath not an American eyes? Hath not an Amer-
> ican hands, organs, dimensions, senses, affections,
> passions? Is he not fed with the same food, hurt
> with the same weapons, (I should think so, just
> now), subject to the same diseases, healed by the
> same means, warmed and cooled by the same win-
> ter and summer, as another man is?

Clapp pointed out that we are human beings subject to the
same nature which affects humans the world over. Thus
whether here or in Europe, the lives of men and women
"must necessarily afford all the varieties of incident, all
the complexities of situation, all the intensities of effect,
that any dramatist could desire--and, this being true, if any
country lacks a national drama it is certainly not for want
of material. "

While Clapp thought there was nothing wrong with the
American playwright's obsession with "local color, " he believed the best dramas deal with matters of the human heart
and are independent of locale and time. He recommended
contemporary French plays as proper models, pointing out
that French playwrights might locate their action in Paris
but the incidents, folly or crimes are universal and might
have happened in Peking or New York.

As a critic of acting, Clapp thought the traditional school absurd. "Give up all this Podsnappian talk about 'classic art,'" he advised William Winter in 1866. "If you wish to reform the stage ... turn your energies toward converting actors and actresses into simple human beings...."[41] Tragedians reminded him of manikins and puppets, not men and women. While they might differ to a degree in their style of elocution, the general conception of their roles was based upon models handed down from generation to generation. He pleaded with them to abandon that "fearful old stage walk, the horrible stage shrug, that dismal stage voice, ... and ... an amount of striding, ranting, bellowing ... the very thought of which is enough to make one shudder." They were so unnatural that they seemed to Clapp like stage properties to be packed away in the storeroom after the performance. "An actor who should give us a Richard III, a Hamlet, a Macbeth, a Richelieu, as simple human beings ... regardless of tradition or precedent ... as if he himself were the character ... would create such a sensation as the stage has hardly known for a century," Clapp prophesied. [42]

In Charles Kean's farewell American tour of 1865, Clapp thought he discovered tragic acting to his tastes: "It stands out in such glaring contrast to everything else we see on the stage; ... it violates so coolly and constantly all recognized useages and traditions--it ignores, with such consummate complacency and sang froid any preconceived opinions on the part of the public--it defies so bravely all critics and all criticism--that on a first experience of it, all other emotions are swallowed up in that of astonishment."[43] Kean and his wife were making a tour of America at the end of their careers. According to George Henry Lewes, Kean had changed from "the stamping, sputtering, ranting, tricky actor" of his early career to one remarkable for his "naturalness and forcible quietness."[44] Clapp had viewed Kean's acting on previous occasions but had never considered him a great actor. Yet the new style was attractive. In playing Cardinal Wolsey, Kean "so identified himself with the character," Figaro reported in the Saturday Press for September 2, "that everybody in the house forgot all about the play and the author, and the theatre itself, and thought only of the character, which was before us as distinctly as if it had crossed our own path, and it was we ourselves who had to do with it."

A week later, after he had viewed the actor's Hamlet, Macbeth, and Lear, he advised young actors and actresses

to see him "en masse, " every chance they could get: "They
will learn more from him in an hour than they could learn
from any other source in a life-time, --and un-learn more,
too, which would be still better. "[45]   Kean's secret to Clapp
was simple: "Everything he conceives, he unadorns.   Kings
and princes count for nothing with him.   It is the total absence of all pretense in his acting that exposes him, sometimes to the charge of being prosy and commonplace. "   His
Lear and Macbeth were so human, "you wouldn't mind taking
a drink with them, or, on a pinch, asking them to take a
drink with you. "   Clapp regarded Kean's Louis XI as his
masterpiece because it offered a king who "might be considered as belonging to the human species. "

     But in the end, Charles Kean did not measure up to
his ideal.   In the May 26, 1866 Saturday Press, Figaro
criticized the actor for being too mechanical--for portraying
Louis XI exactly the same way each performance: "You may
see it a thousand times and you will never find it vary an
iota: every look, gesture, movement, accent, is measured
to a millionth part of a hair. "   Where the performance
showed "consummate knowledge of stage effects (not to say
tricks), " it lacked inspiration and impulse--qualities which
Clapp thought essential for great acting.   Even though he
grew enthusiastic over the performance, he admitted that he
did not care to view it again, "and this tells the whole
story. "

     It seemed impossible for critics of the 1860s to talk
about Edwin Booth without comparing him to Edwin Forrest.
Clapp preferred the older actor (who commanded the "vile
multitude" rather than the "dilettanti"), but thought young
Booth a promising talent.   "Whatever advantage there may be
on the side of Mr. Forrest in certain characters, " Clapp
wrote in the Leader, October 4, 1862, "is probably to be at-
tributed in part to certain physical attributes and in part to
long experience. "   Forrest and Booth both performed in New
York during the fall of 1862--the former at Niblo's and the
latter at the Winter Garden.   This offered the public (and
the critics) an opportunity to judge between the two actors.
Clapp found "not much delicacy" about Forrest's characterizations but thought their "boldness of outline and brilliancy of
color" impressive.   He despised the actor's Richelieu but
found much to praise in his Othello, Hamlet, and Richard III.
Despite all his "ranting and roaring and butting and bullying
and tearing the passions (and everything else) to shreds, he
now and then gives us one of those delicious pictures of real

life which startle and delight one like the sight of a cottage,
or a cornfield among the wild solitudes of the Andes.   And
in fact, throughout, he is essentially human. "[46]   His main
fault, Clapp noted, was that he invested characters such as
Othello, Hamlet and Richard III with "those ferocious attributes which shock us even in a Spartacus or a Metamora.
He has not yet learned that the passions are like unchained
tigers only in the lowest and most brutal characters. "

Booth, on the other hand, anxious not to "tear round
and break things, " had fallen into the opposite extreme.   He
opened his engagement on September 29 with a Hamlet which
Clapp thought lacked "flesh and blood. "   The critic also did
not like Booth's acting of Othello, Payne's Brutus, and Shylock: "[He has] given us a series of hard, dry, woe-begone
characters which (except in a few purely domestic scenes
which he renders at times with great delicacy and sweetness),
are like certain under-toned pictures of mountain scenery
which represent the loneliness of the scene without giving
any idea of its wildness or its beauty. "[47]   His acting seemed
more like a miniature painting than a stage picture.

Clapp pondered the reasons behind the rapid rise of
the actor: "I can't exactly tell you ... what the charm is
about young Booth; but if you have seen him you don't need
to be told.   Ada Clare says that it is his plaintiveness and
pathos.   I shouldn't wonder.   He seems to have tears in his
voice, as the French say.   I think on the whole that it is
his voice which is the great talisman.   His action is rather
too mechanical and elaborate.   There is no unction about it.
He doesn't seem so much to move as to be moved.   You
are on the lookout constantly for the wires.   But his tones
have a witchery about them which is indescribable. "[48]
Booth's intellectual approach to acting did not please the old
Bohemian, who thought inspiration and passion more essential than design for great acting.   He agreed essentially with
Walt Whitman that Booth "never made me forget everything
else and follow him, as the greatest fellows, when they let
themselves go, always do. "[49]

If Henry Clapp could not enjoy the actor's quiet, un-
assuming, intellectual style, he could enjoy his original interpretations of Shakespeare.   In Hamlet and Richard III
Booth excelled, Clapp believed, while in melodramatic roles
such as Lagardère in The Duke's Motto, Claude Melnotte in
The Lady of Lyons, and the title roles in Don Caesar de
Bazan and Ruy Blas he was coarse and vulgar.   Booth should

leave such parts alone and stick to Shakespeare, the critic advised, "about as high a compliment as an actor could well receive."

For actresses in serious roles, Clapp favored the emotional school of acting over the classic, although he cautioned against excessive emotionalism which lacks both dignity and repose. Garff B. Wilson has described the emotional school as possessing three characteristics: "First, the actress of this school actually experiences the feelings and passions of her role and surrenders herself to these emotions. She does not simulate but actively participates in the agonies of the mimic characters. Second, she cultivates a lush, overt display of the passions she is feeling. Her performance is marked by sobs, tears, screams, shudders, heaving, writhing, panting, growling, trembling, and all manner of other physical manifestations. The third major characteristic ... is neglect of technique. In surrendering to emotion and cultivating lavish, overt expression, the emotional actress disregards discipline and control. Her elocution, gestures, movement, and performance of stage business are likely to be impromptu, unstudied, and haphazard."[50]

Clapp wanted an actress to put her own stamp upon the role, to make it her own rather than to follow standard interpretations. And despite the abuses of the emotional school by actresses such as Lucille Western, Maggie Mitchell, and Olive Logan, Clapp thought the success of Matilda Heron amply demonstrated its virtues. He viewed Heron's Camille again and again. "Why? Because she puts so much of herself into it--so much of her strong, impulsive, irrepressible genius--that she could no more play it exactly the same way two consecutive evenings than she could be exactly the same person two consecutive evenings."[51] While her presentation was not entirely free from faults, it did offer two essential qualities--individuality and humanity.

Vitality and energy together with inspiration and naturalness counted much with Clapp, especially if such attributes were joined with grace and dignity. He reviewed the stage debut of Miss Ann Lacoste in 1866 with such standards clearly in mind. Miss Lacoste portrayed the title character in Isaac Pray's Virginia of Rome, which opened at the Academy of Music, February 17, 1866. "The best thing to be said about her first performance," Clapp wrote the following week, "is that she was letter-perfect in her part; that she

evidently knew the meaning of the words (a rare occurrence
even with 'stars'); that she showed no tendency to rant; and
that in some of the impassioned scenes she overcame the
bombast of the language and gave us a touch or two of
genuine womanly pathos. " Clapp continued in the next paragraph: "If I had any advice to give to Miss Lacoste it would
be that she make a special study of the natural school of
acting, as distinguished from the traditional--that she dis-
continue all lessons in elocution--and that before playing
again she go to some tragedy theatre as often as possible
to learn 'how not to do it. '"[52] But Clapp did admit that
there was much humbug to natural acting, and that an actor
could not conduct himself on stage exactly as he would in a
drawing-room except to make an idiot out of himself. A certain degree of exaggeration is necessary, he concluded, to
produce the simplest effect.

He regarded Mrs. John Wood as the finest comic actress on the American stage, and determined that "her
presence alone is enough to save a pretty dull play. "[53] Mrs.
Wood specialized in burlesque comedy and was idolized by the
Bohemians--especially Wilkins--who nicknamed her "Thalia. "
The daughter of Henry Vining, an English actor, Mrs. Wood
established her New York reputation during the 1857-1858
season by creating the role of Minnehaha in Charles Walcot's
Hi-A-Wa-Tha: or Ardent Spirits and Laughing Waters, a
burlesque of Hiawatha. [54] Bayard (F. J. Ottarson) wrote of
her in the Spirit of the Times: "Mrs. Wood is one of the
few artists to whom it is impossible to be indifferent. The
moment her voice is heard from the wing, the ear is attent,
and when her saucy face appears, all eyes are at her service,
watchful lest they miss the comical, or impudent, or ludicrous, or mock-heroic byplay, which radiates over her
features like sunlight on a dimpled sea. "[55] Habitué, in the
Leader of April 21, 1860, called her "one of the best burlesque actresses in this country. " Clapp agreed. After
viewing her in Brougham's burlesque of Pocahontas in September 1865, he called her the "most fascinating burlesque
actress in the land. "[56] Next to Ada Clare, there was no
woman so dearly loved by the coterie of Pfaff's.

Clapp discussed the leading comedians of his age in
the Leader for August 27, 1864. John S. Clarke, William
E. Burton, and Joseph Jefferson he selected as the finest
actors in their lines. Burton he thought the greatest of the
three: "He was more a broad comedian rather than low
comedian. He was broad or nothing. There was infinite fun

in him, but it all ran in one direction and would hardly bear
analysis. He was funny and broad not through study or design but because he couldn't help it. He had only to show
his person to convulse the house. " Clapp ranked Jefferson
as having no equal as an eccentric low comedian: "Genuine
humor he has very little of; but he has a fine sense of the
ludicrous, and in grotesque parts, whether in comedy, farce,
or extravaganza, is really great. " Clarke was neither a low
comedian nor an eccentric comedian, but a combination of
both: "It would be folly to call him as good an actor as Jefferson, while to call either of them as good as Burton would
be sheer nonsense.... He has a great deal of genuine humor, only he is a little afraid to let it loose. His great difficulty is that he thinks too much of elaborating certain specific points. He seems to have the rare fault of studying too
much. His performances smell of the lamp. Moreover, his
sketches are unnecessarily filled out, and consequently fail
in suggestiveness. They always impress his audiences with
the idea that he has done his utmost. These, however, are
good faults, and in time will disappear. Like Jefferson, his
success, thus far, has been in grotesque parts, but he has a
fund of pathos and sentiment which can hardly fail to make
him succeed, if he has a chance, in much higher roles. "
Clapp's detailed comments about these actors provide a clearer picture of their acting methods.

The coterie which Clapp had assembled in the 1850s
began to disintegrate in the early 1860s. Ned Wilkins and a
young Philadelphia journalist, Harry Neill, died in 1861;
Fitz-James O'Brien followed in 1862; Frank Wood, the first
editor of Vanity Fair, joined Wilkins, Neill, and O'Brien in
1864; and George Arnold, Clapp's closest friend and protégé,
passed from the scene in 1865. A poet and journalist, Arnold had briefly replaced him as dramatic feuilletonist of the
Leader from December 12, 1863 to January 23, 1864, when
he wrote a gossip column for the same paper. They shared
a common faith in Fourierism. Arnold was best known for
his "McArone Papers" in Vanity Fair and the Leader which
satirized the reporting of war correspondents during the Civil
War. [57] Clapp's rapid decline in health dates from Arnold's
death.

In 1864 Henry Clapp together with Stephen Fiske edited
the Leader for a period of time after the death of John Glan-
cy, editor and proprietor. A quarrel with Fiske (whom he
disliked) over editorial policy resulted in "figaro" moving his
dramatic column to the New York Weekly Review from Janu-

ary to July, 1865. Edited by Charles B. Seymour and published by Theodore Hagen, the Weekly Review aimed to be a quality literary and critical paper.[58] This was the most prosperous period of Clapp's journalistic career; with the end of the Civil War, he was encouraged to resurrect the Saturday Press.

This paper stopped in 1860 "for want of means," he wrote in his first post-war issue on August 5, 1865; it is revived "for the same reason." The new Press lacked the vitality and brilliance of the pre-war version, however, and never recaptured the interest of the literary world. The sparkling wit of O'Brien and Wilkins might have brought the paper to life had they been alive. William Winter might have given credibility to the publication but he had established himself during the war as a critic for the Albion--a British weekly published in this country--and as literary editor of the New York Weekly Review. And in August 1865, he was beginning his career as theatre critic for the New York Tribune. Ada Clare contributed infrequently to the new Press as she was pursuing an acting career; her place was filled by Olive Logan. Clapp, himself, wrote the dramatic feuilleton from August 5 until November 4, after which Charles B. Seymour (C. B. S.) replaced him for a few weeks. Born in England, Seymour had established his reputation as musical and dramatic editor of the New York Times. William Winter described his style as "tingled with playful humor and ... felicitous with lightness of touch."[59] His easy and graceful style, however, did not long replace the wit and satire of Clapp. On January 6, 1866, the Saturday Press editor resumed writing the dramatic feuilleton. He would be the paper's last theatre critic; it folded six months later.

Henry Clapp, Jr. attempted to organize other journalistic ventures. He wrote to James Russell Lowell on October 10, 1865, "I have many serious things to say on all sorts of topics but they must not be put in a serious form." He wished to start a comic paper, but rejected the idea of a comic paper which had no other purpose "beyond raising a guffaw." He proposed founding a paper called "The Clown" in which "under the most grotesque forms I might set forth the gravest things which can well occupy the human mind."[60]

The Saturday Press ceased to exist after its June 2, 1866 issue. In a letter to William Winter on June 7, Clapp admitted he had made a mistake in re-commencing it and contemplated how he would make a living: "If I can, I shall

go abroad as London or Paris correspondent. Meanwhile, I
may think of some fugitive trifles to write which I shall offer to the Tribune or Times. Also there is always a chance
to do something for Harper. However, nothing has taken a
definite form in my mind, as the death of the S. P. incapa-
citates me for the moment to think of ought else. "[61]

After the debacle of his second attempt to start a
literary weekly, Clapp took a government job at the City Hall
in New York City. In a letter to Thomas Bailey Aldrich on
October 1, 1867, he confessed to giving up literature and
letters as "a bad job." But he had kept informed about the
activities of his Bohemians, noting with pride the success of
William Winter as drama critic of the Tribune and of Mrs.
Winter as a member of Wallack's stock company. He mentioned in his letter that Seymour was in Europe and had married; that Walt Whitman had dropped by to see him; and that
Ada Clare was in Albany "looking lovelier than ever. "[62] His
stint as a bureaucrat, however, was short-lived. On December 7, 1867, he was back at work on the Leader. For the
next two years he wrote the dramatic feuilleton, although his
periods of absenteeism grew more frequent. By 1869 Clapp
had ceased to be a force in New York journalism.

The next few years he lived in a farm house at what
had been the Fourier Phalanx at Red Bank, New Jersey. [63]
He intermittently contributed to the Leader and to the New
York Daily Graphic. Winter describes these years as
"frought with terrible suffering. After the failure of all his
hopes and ambitions, when he had become entirely embittered with the world, broken-hearted by failure, conscious
of his own shortcomings, of the defects that had ruined him,
he took to drink. "[64] According to Winter, Theodore Hagen,
editor of Weekly Review, took Clapp into his home; after he
left, Hagen found empty vials of chloral. In his Garrets and
Pretenders, Albert Parry writes, "there was something So-
cratic in the Henry Clapp of the closing years. The few
friends who understood him supplied him with money to buy
drinks. Herr Pfaff fed him gratis.... George Hall, Mayor
of Brooklyn, printer and temperance worker, sent him several times to the Binghamton Inebriate Asylum, but to no
avail. "[65] In May 1874, Clapp committed himself to the New
York City Asylum on Wards Island. In a letter to E. C.
Stedman on May 14, 1874, he explained that "I had myself
sent up here to get cleansed in the body ... and clothed in
my right mind. Somehow or other, tho' I was dirty as a
pig, and full not only of alcohol but of vermin, (thousands,

literally of these last)."[66] He asked Stedman to send him a
"few dollars to buy tobacco, pipes, newspapers (for I shall
have leisure to continue my contribution to the Graphic),
postage stamps, paper collars etc." And he added, "You
will make me a happier man than I have been for years,
thought I am in a lunatic asylum." Stedman sent the gar-
ments; on May 22, Clapp wrote to thank him and noted that
his health had improved "wonderfully" and he had almost
kicked the habit.[67] He wrote again to Stedman on May 31,
admitting that his situation was not an honorable one but "I
grin and bear it."[68]

When he died on April 2, 1875, the press turned his
obituary into a moral and temperance lecture. The New
York Times on April 11 called his writings "spicy and attractive" but his judgment indifferent. The Daily Graphic of
April 16 asserted that the old Bohemian's life ought to be a
warning for anyone romanticizing the Pfaffian life style:
"From temperance lectures and Sunday-school teaching to
beggary, loneliness, and degradation is a stride that no man
can take without knowing the keen misery of mourning over a
wasted life."[69] Yet, William Winter thought he had rendered
a great service to literature and art. With Stephen Fiske,
Charles Delmonico, George H. Butler, and George S.
McWalters--all friends of Clapp--Winter organized the funeral
and helped defray the cost of removing his body to Nantucket
for burial. Winter wrote an epitaph for a monument which
was never erected.[70]

Clapp's death signalled the end of an era. Of the
poets, critics, and journalists who had joined him at Pfaff's
in 1858 almost all were dead. Ada Clare preceded Clapp in
death by one year. After an unsuccessful career as an actress and writer, and after several scandalous love affairs,
in 1868 she married J. F. Noyes, an actor. While this relationship appears to have brought Ada Clare some measure
of happiness, her death was as tragic as Clapp's. Bitten by
a dog on January 30, 1874, she contracted rabies and died
on March 4. Walt Whitman wrote to a friend, "Poor, poor
Ada Clare--I have been inexpressibly shocked by the horrible
and sudden close of her gay, easy, sunny, free, loose, but
not ungood life."[71]

Writing much later about the Bohemians, William Dean
Howells thought that Henry Clapp had mellowed in his last
years: "I have the feeling that he too came to own before he
died that man cannot live by snapping-turtle alone."[72] While

despondent about his condition during his last years, there is no evidence that Clapp relented for a moment his savage attack upon elitism which dominated official culture in Victorian America.

In 1859 Henry Clapp described the French people in a manner befitting his own epitaph: "They seemed to me alternately the gayest and the saddest, the most profound and the most superficial, the most religious and the most sceptical, the most humane and the most unfeeling, the bravest and the most cowardly, the most polished and the most vulgar, the cleanest and the dirtiest, the best and the worst of all civilized people. "[73]

Clapp resented the worship of tradition and puritanism which permeated mid-nineteenth century American culture. Influenced by his contacts with the French during the 1840s and 1850s, he advocated reform. He inspired an entire generation of writers, many of whom were dramatic critics. But the disruption of the country by the Civil War, the early deaths of his most talented followers, and his own tragic decline reduced his influence. He remains known today as the founder of America's first Bohemia.

CHAPTER THREE

Edward G. P. Wilkins
"personne"

Henry Clapp described Edward G. P. Wilkins as "the
most brilliant of all our dramatic critics" in the period before the Civil War. This position, Clapp pointed out, was
"universally conceded to him."[1] Most of his contemporaries,
including William Winter and Franklin J. Ottarson (Bayard),
agreed with this assessment.[2] In the 1850s, Wilkins established his reputation by writing for Bennett's Herald, and
chic periodicals Harper's Weekly and Clapp's Saturday Press.
In contrast to the serious prose offered by most of his colleagues, Wilkins wrote in a style lightly satirical--similar to
that of the French critic, Jules Janin. He was widely imitated, not only in New York but throughout the country. His
death on May 5, 1861 cut short a very promising career.

Born in Boston on November 11, 1829, Wilkins, like
Clapp and Winter, grew up in the "Athens" of America. He
was the son of a baker. His parents, James and Lydia Wilkins, were of modest means in a household which included
four sons and at least one daughter.[3] Wilkins learned the
trade of a printer before entering the field of journalism, an
apprenticeship in common with many of his contemporaries.
He contributed sketches entitled "Our Ned" to the Spirit of
the Times and wrote the local news for the Boston Daily
Times in 1850-1851.[4] A sensational newspaper, the Daily
Times followed the lead of Bennett's New York Herald in
exploiting the more morbid aspects of the news to increase
circulation.

Wilkins claimed to have attended Columbia University.[5]
Records at Columbia do not support this claim.[6] It is almost
certain that financial conditions in the Wilkins home would
have prevented him from attending college. In his writings,

he also alluded to travel abroad--to Paris and Versailles. While this may have occurred after he left Boston, no hard evidence has surfaced to prove the point either way. Wilkins was fluent in French. William Winter later recalled that he read Montaigne in the original. [7] Whether he lived in Paris, studied the language in school, or learned it on his own is uncertain. A liberal use of French bon mots was in vogue for fashionable writers during the 1850s, so Wilkins had good reason to learn French if he wished to succeed as a journalist. Apparently, he was self-educated. He had a broad knowledge of literature, drama, and music. Winter noted that he enjoyed the later poems of Whittier and the writings of Carlyle. Clapp thought his favorite authors were Thackeray and Dickens. Bennett found his musical tastes developed enough to appoint him music critic for the Herald.

While there is but scant information about Wilkins' early life, he grew up in the midst of the literary and art capital of this country. He could have attended some of the finest concerts and theatre in America. The Tremont offered first class theatrical fare in the 1830s. The establishment of the Boston Museum in the 1840s with a first rate stock company managed by William H. Smith brought to pious Bostonians both classical and modern plays--works by Shakespeare, Sheridan, Knowles, Bulwer-Lytton, and Boucicault. Smith's temperance melodrama, The Drunkard, or the Fallen Saved, opened at the Museum on February 25, 1844, for a run of over one hundred performances, a record for any play at this time. Guest appearances by established stars such as George Vandenhoff, Junius B. Booth, E. L. Davenport, and Mr. and Mrs. James Wallack, Jr. assured audiences of quality acting. Wilkins may have viewed Edwin Booth's stage debut at the Boston Museum on September 10, 1849, when he portrayed Tressel to his father's Richard III.

Wilkins acquired an early interest in theatre. In a Leader article of 1860, he recalled acting in an amateur production to raise money for Ayling, a local theatre manager: "The subscriber was stage manager; and, in casting the pieces, took the smallest parts, in order to give the others who were more ambitious than I, a fair chance. One of the characters which I 'embodied,' on this occasion was the flunkey in 'A Pleasant Neighbor,' and I played it well. "[8] Probably he played other roles but there is no further reference to his "acting" career.

Wilkins moved from Boston to New York in early 1853,

after accepting a position as reporter with the New York
Herald. He gained the attention of his superiors by writing
a vivid account of the New York Crystal Palace Exhibition.
The Exhibition's name and concept were borrowed from London's first industrial fair which had opened in 1851. Built
at the corner of Sixth Avenue and Forty-second Street, the
Crystal Palace covered five acres. Constructed of glass and
steel, it resembled, according to T. Allston Brown, "a half-
disclosed balloon, as large as a cathedral."[9] For the grand
opening on July 14, 1853, President Franklin Pierce, a
crowd of over 20,000 persons, military bands, a grand
chorus, and the Herald reporter were present.[10] William
Winter credits Wilkins' "excellent account" of this exhibition
for his rapid advancement by Bennett to editorial writer,
and musical and dramatic critic.[11]

His association with Henry Clapp began in 1855 or
1856, shortly after Clapp's return from Paris. He was a
charter member of the old Bohemian's group at Pfaff's. He
also joined Fitz-James O'Brien, John Brougham, and the actor Mark Smith in 1856 to form a select club for actors,
writers, and artists.[12] Called "The Bees," the club met
regularly for dinner and conversation. The group came to be
feared by theatrical managers because of their clever ridicule
of plays. Wilkins, together with O'Brien and Smith, also
joined Theta Delta Chi Fraternity. He claimed to have graduated from Columbia University, which made him eligible for
membership in a graduate chapter.[13]

The character of Wilkins is difficult to ascertain: he
died before much was written about him. According to his
friends, he was a strikingly handsome man. In 1865 George
Arnold remembered him in vivid detail: "His complexion was
light; his eyes were intensely blue and expressive, sometimes
twinkling with plenitude of merriment. His features were
sharply cut, and thorough-bred in mould; his skin, clear and
delicate; his hair, which he parted nearly in the middle of a
high forehead, was lustrous and wavy; and his mouth was
partly concealed by a well-grown and becoming mustache,
golden brown in color, and remarkably fine in texture. His
hands were long, thin, and delicate as a girl's. His dress
was always unexceptionable no matter what the occasion or
the season, though his preference was generally for loose,
rough, easy styles, which became him wonderfully."[14] William Winter remembered him in 1909 as being slightly deaf but
still an attractive man with a delicate constitution and fine
features.[15] Thanks to Mme. Cora de Wilhorst, a wealthy

socialite and aspiring opera singer, Wilkins polished his manners and made the acquaintance of New York's young fashionable set--a social group he would satirize in much of his writing.

The daughter of Reuben Withers, a wealthy bank cashier and member of Fifth Avenue society, Cora provided Wilkins with an introduction into high society. She was an attractive woman. The New York Evening Post of January 31, 1857 described her as a "pretty little lady of some twenty-four summers, with a fresh color, black hair and eyes, and an unmistakable air of self-possession and aplomb." She pursued a singing career after marrying her music teacher, M. de Wilhorst, against her father's wishes. Then she made her professional debut in Lucia di Lammermoor at the Academy of Music in January 1857. After studying abroad for a year she joined Maurice Strakosch's American Company. Wilkins became her strongest supporter. William Winter mentions their personal relationship in his book, Old Friends.

Wilkins was also a prolific journalist. Besides writing the dramatic and musical criticism for the Herald, he also contributed to the editorial page. According to his obituary in the Herald, May 6, 1861, "His versatility was such that there were few topics upon which he could not write fluently, forcibly, and suggestively." George Arnold described Wilkins as an "undefatigable worker" who "rose at six in the morning, and wrote till breakfast-time,--between nine and ten. With the product of this healthy fresh, early-morning labor in his pocket, he could breakfast with elegant idleness, and saunter down town as if time-killing were his only object in life. In the Herald office he usually wrote something more, and returned home to dine at dusk, with nothing to think of until the theatres opened, when he went about from one to the other, wherever there was anything new going on, making mental notes for the amusement paragraphs which he usually wrote immediately on going home, and sent to the paper by a messenger."[16] While such a schedule might have occupied a less able man, Wilkins found time to serve as a correspondent for the London Morning Chronicle and for the New Orleans Crescent. From November 7, 1857 to April 3, 1858, he contributed a column, "Bohemian Walks and Talks," to Harper's Weekly under a pseudonym "Bohemien." And from February 5, 1859 until May 12, 1860, he wrote dramatic feuilletons for the Saturday Press under the name of "Personne." After covering the

Republican Convention in Chicago for the Herald in May 1860,
he again used "Personne" for the New York Leader. An organ of the Democratic Party, the Leader carried his column
beginning June 2, 1860. At the time of his death, Wilkins
was writing for the Herald and the Leader.

There are several obstacles to evaluating his dramatic
writings for the Herald. James Gordon Bennett, the elder,
like other powerful editors of the period, exercised dictatorial
control over his paper and allowed no by-lines by his staff.
While Wilkins was dramatic editor and major critic for eight
years (1853-1861), it is doubtful if he wrote every review
that appeared in the Herald. Stephen Ryder Fiske, who followed him as Herald dramatic critic, also suggests that he
may not have attended all the productions he reviewed. Fiske
recalled an occasion when Wilkins had to "look after" two
performances in one evening. He attended a new play at
Wallack's Theatre and wrote up Forrest's performance at the
Broadway Theatre from a playbill. Unfortunately, Forrest
did not play that evening.[17] Such practices were common in
the 1850s because editors did not regard theatre as an art
worthy of knowledgeable criticism. Frequently they assigned
untrained reporters to cover the opening of a play as they
would a murder, fire, rape, or social event. Such reporters
were journalists first and critics last. The event was more
important than its quality.

The known prejudices of Bennett provide other obstacles to considering Wilkins' standards and tastes. F. J.
Ottarson, city editor of the New York Tribune and dramatic
writer (Bayard) for Wilkes' Spirit of the Times, thought that
Bennett exerted considerable influence over his dramatic
critic: "While the responsible Rhadamanthus of a daily newspaper, he [Wilkins] was generally reserved and cautious; it
seemed that he was under some restraint by a higher power
that forbade the free utterance of his convictions."[18] The
Herald editor held strong opinions about every subject, and
no reporter or critic dared challenge his authority. For example, he considered it his patriotic duty to defend American
principles and personages when in conflict with those of Great
Britain. Consequently, he took sides against Macready and
for Edwin Forrest during the Astor Place Riots in 1849.
Throughout the 1850s, Forrest received strong support from
the Herald; at the same time a definite anti-British bias is
evident on both the editorial and dramatic pages. For instance, when English actor James R. Anderson returned to
New York in 1853 after five seasons on the London stage,

the New York Herald of October 23 asked why, when he managed
the Drury Lane Theatre, had he allowed visiting American actors
to be called "Her Majesty's Servants"? And by suggesting that
Anderson was too much like Macready in style, the paper
sought to discredit him with New Yorkers who had sided
against the English star during the Astor Place incident of
1849. In addition to his anti-British prejudices, Bennett
maintained a pro-Southern attitude until the outbreak of the
Civil War. Neither in the dramatic column nor on the editorial page were plays such as Uncle Tom's Cabin and Boucicault's The Octoroon favorably received.

While we must tip-toe carefully through the Herald
files to find the real Wilkins, we have both internal and ex-
ternal evidence to assist our search. His penchant for
French words, his favorite expressions (e. g. , "dry goods, "
"vigor, " "Peoria, " "good gracious"), his cynical wit, and
his smooth and urbane style are helpful in identifying him as
the probable author of editorials about the theatre as well as
reviews. And his known writings for periodicals--Harper's
Weekly, Saturday Press, Leader--provide a more reliable
guide to his tastes and standards. Contemporary evidence
suggests that while his opinions in the Herald were filtered
through Bennett's office, he had free rein in the periodicals.
In commenting on the subject in 1861, Henry Clapp noted that
"On the dailies a writer is not so much himself as the paper's--and the paper is generally stupid, and never sincere. "19

Employment on Bennett's Herald meant that Wilkins
would be read by more people than any other dramatic critic
in New York. The paper provided lengthy columns of theatrical news, readable reviews, and occasionally an editorial
discussing, for example, a performance of Edwin Forrest's
at Niblo's, the opening of Laura Keene's new theatre, or the
controversy over Dion Boucicault's The Octoroon. The scandalous reputation of the paper, however, meant that the reader might not be among the social and intellectual elite. Mott
describes the Herald as the most controversial newspaper of
the period: "Its columns sparkled. Everything was personal-
ized. Wit supplanted dignity; recklessness took the place of
conservatism. Objective reporting suffered and news reports
were editorized. "20 The paper "came to be thought of as
'spicy' and 'saucy. ' " The cultured classes did not profess
to read it. Writing for Harper's Weekly and Saturday Press,
therefore, offered Wilkins an important opportunity to get his
work before the chic crowd. His "Bohemian Walks and

Talks" in Harper's combines society gossip and theatrical
chit-chat in an amusing style much like George W.
Curtis's "Lounger" column in the same publication. He introduced
into his weekly essay a society belle, Ethelinda, who is
called upon from time to time for her opinion about the
latest fashion or play. For instance, in the November 28,
1857 "Bohemian Walks and Talks," Ethelinda describes The
Maiden Wife: or, Romance After Marriage, the new comedy
at Wallack's:

> In the beginning there's a wedding with illuminated
> gardens, and all that sort of thing very nice. Er-
> nest, that's Mr. Lester (what nice dress-coats he
> does have to be sure!) is the bridegroom, and
> Louise (that's Miss Stevens--who has a bad figure
> and dresses horridly, besides being nearly frightened
> to death, poor thing!)--Louise, like a little fool,
> has gone and fallen in love with her husband, and
> has built all sorts of chateaux en Espagne about
> their wedded life. Her sister, that's Mrs. Hoey
> (I wonder what she would be without crinoline?),
> says that marriage is a rascally invention (that's
> because she wasn't married), and how she believes
> that Ernest will turn out to be a humbug after all.

After relating the plot for Act One, Ethelinda points out that
the second act is "nice too" but "hasn't anything to do with
the first that I could see." Of course Wilkins regarded The
Maiden Wife as a silly comedy and ridiculed it through the
observations of his hair-brained fictitious companion.

"Bohemien" contributed numerous light and satirical
articles to Harper's Weekly. He commented upon clothes,
walking in the park, the disgrace of the American kitchen,
the effect of the new copyright law (1956), deadheads at the
opera, Bohemians at Thanksgiving, and Mrs. Frances Anne
Kemble's readings from Shakespeare. On November 21,
1857, his "Bohemian Walks and Talks" suggested that "The
important questions of ethnology, philosophy, physiology, and
other ologies, which are settled by this little paragraph,
have puzzled the savants for centuries. The difference is
all in clothes. Hereafter let no man sneer at young Fastboy
because he adorns himself with gay waistcoats and stunning
trowsers, or make sarcastic remarks at Ethelinda's crinoline.
They are important agents in bringing about the civilization of
the nineteenth century; and it is a logical conclusion that if
we could all have such waistcoats and trowsers, and skirts,

the world would rise to a pitch of civilization heretofore unknown. " "Bohemian Walks and Talks, " while of ephemeral
value, is entertaining to read, even today.

Wilkins' dramatic essays for the Saturday Press and
the Leader are similar in style to his Harper's Weekly writings. Now signing his reviews "Personne" and calling them
dramatic feuilletons, Wilkins became the "desire and the
dread of the profession. " "He was the oracle for whose
lightest syllable the scribbling tribe trembled in expectation, "
Ottarson suggested, "and whose nod decided the fate of plays
and players as that of Jupiter does the fate of greater affairs
among the gods. "[21] Such a statement seems an exaggeration.
No critic had that much power in the 1850s and 1860s.   But
a number of writers took their cue from Wilkins; thus his influence transcended his own reviews.   Ottarson concluded that
Henry Clapp allowed his critic "full independence in expression as well as in thought. "

William Winter credited Wilkins with introducing to
this country the French dramatic feuilleton.   Henry Clapp,
who thought he had imported it himself, naturally disagreed.
He argued that Wilkins was more Yankee than French and
chided those who compared him with Jules Janin.   An editorial
(almost certainly by Clapp) in the Leader of May 11, 1861
called Wilkins' literary style "as purely American as Jack
Downing's Letters, or the Bigelow Papers, both of which, by
the way, he greatly admired.   French literature he neither
imitated nor to any great extent studied. "   The editorial drew
the conclusion that Wilkins' style resembled Jules Janin's
"about as much as Burgundy resembles Champagne.   They had
a depth and richness of humor in them which the French
feuilletonist never approached--never even attempted. "

Despite such statements, Wilkins knew Janin's work and
borrowed from it.   He mentioned Janin frequently in the
Herald; and according to Spirit of the Times, May 25, 1861,
he "did on more than one occasion admit that it was from
reading the little Frenchman's gossipy lucubrations while so-
journing in Paris, that he first conceived the idea of doing
them in New York. "   The same writer remembered that Wilkins had often "confessed to a great appreciation of Janin's
talents and style. "   Yet Clapp made a strong case for the originality of Wilkins' style: "The secret of Wilkins' wit was its
homeliness--its common sense--its nack of hitting the nail on
the head.   It made you exclaim not 'how smart!' but 'how
true. ' You always felt as if you might have said the same

thing yourself--if you had only thought of it. And so you might. When he described Jersey City as 'a place where people go to see other people off to Europe,' he uttered a piece of satire which might indeed have occurred to any of us--only it didn't." We might conclude that Wilkins adapted the feuilleton to his own style, and made it more satirical than the French. But like Janin he frequently digressed from the subject. He called "old-fashioned" people who "still cling to the absurd idea that when a man commences to write about a special subject, he ought to adhere to it, and not sail off into the quagmires of digression."22

For his Saturday Press feuilleton, Wilkins created another society belle to comment upon fashionable events: Anna Maria, daughter of a New York banker and a member of Fifth Avenue society. This persona supplied him with memorable opinions on serious matters of taste. Her letter in the June 4, 1859 Saturday Press, suggests the target of much of Wilkins' satire. It is addressed to "Mon cher Redacteur."

> But, oh! if you won't take and put it in your paper, I'll tell you something that Personne nor none of those men [writers] know, because Charles Henry ['that's the young man Pa just got into the bank, and he's been to Paris'] says that literary people ain't asked out anywhere of any consequence. Well, it's about Miss T____n that was, and the Countess Blank she is now. Don't you know she was maid of honor--no, dame d'honneur, that's it--to the Empress, and was the handsomest of all of them, so they say; and her picture is in the one that what's his name--something about Winter--painted. Well, she is going to sing at the Academy in the Puritani, for the thing they are going to have for the French, or the Austrians, or somebody that's going to war, or been, or something. And it's going to be real nice, and all the people in society are in it, and the men that write for the papers ain't to have anything to do with it. How will Mr. Personne like that, I'd like to know?
> Now I must stop, because here comes that awful Manzocchi, and he asks two dollars a lesson, and Ma says I can't do anything in music, because I talk all the time, and don't get the money's worth.

Anna Maria signed her letter "Votre bien dévouée" and "Tout-à-vous."

While Anna Maria's letters cleverly satirized the so-cial climbing nouveaux riches of Fifth Avenue, they also ridiculed society journalism, which Bennett had perfected in the Herald. In the 1830s, the editor realized before any of his colleagues the widespread interest in the comings and goings of New York's "better families." He wrote on March 17, 1837: "No one ever attempted till now to bring out the graces, the polish, the elegancies, the bright and airy at-tributes of social life."[23] To add an air of mystery and ex-citement to such news, Bennett would print only the first and last letters of the names, separated by dashes. Willard Grosvenor Bleyer, in his history of American journalism, notes that "However little New York society may have relished having their receptions and balls described in the tasteless manner in which the Herald treated such events, they feared to incur the displeasure of an editor who had it in his power to abuse and ridicule them if they refused him or his re-porters admittance to these affairs."[24] Anna Maria alludes to much of this in her letters. Personne offered additional society gossip in an occasional essay from Saratoga or New-port--the summer watering holes of the rich.

Wilkens' terse and epigrammatic style distinguishes his dramatic feuilletons from those of his contemporaries. Note his verve and wit in commemorating the opening of the Winter Garden Theatre in September, 1859:

> The Event has eventuated.
> The Winter Garden is open.
> Le Chauve absolutely radiates with triumph.
> The Oldest Man [Clapp] likes it.
> I like it.
> It is a success. Grand, veritable, extraordinary
>   success.
> Without doubt, the dollar-crop in the Winter Garden
>   will be equal to the cotton-crop in Texas.[25]

This is "hot criticism" meant to provide impressions of an event--not to analyze it in any depth.

Numerous parodies of his style attested to his influ-ence. After viewing Wilkins' play Henriette, Winter wrote in the Albion of February 14, 1863:

> I went to see the play.
> I liked it.
> Afterward I went to the Green Room and drank beer.

> I liked that too.
> The play and the beer had much in common.   They
>   were amber-coloured, frothy, exhilarating. --

By cutting his copy into short paragraphs, Winter teased, he could also sparkle in the French style.

Forty-six years later Winter would observe: "Many writers of this period are, --without being aware of it, --following an example that was set by him [Wilkins]; writing about the stage and society in a facetious, satirical vein, striving to lighten heavy or barren themes with playful banter, and to gild the dreariness of criticism with the glitter of wit.   Wilkins not only attempted that task, but he accomplished it."[26]   Such statements are difficult to confirm. The proliferation of newspaper criticism led writers to adapt a light and gossipy tone.   That Wilkins first made such a style popular may not mean he unduly influenced the course of events which followed.   There is no hard evidence either way.

Wilkins was a playwright of some reputation.   Frank Bellew, a graphic artist and fellow Pfaffian, included him with Brougham, Boucicault, Cornelius Mathews, Charles Gayler, Fitz-James O'Brien, and Benjamin A. Baker in a Picayune cartoon (September 20, 1856) depicting playwrights registering their dramatic works before the first copyright law went into effect.   His first dramatic effort, a one-act sketch entitled My Wife's Mirror, opened at Laura Keene's Varieties, May 10, 1856, to favorable reviews.   Stuffed with topical allusions, the piece dramatized the marriage difficulties of Mrs. Racket (played by Laura Keene) in coping with the tastes of her husband (played by George Jordon), a gambler, gourmand, duelist, and man-about-town.   She resolves to make herself a mirror of his defects in order that he will become disgusted with his life and reform.   The play delighted an opening night audience with its playful satire on New York society.   Mrs. Racket reads in "The Legend of the Devil's Mirror" that Satan lives at City Hall; and that Beelzebub has been admitted into the very best of society and is being cultivated by Brown.[27]   The characters are all types: Mr. Racket, Mr. Peaceable, Mrs. Racket, Mrs. Torpedo, and Mr. Vingt-un.   Mrs. Torpedo is the widow of Colonel Torpedo of the 1st Utah Dragoons.   In Scene Two she defends her late husband's profession: "I like to cultivate a taste for the militia.   It preserves the public peace, and makes Broadway look pretty--sets up target companies, en-

courages the plated cake-basket trade, and is the best school
of the soldier...." The New York Times of May 13 described My Wife's Mirror as a bright little piece which
avoided such clichés of fashionable plays as "monstrous par-
venues in fifth-avenue drinking blacking for claret, or British
bricklayers mistaken for Neapolitan Princes." The production ran for two weeks without a break, attesting to its popularity.

Wilkins followed this minor success with his first full-
length play, Young New York, which opened at Laura Keene's
new theatre on November 24, 1856. Like his earlier dramatic sketch, Young New York also depicted the foibles of New
York society. The plot is roughly based upon Cora de Wilhorst's marriage. The Ten-Per-Cents (New York million-
aires and society types) want their daughter Rose to marry a
wealthy fashionable clergyman, the Reverend Needham Crawl.
She rejects Crawl, however, for an itinerant Count Signor
Patrici Skibberini, her music teacher, and first tenor of the
Italian opera. Disowned by her family, who chase away her
husband, Rose makes her living by sewing and giving successful concerts. Meanwhile, her father is persuaded by the
Reverend Crawl to run for Congress. Not only is he de-
feated, but he loses his fortune. One day he discovers that
Rose is giving a concert and attends. Her singing softens
his heart and reconciles the family. Rose gives a curtain
speech which asks that "the rich are not to be censured by
the poor for being rich, nor the poor by the rich for being
poor; but that every man and woman is to be tried by the
standard of their acts alone; and upon them is to stand or
fall."[28] A fine cast was headed by Laura Keene, who played
Rose.

Once again, Wilkins satirized the social-climbing Fifth
Avenue crowd. Mr. Ten-Per-Cent complains about the customs of the rich: "Fashion keeps us out of our comfortable
homes three months in the year, and sends us here to Saratoga, where we pay two hundred dollars a week, for a dog-
kennel, which they call a parlor, and three dry-goods boxes,
impudently termed bed-rooms; get nothing to eat--drive over
dusty roads--and drink water, flavored with old iron, boot-
heels and brimstone--bah!" Mrs. Ten-Per-Cent is addicted
to "fashionable society and four parties a week." A son,
Adolphus Washington, wants "billiards, brandy and water, and
the corps' De Ballet." The Reverend Crawl needs "Bible Societies, religious anniversaries, Christian Associations, Oxford Prayer Books, and two per cent per month; with one eye

in Wall Street and the other on Grace Church." Wilkins
lampooned politicians, intellectuals (from Boston), Italian
tenors and the theatre profession. In Act III, Nutgalls, editor
of the Daily Scorcher, and Mr. Airy Froth, "an ex-politician,
ex-diplomatist, ex-musical agent, ex-journalist, ex-artist,"
discuss the tour of actress, Miss Pauline De Vernon, Cide-
vant Jenkins.

> FROTH: Went out West with the tremendous
> American actress, Miss Pauline De Vernon, Cide-
> vant Jenkins. Went to Albany, Chicago, Buffalo,
> and lots of high old places. De Vernon is a great
> card for circus business-rolls herself up in the
> American flag, and all that sort of thing. I believe
> she would have stood on her head, if it hadn't been
> against the law. When she dies, tumbles all over
> the stage; sometimes dies five or six times. Im-
> mense creature, but she didn't pay.
> NUTGALLS: Why? didn't you do all your infal-
> lible dodges?
> FROTH: Yes, everything: had long extracts out
> of the New York papers--advertising columns--asked
> all the country editors to drink, and the cleanest of
> them to dinner; illuminated the theatre on the bene-
> fit night; set off twenty shillings worth of rockets;
> got up a romantic story about her early history and
> trials (she ought to be tried for getting people's
> money on false pretences); had the same set of dia-
> monds (California ones, from the original Jacobs),
> presented to her in seven cities, by seven different
> public spirited citizens; serenaded by six amateur
> brass bands; twelve four shilling bouquets every
> night; two complementary benefits, tendered by the
> Mayor and principal nobs of each one horse town,
> every week--but it wasn't a go.
> NUTGALLS: (Laughing) No? Why not? If
> there's any virtue in humbug, all that ought to suc-
> ceed.
> FROTH: There is virtue in humbug, my boy,
> but you must have something to work on. That
> French joker, who made fifteen different kinds of
> soup out of an old boot, had to have the boot to do
> it with. We 'busted,' simply because the Vernon,
> née Jenkins, though a very neat washerwoman,
> hadn't the slightest talent for the stage. I couldn't
> make the soup, because I didn't have the boot.

The New York Times thought the objective of Young New
York was to convince parents of the "impropriety of bringing
up their children in an extravagant and useless way. "[29]
The same reviewer praised the piece as "agreeable ... per-
fectly local, and perfectly up to the moment. " Young New
York was Wilkins' most successful original dramatic work.

Not everyone found the play agreeable. A letter to
the Editors of the Atlas (November 30, 1856) complained
that the writers of "these local plays" have no actual knowledge of the upper classes; thus, their presentation of
fashionable frailties and follies are purely imaginary. The
letter also complained that the excessive slang and lack of
a moral made these plays poor models. The critic of the
Atlas found the plot "flimsy" but the satire excellent.

An American comedy of manners, Young New York
belongs in a class with Ann Cora Mowatt's Fashion (1845)
and Mrs. Sidney F. Bateman's Self (1856). Mrs. Mowatt
intended the former as a "good-natured satire upon some of
the foibles incident to a new country where foreign dross
sometimes passes for gold. "[30] Her Mrs. Tiffany worships
everything foreign, particularly French titles. Mrs. Bateman's comedy is intended as a satire upon extravagant ex-
penditure thought characteristic of wealthy persons. Her
Mrs. Apex spends money to keep up with fashion, causing
Mr. Apex financial difficulties. A daughter, Mary Apex, and
a kind old Godfather help straighten out the family problems.
Like these plays, Young New York offered sparkling dialogue
and clever jokes.

Wilkins' association with Laura Keene continued
through 1857. On February 21, 1857 she gave him a benefit,
playing both My Wife's Mirror and Young New York. To
open the 1857-58 season on September 28, she staged his
next dramatic piece, The Siam Light Guard. Titled a "musical and military burlesque, " the play, as adapted from the
French, depended upon the military maneuvers of the Siam
Light Guard--a company of pretty young ladies in uniform.
The piece was lively and fun with songs and dances. Wilkins
again drew upon local events to satirize the audience. Laura
Keene played the leading role of Mrs. Catchmug, with Joseph
Jefferson portraying her husband. The New York Times of
September 29 thought Jefferson's Catchmug very funny, es-
pecially his timid bashfulness when confronted with the young
ladies of Siam. His imitation of tightrope dancing also drew
praise. The Herald of the same date called the piece "good

extravaganza. " If it has a fault, the reviewer stated, "there
is too much fun in it. " Wilkins, of course, was the regular
critic and dramatic editor of the Herald. The Tribune noted
that The Siam Light Guard was well received, "with considerable approbation, " although it mentioned that there was no
call for the author. 31

The Siam Light Guard marks the end of Wilkins' professional relationship with Laura Keene. While there is no
record of a formal break in their relationship, his increased
criticism of her acting and managing indicates some disruption in what had been a mutually beneficial arrangement. He
accused her of preferring foreign to native plays because she
could obtain the former free of charge. On March 10, 1860,
he wrote in the Saturday Press that comic writers are "too
well paid elsewhere to think of writing for the theatres, the
managers of which fancy that paying money to authors is equi-
valent to throwing it out the window. " Other statements of a
similar nature during his tenure as Saturday Press critic suggest that he had not been well paid by Miss Keene for his
contributions to American comedy. An article in the Leader
for January 16, 1864 hints that she cheated him out of one
hundred dollars, but no further evidence is available.

In early 1861, Wilkins with the help of a friend translated Sardou's Les Pattes de Mouche and re-named it Henriette. It was not to Laura Keene, however, that he offered
the play. On March 27, 1861, Henriette opened at Wallack's
Theatre to favorable reviews. Both the Herald and the Times
called the production a brilliant success and commended Wilkins on his excellent adaptation. Sardou's Les Pattes de
Mouche had opened the previous year at the Porte Saint Martin Theatre in Paris, and Wilkins had worked quickly to prepare his version.

The plot turns upon the existence and discovery of a
love letter written by Rosalie Latour while a young girl to
Emile Lefevre. Emile, wounded in a duel, does not receive
it. Later, Rosalie, in obedience to her parents, marries a
jealous M. Latour. She forgets to check whether Emile has
removed her letter from a hiding place they have used as a
post office. Hearing that she has married another, Emile
does not return to her chateau. Three years later, when he
is required by his uncle to marry, he asks M. Latour for the
hand of his sister-in-law, Marianna (Rosalie's sister). At
this time he learns of the missing letter, obtains it, and
threatens Rosalie with blackmail if she does not help him win

Marianna. In despair, Rosalie confides in her old friend
Henriette (a cousin of M. Latour), who becomes involved in
a plot to steal the letter. The rest of the play is devoted
to the struggle between Emile and Henriette for possession
of the letter. After numerous complications, Emile falls in
love with Henriette and eventually marries her. [32] The letter
is destroyed and Rosalie's reputation is saved.

Although advertised as a comedy, the play, with its
multitude of improbable events, is obviously a farce. The
New York Times of March 28 described it as "one of the
best adaptations from the French which have been placed upon
our stage of late years." While pointing out that the first
act needs some judicious pruning, the Herald reviewer (Wilkins himself?) thought the comic effects kept the audience "in
a perfect gale of laughter." "The adaptation is admirably
made," the Herald continued, "the language is brilliant, and
perfectly free from slang, and all the local references and
allusions are appropriately made, and not dragged forcibly
with malice...." [33] While not an original work, Henriette
firmly established Wilkins as a clever and popular dramatist.

The play was revived on February 10, 1863 by Lester
Wallack. Mercutio (William Winter) in the Albion of February 14 called it a charming comedy of social intrigue: "It
holds the mirror up to French nature, and amuses us with
the eccentricities of a number of frivolous but not the less
interesting people." While admitting that the plot was somewhat hackneyed, Winter thought the character sketches excellent and the style of writing "vivacious, witty, and uncommon-
ly pure." The play did not distract Winter's attention by
"raising questions of naturalness, taste, or propriety." After
this revival, Les Pattes de Mouche would be known as A
Scrap of Paper and viewed in other translations.

The Tribune as well as the Herald lauded the playwright's candor in admitting that he was but the adaptor, not
the author. While such honesty was unusual for the time,
Wilkins had launched a campaign to expose what he called
"filibusters"--plagiarized scripts which kept being passed off
as original work. In the February 12, 1859 Saturday Press,
he reprimanded Laura Keene for presenting three such pieces
in one month. In order to embarrass her, he printed both
the French and English titles to what had been claimed as
original farces:

Edgar[d] et sa Bonne	Aunt Charlotte's Maid
La Saur de Jocrisse	The Bonnie Fishwife
La Fille Térrible	The Little Savage

Wilkins warned, "Filibuster as much as you please, ladies
and gentlemen; success is nothing but success. But full
houses will not buy literary reputation for borrowed
plumes. "

With his knowledge of dramatic literature and fluency
in French, Wilkins served as a self-appointed watchdog over
Gallic imports--especially if they were produced by Laura
Keene. In his feuilleton for September 3, 1859, he chided
Tom Taylor for going play-shopping in Paris: "Since last
Spring he has 'run in' no less than three invoices, one of
which is Octave Feuillet's Périls dans la Demeure, which
Mr. Taylor rechristened, The House; or the Home, and produced last April at the Adelphi. " A double crime was committed, however, when Laura Keene, "who has that intense
affection for Tom Taylor which only managers can feel
towards an author whose pieces they get for nothing, " went
shopping in London and returned with his latest "two-act
larcency. " Such dramatic fare attracts audiences from everywhere, Wilkins wrote sarcastically, especially from Peoria,
Tar River, Attakapas, and Barkhampstead.

Laura Keene was not his only target. On September
10, 1859, he pursued an argument with Charles Gayler which
had been brewing for some time over the authorship of Many
a Slip Twixt the Cup and the Lip. Gayler claimed that he
had written an original play by that title; Wilkins pointed out
the similarities between his play and a French comedy, Les
Crochets du Père Martin. Gayler, in rebuttal, noted that he
had never seen the French comedy, either on stage or in
translation; also that his own play was written much earlier
than the French piece. "If Mr. Gayler will read the analysis
of the plot of Les Crochets, printed the other day in the
Evening Post, " Wilkins teased, "he will see that the rascally
Gauls have stolen his main ideas--as I stated. "[34] Like Henry
Clapp, Wilkins understood that wit and satire are preferable
to seriousness in opposing folly.

He thought The Poor of New York an "extraordinary"
drama, but reminded his readers (and the author) that a play
which claims to be local should be original, not adapted from
"one of those curious melodramas which so delight the frequenters of the theatres on the Boulevards. "[35] Despite his

criticism of Boucicault, Wilkins considered him a major force in the American theatre: "He knows the theatre as thoroughly as any actor-manager, and has the superior advantages of education and mental cultivation." In looking over his career in 1860, Wilkins concluded that Boucicault had "entirely changed the character of the New York theatricals"; that he "ought to be canonized for breaking up the old star business, The Hunchback and Lady of Lyons style of things, which the dear public had crammed down their throats continuously for twenty years before his time."[36]

    With an eye for the sham and the false, Wilkins wrote extensively about the New York theatre. He had witnessed on numerous occasions the stage debuts of young women of society "who believe they have a call to gush in white satin or book muslin...." In the Leader of December 22, 1860, he described their short road to ruin. First a young lady appears in amateur theatricals; then she acts "very nicely" at Mrs. Dash's party. At this point she is encouraged to hire an acting teacher to prepare her for a professional debut.

    Who so good as Mr. Splutter? Splutter is an actor--Splutter is one of the old school. Splutter was a member of the old Park company, when there was a theatre in New York, sir. Splutter remembers George Frederick Cooke and Tom Cooper. Splutter is an 'elocutionist,' and would be considered a splendid actor were it not for the critics who know nothing of the drama, and who insist that Splutter's 'elocution' is all fudge, and that he macadamizes the text with the hammer of his emphasis, which, as Splutter remarks, may be blasted fine writing, but he'd be blessed if he knows what it means. However, Splutter is 'experienced.' Splutter knows where people ought to enter and exit, how they should get on and off the stage, what sort of gesture they should use when they appeal to Heaven, and all manner of other useful things.

    So Splutter shall be paid roundly to give the little girl lessons.

With the lessons underway, managers are besieged by friends and admirers of the young lady until the desired "appearance" is arranged. Critics are requested to "let the lady up lightly--she's only a woman, you know." After Splutter finishes his instruction, the young lady chooses the role for her debut. It will be Julia in The Hunchback, Juliet, or another major part "which experienced actresses approach with fear and trembling." On opening night, the debutante will have plenty of applause--her friends are in the audience. But her future is not bright. The profession considers her as an interloper. She will be sent to "Peoria" or anywhere "out West" to find engagements. Her chance of being accepted by the public is slight. "This would seem to warrant the dictum of the theatre," Wilkins concluded, "that acting is an art which must be studied earnestly and practiced diligently, and that the beginner should not attempt the highest rank by murdering the most important characters."

Wilkins' Herald, Saturday Press, Harper's Weekly, and Leader essays suggest that he was a perceptive critic of acting, capable of dissecting a role with precision, authority, and candor. Some dissatisfaction with the Forrest school of acting is evident in his September 12, 1854 Herald review of E. L. Davenport's Othello. Davenport had just returned to New York from an extended engagement in London. Wilkins praised his departure from an exaggerated style which pleased the multitude but offended finer tastes. And the critic suggested that Davenport belonged more to the French school of tragedians than to the English.

He was impressed with Mlle. Rachel's acting the following year. The celebrated French actress visited New York in September and opened her engagement on the 4th with Camille in Corneille's tragedy, Horace. Wilkins praised her performance as the "only piece of great acting" that he had ever seen. "She did not seem to endeavor to produce great effects, and yet they were produced."[37] She chose Phèdre for her second appearance. "She produces effects without the odious physical display which is the distinguishing trait in the most popular school of American acting," he observed, "and which is so disgusting to the refined mind." Rachel had discovered the secret of acting, he thought, by producing "great dramatic effects without apparent effort; and without overstepping the modesty of nature."[38] Up to this point Rachel had attempted to win the New York audience with French classical tragedy. She next chose Adrienne Lecouvreur, a role to convince critics of her versatility and power. Wilkins was impressed and described her final scene in detail:

> Her death scene, they say, was studied gasp by gasp, and groan by groan, in the Parisian hospitals;

whether this be true or not, the fact that the death
is eminently natural remains the same. The king
of terrors is brought before your lorgnette as the
skeleton was introduced at the Egyptian festivals.
The ineffectual struggles for freer respiration--the
action of the nerves strained to the highest ten-
sion--the sudden reaction, and consequent weak-
ness--the wandering of the mind to the theatre, and
the fit of delirium when she thinks she sees her
lover sitting with her rival--the ineffectual attempt
to brush away from her eyes the shadowy film of
the dark valley, and the final passing of the spirit--
are all interpreted with the most terrible truthfulness. [39]

Personne later noted that he had "never seen any actress except Rachel who could play Adrienne Le Couvreur." While
the actress was not as successful in depicting quiet and tender emotions, Wilkins concluded that she was so great that
she must be judged "carefully, considerably, and impartially.
She invites the closest criticism and the most searching analysis."

He followed closely that other French phenomenon of
the 1850s, Dumas fils' La Dame aux Camélias. Jean M. Davenport's version, Camille the Coquette, he found filled with in-
consistencies due to her removal of all references to sexual
improprieties. But he praised her acting as a "purely artistic effort--a full embodiment of the part; a picture vividly but
not too highly colored."[40] Laura Keene made the offensive
portion only a dream and was able to offer her version,
Camille: or the Moral of a Life, to crowded houses for three
weeks. Wilkins welcomed her representation, calling it
"fresh, natural, unconventional, and vigorous.... She took a
new view of the part, and we like originality when joined with
true genius."[41] On January 22, 1857, Matilda Heron's controversial rendition of the piece opened at Wallack's Theatre.
The play, as well as Heron's acting, prompted lengthy discussion by Wilkins in the Herald, both in the dramatic column
and on the editorial page. Wilkins thought the title absurd,
noting that Camille was "one of the attendants upon Diana, a
chaste goddess, while this play illustrates the erratic life and
miserable death of a consumptive lorette." He then compared
Heron's interpretation with Davenport's and Keene's. "Miss
Davenport played Camille well. She was like a safe, strong
ocean steamer, well constructed in every part, carrying just
enough steam to make good time, and bringing her passengers

safe into port. " Keene's Camille "resembled a nicely built, beautifully fitted up yacht, gliding among pleasant scenes, giving you glimpses of Etruscan vales and Claude Lorraine landscapes, throwing vivid color over all around. " Matilda Heron's portrayal differed. "Miss Heron we should describe as a high pressure first-class Western steamboat, with all her fires up, extra pounds of steam to the square inch. The effect is fine, but the danger of an explosion is imminent."[42] Wilkins concluded that Heron's acting was a "little too broadly colored to suit our individual taste, " but that she deserved to rank as a grand tragedienne. Her success is "un fait accompli. "

The morality of the play, however, prevented him from enjoying her success in the role. Camille he regarded as a low class courtesan: "Her dress is flashy in the extreme, her manners those of the streets, her appearance strikingly similar to the poor creatures who flaunt in the promenades of every great city. She makes love to Armand in a manner which would disgust any man of refinement; and it is morally impossible that such a person as she represents could have made such a sacrifice as she is supposed to make...." The same paper on April 12 further described her character as a "deification of prostitution" and concluded that the play appeals directly to the "worst passions of the human heart. "

Personne's comments about the same subject in the Saturday Press and in the Leader agree basically with the Herald both in tone and style. Heron's Lesbia, at the Winter Garden Theatre in January 1860, seemed to him "a dull melodrama, which neither interests, nor entertains, nor thrills you in any way.... It is cheap theatrical trash, from the beginning to the end. "[43] While he did not believe in Sunday-School drama he did believe that "art does not require a sacrifice of all the proprieties. " Heron, he observed, "moans and howls" a little more in Lesbia than as Camille. In addition "her costumes are in the worst taste, and make her look much heavier than she is; ... the little touch of nature, which was the chiefest of her charms, has disappeared. " He concluded that she had been spoiled by the outrageous puffing of the critics. Editorials in the Herald had offered the same conclusions. Despite Wilkins' professed rejection of New England Puritanism, the tone of his writing was moralistic and conservative. Such contradictions seem to characterize the age.

Wilkins' evaluation of the acting of Edwin Booth was favorable, with reservations. In April 1858, he described Booth as "a true tragic artist of great merit, but of greater promise. " The actor possessed "the true fire of genius, " he concluded, "which needs but time, industry, and study to place its possessor in the very rank of living tragedians. "[44] Charles Shattuck has called "illuminating" Wilkins' November 29, 1860 review in the Herald of the actor's Hamlet.

> We perceive in Edwin Booth many of his father's fine qualities, to which the former adds youth, a handsome person, a very sympathetic and musical voice, a thorough knowledge of the stage, and complete mastery of the tricks by which actors tickle the fancy of the public. Mr. Booth's Hamlet is a very clever performance. In certain scenes, such as those of the play and the interview with the Queen (third act), he was very fine. The scene with the Ghost (first act) was well managed; and that where he introduces the recorders to Rosencrantz and Guildenstern was also exceedingly good. Mr. Booth's prime quality--and we wish that all actors and actresses would note this--is that he appears perfectly unconscious that there is any audience before him. He seems to us to possess this very important power of losing himself in the play to an eminent degree. We do not altogether fancy Mr. Booth's elocution. He reads the soliloquies intelligently and effectively, but has not yet mastered the art of speaking dialogue in a level natural offhand manner.

Wilkins added, "In Hamlet we naturally look for more repose than Mr. Booth is at present capable of giving us. " Shattuck concludes that Wilkins was but "echoing Booth's intentions, charging him with falling short of his own aims. "[45]

During this engagement, Booth followed Hamlet with Richelieu, an old war-horse which actors of the period unharnassed from time to time to "tickle the fancy of the public. " On the eve of the Civil War, Bulwer-Lytton's melodrama ignited the right sparks with its patriotic sentiments and loud rhetoric. Booth usually drew rave notices when he played the wily old Cardinal, and Wilkins was not immune from his magic. In the Leader of December 8, 1860, he described Booth's Richelieu as "a superb performance and ... a great sensation"--one of the finest pieces of acting that

he had seen in some time. But when Booth followed with
Romeo, the critic called his performance "a high place among
the worst I have ever seen. He absolutely chanted the words,
and very rarely spoke, or walked, or stood still like a human being."[46] The actor, of course, had no success playing
Romeo and later dropped it from his repertory. After he
closed his engagement, Wilkins concluded that he had "wonderfully improved" in two years and predicted that he could
be great: "All that he requires is patient, earnest study, and
the finish which comes by practice. He is the incarnation of
young America in the coulisses."[47]

While Edwin Booth's quiet and intellectual style seemed
attractive to Wilkins, he followed Henry Clapp in determining
that Edwin Forrest was the better actor. In the late 1850s
comparison of the two men, however, seemed silly to the
critic. Booth was but beginning his career while Forrest had
established himself as the premiere American tragedian.
While not blind to the latter's faults, Wilkins still enjoyed his
"great, grand, thrilling touches," especially in roles such as
Virginius and Spartacus. He admitted that Forrest could
never lose his individuality in a role. As Othello, he could
not show the transformation from warrior to lover; his voice
was too "deep and guttural, and has too ventral a source";
and he irritated playgoers by grinding his teeth and empha-
sizing the word "sieges" in a harsh manner. Despite such
flaws, Wilkins regarded Forrest as a "great artist and sublime tragedian."[48]

When it was rumored that Forrest would retire from
the stage, an editorial in the Herald of November 4, 1858
called him "essentially an American actor." His style was
"massive as our mountains, broad as our prairies, grand as
the rolling of our mighty waters.... He is the last of the
Titanic school of artists, and in the bold original individuality
of his style has defied imitation and distances rivalry."
While these sentences about Forrest may have been written
by Bennett, they seem a fair summary of Wilkins' high regard of the actor in 1858.

By 1860 Wilkins believed that Forrest could not receive a fair hearing in New York. He was not a favorite
with other actors. "I never knew a case where a man whose
position overshadowed that of all his confreres was liked by
them," Personne mused. As a result, "a most persistent
artistic clique is against Forrest, and the influence of that
clique reacts upon the 'critics' who rarely have pluck enough

to judge for themselves.... "49 This "clique" included William Stuart of the Tribune, Adam Badeau of the Sunday Times, George William Curtis of Harper's, and William Hurlburt of the Albion. These critics found Forrest's style of acting and choice of plays embarrassing to refined and educated tastes. In the Leader of December 29, 1860, Personne noted that Forrest drew a "popular and populous" audience for his Spartacus, and chided those individuals who "pooh-pooh at the actor who appeals directly to the popular heart, and stirs sympathies as the storm agitates the ocean. " And Personne could not understand why these individuals "persist in going to see plays which they condemn. " The majority of the Bohemians saw flaws in the old actor's style but regarded him as representative of the primitive and earlier American civilization. They refused to judge him on his personal life. Wilkins regarded Forrest with respect but also enjoyed the more refined acting of Edwin Booth.

His attitude towards Charlotte Cushman remains unclear because of the wide variance between his newspaper and periodical opinions. While his critical estimation of Booth's and Forrest's talents remained consistent in all of his writings, he praised Cushman in the Herald and damned her in Harper's Weekly, Saturday Press, and the Leader. Ottarson's line of reasoning, that Bennett muzzled his critic in certain areas, might be a possible explanation for this lack of critical integrity. Cushman was extremely popular with the masses--the main audience of the New York Herald. She was an American actress with some international standing and the Herald praised her with patriotic fervor as it praised Edwin Forrest. Apparently (if we can believe his periodical reviews), Wilkens never favored her acting style, however. When given free editorial rein in Harper's Weekly or Saturday Press, he spoke harshly of this country's most respected actress.

He first reviewed her acting during the autumn of 1857. Cushman had returned from a five-year stay in Europe. She chose to open her engagement in New York with Bianca in the Reverend Henry Hart Milman's Fazio, or the Italian Wife--not a great play but one offering a role in which she could demonstrate her histrionic fireworks. "The marked peculiarity of her acting is its wonderful intensity, " the Herald raved. "There is fire in every word she utters, and the coldest auditor is carried away by the vivid and painful reality of the scene. "50 The reviewer concluded that she "belongs to the old school of acting, and the admirers of the

modern school might take exception to her redundant action
and violent gesticulation, but all must admit its exceeding
effectiveness. " Three years later when she appeared at the
Winter Garden Theatre in her standard repertory, the
Herald (October 9, 1860) found her intense dramatic powers
unequaled by any living actress. Her Meg Merrilies evoked
the following: "There is no artist who can better convey
the value of a work, by throwing her whole soul into utterance, look and action--thus striking at the same time the
senses and the intellectual perceptions, without sacrificing
dignity to intensity or judgment to passion. " She revived
Lady Macbeth on October 29 in a performance which the
Herald called "a superb effort, her rendering of the sleeping
scene being perhaps, one of the finest pieces of acting with
which she has ever enthralled an audience. "

During these engagements, Wilkins was the acknowledged dramatic critic of the Herald. In 1857 he was also
writing "Bohemian Walks and Talks" for Harper's Weekly.
While the Herald was bestowing unqualified praise for Cushman, "Bohemien" was ridiculing her in Harper's. Her Lady
Macbeth was too ugly to tempt Macbeth: "Why, Sir, if Macbeth had had such a wife in these days he would have removed
to Illinois and gotten a divorce from her at once."[51] Mainly,
he charged her with lack of control: "Of the grand repose,
which is the secret of tragic acting, Miss Cushman knows
nothing, and the constant movement of the muscles of her
face, though disagreeable at first, becomes at last intensely
ludicrous. " Bohemien concluded his remarks by asking,
"Who will find us an actress? The English stage has none. "

When Cushman re-appeared at the Winter Garden in
October 1860, Wilkins was "Personne" for the Leader in addition to his regular duties as critic of the Herald. While
the latter publication had nothing but praise for her acting,
Personne thought her performance after the "anatomical museum style. " Her poses were awkward, her effects "thrilling" and "vulgar, " and her characterizations lacking in finish
and delicacy. Where he called her Queen Katharine "prime, "
he thought Meg Merrilies showed no improvement over her
last engagement. "Did her artist friends tell Miss Cushman
to hold her arms like the broken wings of a turkey, with
pendant eagle claws?"[52] Personne complained. "Did they
tell her that, because Meg was an old woman, and a gypsy,
that all her attitudes should necessarily be angular and awkward. " The critic thought she should have viewed pictures
of the Bohemian race in the art galleries of Europe while

she was abroad. His remarks were insulting and intended
to be so.

In the Leader, November 24, 1860, he accused Miss
Cushman of taking no risks to improve the quality of the
American theatre: "Miss Cushman prefers to travel in the
old tracks, everything for the 'star,' no matter about the
author; never mind the public, hire Jones, Nokes, Stokes,
and Mokes for five dollars a week; push them on the stage,
they'll remember the cues and that is all the star wants."
Wilkins opposed the star system and with it, Charlotte Cushman. He seemed less enraged by her style of acting than
by her lack of artistic development and her selfishness
towards the rest of her profession.

Like Clapp and, later, Stephen Fiske, Wilkins' favorite
actress was Mrs. John Wood, whom he named "Thalia" after
the comic muse. "She is an exceedingly pretty woman, sings
well, dances well, talks well, acts well," he cooed after
viewing her in the burlesque of Hiawatha in December 1856. [53]
"She has a quick perception of every funny thing she utters,
and has a peculiar knack of making the audience know that it
is funny, and that they are to laugh, and they do laugh." In
1860 he suggested that the introduction of a little wood into
the Winter Garden was the only thing that was required to
make that horticultural institution the nicest place in town.
And when Mrs. Wood finally opened at that theatre in Ivanhoe,
his feuilleton sparkled: "Fellows who had been bored to death
by their wives, or snubbed by their governors, or set out in
the cold by their Anna Marias, or worried by their creditors,
dropped in upon Wood and had to laugh in spite of all their
sorrow." [54] He was not objective about her talents. She
could make people laugh, even against their will. He was impressed that she never lost her self-possession: "If she gives
the audience a joke, and they don't see it, she doesn't waver,
but goes straight on to another. Her impudence, I really
can't call it anything else, is colossal. It is the here-I-am
style, now laugh, or I'll know the reason why! And they do
laugh hugely." Wilkins promoted her career, pleaded for her
a theatre, and defended her from attacks by other critics.
He found her a bright light in a society "where everybody is
so infernally respectable and awfully dull." [55]

Wilkins insisted upon critical independence when he began his column in the Leader. "I intend to write about the
opera, theatres and kindred topics, just exactly what comes
into my head; to do it my own way, and in such style as may

be found most agreeable to the public whose obedient servant
I am, " he explained in his first dramatic essay for that paper on June 2, 1860. "I shall neither ask, nor expect, nor
show favor to managers, actors or others. I shall treat
public performers as public property, and shall discharge the
duties of a critic in a manner perfectly independent of any
rules or usages. " He concluded in a manner typically Wilkins: "These papers will be egotistic. They could hardly
be anything else. With the sole exception of the brightest
and best of her sex [Anna Maria] I am rather more fond of
myself than of anyone else in the world. " In June 1860, the
Hudson County Chronicle devoted nearly a column to dramatic
criticism in New York, concluding that "Personne has no superior on the city press. "[56] Although such praise by contemporaries may not be objective, it does point to Wilkins' reputation in his day. He welded French critical practices to
those of mass journalism to offer a fair amount of Yankee
wisdom about the theatre.

Having reached the top of his profession, Wilkins had
little time to enjoy it. He died on May 5, 1861, from pneu-
monia at age thirty-one. To George Arnold his death seemed
like a great mistake: "His position was just assured and
ripening. He was just coming into a handsome income from
his manifold labors.... Everything smiled upon him, and
fortune was turning her wheel in his behalf, when--poof!--
the candle is out!"[57] Funeral services were held in St.
Thomas's Church in New York, after which the body was returned to Boston for burial in the family plot at Woodlawn
Cemetery.

"Ned" Wilkins had become a popular personality of the
period. On May 11, some verses in the Leader by Juliette
H. Beach seemed to sum up the shock and dismay felt among
Wilkins' readers. Here are two stanzas:

> Sitting last night in a thronged concert room,
> Gay with bright flags, and sickly with perfume.
> Waiting the singer's coming on the stage,
> I read upon the evening daily's page:
> 'New York, May 6, died yesterday, Personne. '
>
> I heard the clear notes of the opening song,
> And saw the singer's pretty painted face,
> And all her well conned ways of wavy grace;
> I heard the volunteers' slow, heavy tramp,
> And in the gallery the call and stamp,

Then looked again upon the page that said,
In one brief, sorrowing line, 'Personne is dead. '

It is not the quality of such doggeral but its sentiments which
are important. Personne's warm and chatty column had entertained a wide audience who now mourned his passing.

Some eighteen months before his death, Personne sent
New Year's greetings to his fellow Bohemians. His letter
seems to express well the social role--the public persona--he
had tried to play.

> And to Bohemia, all hail!
> It is your Carnival. You are wanted at dinners
> and suppers, and receptions without end. You are
> the crême de la crême when there is any fun going
> on. To the men I will suggest the propriety of
> preserving a proper dignity when associating with
> people in trade, and never look at a man under a
> hundred thousand. You will be careful to impress
> upon the minds of such a person the littleness of
> all earthly possessions, and to let him know, while
> you drink his Lafitte and eat his pâté de foie gras,
> that there are some things which money cannot
> buy.
> And as for the Bohêmiennes, I will leave them
> to the Queen [Ada Clare] of that land, the only
> free community on the face of the earth. Free,
> because released from the shackles of conventionali-
> ty; free, because recognizing no divine right, ex-
> cept that of mental superiority, which is really di-
> vine; free, on account of a variety of other things
> I haven't time to mention.
> Vive Bohemia!
> Vive La Reine!
>   Tres devoué,
>
>   Personne. [58]

Wilkins challenged the prevailing notion among the
educated classes that to be profound, criticism must be scholarly, serious, and English. He founded, with Clapp and
his fellow Bohemians, a lively impressionist school of theatre
criticism.

CHAPTER FOUR

WILLIAM WINTER
"mercutio"

On October 23, 1859, the Pfaffians celebrated a successful first year of publishing the Saturday Press. For a year they had thumbed their noses at reigning figureheads in literature, theatre, and art, with enthusiastic response from the periodical press. They were the cause célèbre of the young intellectuals and the talk of Fifth Avenue parties-- heady stuff for young "turks" who believed they could reshape the image of society and its literature. Confident of their abilities, during Christmas week, 1859, they launched Vanity Fair, a new comic weekly, with nineteen-year-old Frank Wood as editor. The Pfaffian coterie--at least all who wrote--contributed to the new weekly and it quickly gained a reputation for its urbane wit and pro-Southern political stance. The Bohemians now divided their days between the editorial offices of Saturday Press and Vanity Fair, and assembled in the evenings at Pfaff's to destroy reputations and launch attacks against "philistines, " "commonplace morality, " and the "Boston Mutual Admiration Society" (the editors of Atlantic).

While the Pfaffians were celebrating their publishing success, William Winter, a twenty-three-year-old poet and journalist, set out from Boston to seek his fortune in New York. He had been unable to establish himself as a writer in the closed literary circles of New England, and in Henry Clapp and his coterie saw kindred spirits of rebellion. He was greeted cordially. Clapp soon regarded him as a protégé; Wilkins thought of him as a friend as well as a colleague; Ada Clare included him among her Sunday-night circle. Only Walt Whitman among the group found his friendship and talents distasteful: "'Willy', he said, 'is a young Longfellow, '" and did not mean it as a compliment.[1] But in December 1859, Winter was welcomed to the inner circle at Pfaff's.

Clapp hired him to write for the Saturday Press. He was to become the most famous and influential critic of the nineteenth-century American stage.

He was born on July 15, 1836, in Gloucester, Massachusetts, of Charles and Louisa (Wharf) Winter.[2] His mother died before his fourth birthday; he and his brother Charles stayed with family friends and an elder sister of his mother's. Until he was twenty-three years old, he was to live an "unsettled life" in the Boston area. His father, a sea-going captain, remarried sometime in 1842 or 1843 to provide a home for his two sons. But the stepmother disliked the two boys and failed to establish a happy relationship with Captain Charles. Numerous quarrels and disturbances shattered the tranquillity of their lives. Winter complained bitterly about his upbringing in a letter to Longfellow, January 26, 1855: "I have always wanted a mother's care--have rarely known human sympathy--have been cursed with a most unhappy home, and have been obliged to struggle with poverty to a considerable extent."[3] Yet he later described his boyhood as "rough and neglected" but happy.

For his formal education he attended a public school in Boston and later Cambridge High School where he graduated at age sixteen. On March 1, 1856, he entered Dane Law School at Harvard.[4] He had planned to begin his studies earlier but ill health and financial problems deferred his law education.[5] While he received some aid from his father, he mainly earned his own living as a collector for a tugboat in Boston Harbor, and from his literary efforts. While attending classes at Harvard he continued submitting verses and book reviews to Boston newspapers, including the Transcript, the Olive Branch, and the Saturday Evening Gazette.

During the national elections in 1856, in an atmosphere charged with moral righteousness over the slavery issue, Winter flirted briefly with politics. He opposed slavery and campaigned for Republican John C. Fremont. Yet he opposed radical behavior more and wrote with distaste about the "effusive, hysterical novel of Uncle Tom's Cabin" which "aroused and inflamed thousands of hearts." Thomas Bailey Aldrich warned him in 1858: "Be a good boy and don't get excited on the slavery question."[6] Winter took this advice. He followed Rufus Choate, who opposed human servitude on moral grounds but never advocated abolition. Winter defended Choate from charges that his defense of the South was an act of moral atrocity. Choate should not be judged by "petty standards" of commonplace morality, Winter argued. The moralist wants "not genius, not intellect, not great ideas, not in the largest sense a powerful and splendid life; but 'moral instincts and purposes'--according to his idea of them, no matter how contemptible that idea may be. " It is erroneous to believe that "no man is great unless he is good, " Winter concluded; "That no man is good unless he is great, is a larger and better statement of the truth. "[7] Winter's views on this point were later to change.

After graduating from Law School in 1857, Winter worked in the Boston Law Offices of Lyman Manson and Aurelius D. Parker. Later that year he was admitted to the Suffolk, Massachusetts Bar. But he never practiced law. According to his son, Jefferson, when a woman seeking a divorce told him her side of the case, Winter's sympathy went out so strongly to the husband that he referred her to another attorney and gave up the legal profession. Whether true or not, this story does suggest the lack of commitment which Winter felt toward the legal profession. Professor Theophilus Parsons of Dane Law School had warned him against such a move. When Parsons discovered that Winter was publishing poetry in Boston newspapers, he advised him: "Don't think of living by your pen. Stick to the law! You will be an excellent lawyer. You will have a profession to depend on. You can make your way. You can have home and friends. Stick to the law. "[8] These words may have haunted Winter many times throughout his career--especially during his first year in New York. But in 1859, giving up his profession for the uncertain life of a writer seemed to him a fine and noble gesture.

His friendship with Henry Wadsworth Longfellow exerted a strong influence upon his life. They first met in the spring of 1854. William wanted to publish a slender volume of his poetry and wished it dedicated to Longfellow. The old poet accepted the dedication by letter on April 16, 1854, and invited Winter to his home. [9] From this meeting grew a warm relationship which spanned the next twenty-eight years, ending with the death of Longfellow on March 24, 1882. At first, Winter's awe of the poet and his need for favors reduced his attempts at friendship to fawning. [10] But the young man's respect and affection for Longfellow was genuine: "He knew my love for him, and he trusted it, " Winter eulogized. "I saw him as he was; and within my observation and knowledge of men, which have been exceptionally wide, a man more noble, gentle, lovable, and true never lived. "[11] In

1864, Winter wrote in the Albion that Longfellow's works "are pure and beautiful in spirit, artistic in execution, and adapted to exercise a wholesome influence over the mental and moral growth of his countrymen, and thus over the literature of his country."[12] In his writings Winter sought much of the same ends.

His interest in leaving Boston for New York may have been kindled as early as 1854 while he was reviewing books for Daniel N. Haskell's Boston Transcript. Haskell asked him to comment on The Bells: A Collection of Chimes by T.B.A., a volume which Winter read with pleasure. The author was Thomas Bailey Aldrich, then writing for N.P. Willis's Home Journal in New York. Aldrich was pleased with Winter's review, and in turn dedicated a poem to "W.W." in the Home Journal. They exchanged letters. Finally, in 1855, Aldrich came to Boston, dined with Winter and Haskell, and established a friendship with the former which lasted throughout their lives. A charter member of Pfaff's and the first literary editor of Saturday Press, Aldrich shared many of the same ideals as Winter--a love of beauty and sentiment, and a strong moral bent.

The arrival of Fitz-James O'Brien in Boston during September 1859 may have further kindled Winter's ambitions to seek greener pastures. O'Brien had been the "toast of New York" the previous year with his short story, "The Diamond Lens," in Atlantic magazine. He now spent a month in the city as literary assistant and press agent for H. L. Bateman, tour manager for Matilda Heron. Winter viewed the flamboyant young actress's repertory: Geraldine, Camille, and Medea. Introduced to Fitz-James, he noted that the fiery Irishman "astonished some of the quiet literary circles of that staid and decorous region by his utter and unaffected irreverence for various camphorated figure-heads which were then an incubus upon American letters."[13] No doubt O'Brien was attacking his hated rivals--Martin Farquhar Tupper and George P. Morris--considered in some circles as the greatest living English and American poets. Winter admired his frankness; the two men became friends, and remained so until O'Brien was killed fighting for the North in 1862.

It was clear to Winter that New York's literary climate offered more hope to an unknown poet than its counterpart on Beacon Hill. Before moving there in late fall of 1859, however, he visited at least twice. In 1858 he came for "one or two nights," and the following summer he stayed for about a

week with his father, who "had temporary charge of a ship."
At this time he met Henry Clapp and "some of his associates."[14] No doubt he had corresponded earlier with Clapp:
his poem, "An Ideal," appeared in the Saturday Press on
May 28, 1859. Five other poems followed in the next eight
months. Thus Winter did not seek his fortune blindly; he
already knew a number of New York writers and editors.
Before leaving Boston, he published his second volume of
poetry, The Queen's Domain and Other Poems. During the
next year, he would reprint several of his verses in the
Saturday Press.

With a law degree, two published volumes of poetry,
and several years of journalistic experience, William Winter
began his career in New York. His experiences in journalism left him well acquainted with the world of magazines and
books. His knowledge of literature (including drama), gained
from attending literature classes at Harvard, was first-rate.
He had been interested in the theatre since his youth. In
1862, he remembered that as a small boy he went early to
the theatre in Boston to get a good seat in the gallery.
There, "enraptured," he beheld "gorgeous scenic spectacle ... adventures by land, storms at sea, and darksome
gropings in dim caverns under the earth ... where the most
surprising events occur in the most natural manner."[15]
When the curtain fell, he rushed into the snow-covered street
to greet the "merry jingle of sleigh-bells." William Winter
always remembered the theatre of his youth with nostalgia.

Jefferson Winter also suggests that his father's legal
training served him well in the critical arena: "It fully and
early developed one of his strongest natural traits--namely,
the judicial quality of mind. It taught him in criticism--
which, he frequently said, is judgment, not censure--to go to
essentials and to base his conclusions wholly on justice and
the facts."[16]

His first year in New York was difficult. On October 26, 1859, he wrote to Longfellow: "There are no vacant
places. There is no prospect of finding a permanent position.... Probably I will have shortly to decide whether to
stay and live the Bohemian life here, or return to Boston
and live it there."[17] He contacted Harper's Publishing Company and found that he could write for both the magazine and
the weekly as a contributor, but no regular employment was
available. In reply to his request for help, Longfellow sent
him a letter of reference dated November 10, 1859: "I have

known Mr. William Winter for several years and consider him a young man of marked ability, both in prose and verse ... and I consider him well qualified to take charge of the Editorial Department of a newspaper."[18] Henry Clapp evidently agreed. From early January to December 15, 1860, Winter worked as assistant editor and book reviewer for the Saturday Press. [19]

Money was always scarce. Clapp paid Winter a salary when he had money, but there were long dry spells. And royalties for poetry and short stories were paid even less frequently. Winter received $15.20 for his poem "Orgia: A Song of a Ruined Man" which Clapp published in the Saturday Press, January 7, 1860. In a letter to Winter on the same date, the editor noted that the amount was all he could afford "for it is a sum due me by ... Nichols and Co., Boston."[20] But while money might be scarce, praise was bestowed freely: "We all like the poem very much. I particularly, or in my present crooked circumstances I couldn't offer you a dollar for it."

Designed to whet the appetite of an old cynic like Clapp, "Orgia" no doubt created a stir around the table at Pfaff's. In fifty-eight rhyming lines it relates the decline and death of a wastrel. The first stanza should demonstrate its literary worth:

> Who cares for nothing alone is free.
> (Sit down, good fellow, and drink with me!)
>
> With a careless heart and a merry eye,
> He will laugh at the world as the world goes by.
>
> He laughs at power, and wealth, and fame;
> He laughs at virtue; he laughs at shame.
>
> He laughs at hope and he laughs at fear;
> At Memory's dead leaves crisp and sere.
>
> He laughs at the future, cold and dim;
> Nor earth nor heaven is dear to him.
>
> O, that is the comrade fit for me!
> He cares for nothing! his soul is free!

Ada Clare did not agree with Clapp about the value of the poem. "I hear Winter's 'Song of the Ruined Man' much eulogized, " she wrote in the Saturday Press of January 14, 1860. "I cannot admire it. With the text he begins with, a practised versifier might go on rhyming until the seas were dry. All you have to do is to conjure up all the things that one should not laugh at, and then laugh at them, and there's your poem. " She compared Winter's poem with Whitman's "Child's Reminiscence, " which "could only have been written by a poet, and versifying would not help it. I love that poem. " While showing no evidence of poetic genius or even talent, Winter's poem suggests a certain youthful reckless-ness and zest for life. Winter hoped to gain recognition as a poet. In the Preface to The Poems of William Winter (1881), he confessed that poetry had been the "Main motive and object of his mental activity. " In his career, he was to publish eleven volumes of verse; most were received poorly or ignored by critics. Thus it must have caused him undue pain to write Thomas Bailey Aldrich on January 5-6, 1891, "I'm not much of a poet myself, but I know something about it in other people. "21

While he enjoyed week-night dinners and drinking bouts at Pfaff's, and Sunday evening crackers and lager beer at Ada Clare's, William Winter's "salad days" in New York were relatively brief. Before the end of December 1859, he was linked romantically with a young Scottish authoress, Lizzie (Elizabeth) Campbell. Lizzie had come from Toronto to New York in 1859 to seek a career as a writer. Befriended by Ada Clare soon after her arrival in New York, Lizzie later rented quarters at Ada's home. It was there that she and William first lived after they were married on December 8, 1860.

The new Mrs. Winter maintained her literary career after marriage. She published several novels and numerous short stories under various names: Elsie Snow, Esabella Castelar, Mrs. E. C. Winter, and E. C. W. She contributed Gothic romances to the New York Ledger; adapted plays for leading actors including Helena Modjeska, Minnie Maddern Fiske, Maud W. Goodkin, and Richard Mansfield; and enjoyed some success herself on the stage, making her debut as Julia in The Hunchback at Rochester, New York, November 3, 1863. She later made her New York debut at the Olympic Theatre, April 11, 1864, as Rosine in J. Maddison Morton's Our Wife. Apparently, she was considered a promising enough novice to play Katherine to Edwin Booth's Petruchio at a matinee on March 14, 1866. She appeared with the companies of Booth, John Brougham, Lester Wallack, and Augustin Daly before re-

tiring from acting to resume her writing career. [22] Lizzie
was under no illusions about the theatre, and held no sentimental ideas about the position she would occupy on the
stage: "I am perfectly aware that it is the hardest profession which a woman can undertake," she wrote Edwin Booth,
June 2, 1869. "At the same time it is almost the only one
accessible to a woman who wishes to earn an independent
livelihood by the exercise of her intellectual faculties." [23]
Despite her efforts to attain a successful career on the stage,
her acting rates only an occasional note in Odell's Annals of
the New York Stage.

The terse and epigrammatic Saturday Press prompted
Winter to write some of his most savage satire. Henry
Clapp believed in cutting his victims swift and deep, and his
assistant attempted to emulate his style. "Whenever old
Clapp knew I was at work on a bit of satire," he later told
his son Jefferson, "he would keep vigilant guard, like a sort
of grim old bird over a nestling, fending off intruders and
interruptions, sucking away at an ill-smelling pipe while we
were alone, and furtively and eagerly watching me out of the
corner of one of his bright, glinting old eyes. He was terribly embittered, and the sharper the satire the more he liked
it. If he thought what I wrote was especially good he would
himself take it over to the printers and order it set up in
type." [24] Winter's diatribe against the North American Review and newspaper criticism in general, in the August 11,
1860, Saturday Press, should have pleased the old cynic.
He accused "all provincial and nearly all the metropolitan
papers" of puffing celebrities. In Europe, he pointed out,
"advertisers do not carry the price of every editor in their
breeches-pockets; the public is not regaled with servile syco-
phancy and purchased adulation; no writer is protected by any
divine hedge of respectability; and ignorance and meanness
are not the passports to journalistic success." On the other
hand, the press of this country held different standards:
"There is literally no limit to its ignorance, its servility,
and its corruption. There is scarcely an editor in the land
that will not sell himself any day for any purpose. There is
scarcely a newspaper that has any character--except a very
bad one--or is believed in by any intelligent person. The
practice of puffery has been carried to such an extent that
at last it promises to become its own antidote and mercifully
work its own ruin." He ended his essay with a flourish
worthy of Henry Clapp: "And the least word of honest criticism, directed against whatever weakness, folly, or fraud,
is greeted with a general howl of execration from the entire

pack of toadeaters throughout the nation." This is straight-
forward hyperbole, certain to attract attention. It is to the
Saturday Press and its editor that Winter owes the beginning
of his professional career.

The collapse of the Saturday Press after the December
15, 1860 issue left Winter unemployed. Both Henry Clapp
and the paper had meant a great deal to him. Later he
would defend them against slanderous statements. He admitted that the Press had weaknesses: "It sometimes mis-
took eccentricity for originality.... In its hatred of the pre-
tence of virtue, it sometimes seemed to condemn even virtue
itself."[25] But he concluded that poverty, not the lack of
brilliance, had brought it down. Events leading up to the
Civil War had tightened purse-strings in the business community, and advertising and sales had declined. On December 15, 1860, however, the young bridegroom was more concerned with finding a job than with debating the economics of
commercial journalism. Henry Clapp came to the rescue
once again. He had accepted a position on the editorial staff
of the New York Leader and found William a temporary position for $10.00 per week--an amount which paid for board
and room at Ada Clare's.[26] The lack of money became so
acute that on April 9, 1861, Winter wrote to Longfellow asking for a loan of one hundred dollars.[27] He mentioned his
considerable losses on the Saturday Press which he had been
unable to recover.

After the firing upon Fort Sumter and the beginning of
the Civil War, the Winters spent part of the summer in Cambridge with Captain Charles. Lizzie was pregnant and returned only briefly to New York before moving to Toronto,
where their first child Percy was born on November 16.
William continued to live at Ada Clare's, making several
trips to Toronto during his wife's pregnancy. "Offer my
warmest congratulations to Lizzie," Ada wrote after the birth
of Percy. "I knew she would go through with it spendidly.
Does he talk yet? If so, mention my name to him."[28]

Lizzie returned to New York with Percy in April
1862. The family was forced to find new lodgings soon afterwards when Ada Clare's property in South Carolina became
a casualty of the war, a loss which forced her to give up
housekeeping and servants. Much later, in 1908, Lizzie recalled these Bohemian years, remembering how they struggled
to make ends meet by taking their dinner at a small cafe,
eating no lunch, and having "anything we could get" for break-

fast.[29] Depressed with life in general, Winter wrote Stedman on May 1, 1863: "I seldom see any of the people that
you know, and never go into society at all. I am, as I
ever was, something of a black sheep and none of our
friends care to acknowledge me socially."[30]

During the war, he wrote for numerous publications
to make a living. He was editor of the Petroleum Monitor,
managing editor of Frank Leslie's Magazine, and literary
editor of the New York Weekly Review. He contributed to
the Round Table, Philobiblion, The Galaxy, Harper's Weekly,
and Wilkes' Spirit of the Times. He also published poetry
under the name of Mark Vale. Despite his arduous labors,
money was scarce. He and Lizzie were pursuing separate
careers and each supporting a parent besides caring for
their son Percy. Three more sons and a daughter--Arthur
(1872), Louis (1873), William Jefferson (1878), and Viola
(1881)--would add to family financial difficulties. Winter
borrowed money continuously throughout his life to meet his
financial obligations: frequently from a personal friend,
William A. Seaver; at times from colleagues such as Edwin
Booth and Augustin Daly--men he reviewed in his dramatic
column. Questions about his character and critical integrity
remain unanswered because it is difficult to know how lender
and borrower regarded these loans.[31]

Winter left the Leader in December 1861 to take
charge of the Albion's dramatic department, replacing Inigo,
a personal friend named Harry Neill, who had died the previous month. After the obligatory remarks praising Neill's
integrity, grace, and courage, Winter settled in for a four-
and-one-half-year stint. He added the literary column in
1862; and from April to June 1866 served as editor. While
he was paid but $10.00 per week as dramatic editor, he had
his own department and his own column. Under the signature
of Mercutio he penned some of the most perceptive criticism
of the Civil War years. Why a character from Shakespearean drama for his pen-name? He explained in the Albion for
July 23, 1864. "It seems to me that Shakespeare's Mercutio
is the best type that literature affords of the brilliant men of
the world," Winter suggested. "I fancy him, in brave attire
walking about the streets of the old Italian city, or in comfortable inns, drinking wine with gay companions.... He was
always merry and he took the world easily, with laughter for
everything. And yet there was a serious vein in his nature.
He was a true friend. He was ardent, alike in his love and
in his aversion. He had scholarship, at least in belles

lettres; and he was, in his off-hand way, an excellent critic
of manners and of character. " In other words, to Winter,
Mercutio was the ideal Bohemian.

It is unfortunate that Winter did not continue to write
in the terse and epigrammatic style which Clapp had taught
him. A vagueness and naive poetic quality dooms some of
his Albion prose to incomprehensibility. But during his
tenure on the Albion, William Winter developed critical
tastes which would change little for the rest of his career.
Several of his early opinions suggest the direction in which
he was moving and are noted here. In his fourth essay
(January 18, 1862), he condemned the rant and artificiality
of tragic acting (no doubt with Forrest in mind) and praised
the fine intellectual style of E. L. Davenport. The following January 3, he found a "certain symmetry and esprit in
French acting which atones for much of the trash. " On
March 15, 1862, he joined the Pfaffians in praising Matilda
Heron as the "most characteristic actress on the American
stage, " and described her as possessing "a peculiar genius
and natural power for acting. " He would later come to pre-
fer a balance between emotional and intellectual acting.

Although not remembered as a critic of much wit,
William Winter demonstrated in the Albion a wry sense of
humor. On March 29, 1862, he noted that managers were
clamoring for tears, and that the "leading questions in life
are 'How do you like Booth?' and 'What do you think of
Camille?'" He had learned how to turn a phrase--a required talent if one were to survive the banter of Pfaff's.
On April 19, 1862, he expressed his dislike for the "school
of limb and larynx"--referring to the Edwin Forrest acting
style. Later that year, on November 8, he thought that
"tears may be crystallized into currency" through Camille.
And on April 1, 1865, he described Corporal Cartouche at
the Winter Garden in an amusing manner: "It was written
by a Frenchman, brought to these shores by Mr. John Sefton,
translated by an unknown, adapted by Mr. S. R. Fisk [sic]
and advertised as 'an original military and domestic
drama'.... " It appears that Winter attempted to follow Clapp
in combining satire with serious criticism.

He began his career at a time of great national crises.
He watched his friends ride off to war. Several, including
Fitz-James O'Brien, did not come back. Yet Winter wrote
very little about the conflict. On occasion he deplored the
war's effect upon the country. "Emotion, in the mass of hu-

man beings, predominate over judgment, " he concluded in
the October 10, 1863 Albion. Because men wanted "thunder
clouds and a tempest" instead of peace, a "grim sensation
convulses the western world, and a republic whirls onward,
in a red tide of slaughter, toward that despotism which
Hamilton loved and Jefferson dreaded. This is the grand excitement of the hour; and, in order to be recognized at all,
literature and the drama must compete with this. " Discouraged and disgusted with the world, he called for art to "afford a permanent refuge from the insane wickedness of this
epoch. " Yet the theatre, like the war, offered sensationalism, excitement, immorality, and vulgarity. On September
3, 1864, he expressed his disapproval: "Will there ever
come time, when players will understand that the atmosphere
of the stage should be that of the drawing room where refinement prevails and where oaths and innuendoes and coarse
jokes are never permitted. " Winter regarded himself as an
eighteenth-century man, living out of his time in a vulgar
age. In the March 7, 1863 Albion, he longed for the pic-
turesque London of his ancestors, where "dashing Cavaliers
swagger in the streets" and coffee houses flourish.

The assassination of President Lincoln by John Wilkes
Booth on April 14, 1865 engendered a stronger response.
William Winter endeared himself to the theatrical profession
by strongly defending it in the press: "How deeply they [the
profession] feel about this calamity, " he wrote in the Albion
of April 22; "how thoroughly they sympathize with the suffering family of the deceased President, how profoundly they
abhor the crime ... will be understood and appreciated by
all who know them--as I know them--to be, for the most
part, high-minded and warmhearted men and women, true
lovers of their country, of Freedom, Justice and Right. "
He asked the New York Chief of Police to apologize to the
public and to the players for "his illegal and entirely superfluous order ... to close the theatres of the city. " And
Winter thought it unjust to blame the crime on the Booth
family: "The agonized mother, the brothers and sisters,
whose hearts are well nigh broken, whose lives are blighted,
by the horrid deed of that dark and lonely man, whose name
I leave unwritten! Surely their anguish should be sacred. "
As for the criminal: "He is an actor no longer: he belongs
no more to the family of man. He is alone. For him there
is no thought of mercy, save--let it be spoken humbly and
with awe!--in the All-Forgiving Mind. There is something
inexpressibly solemn in the idea of such isolation from human
sympathy. " At a time when the institutions of this country

were damning the theatre for the act of one man, Winter
protected it.   The New York Herald printed vicious editorials
(Winter suggested they were written by Stephen Fiske)[32]
against John Wilkes Booth and the Booth family; Winter defended their best interests in the Albion.

An opportunity to improve his career came on July
13, 1865, when he substituted for Edward H. House, dramatic editor and critic for Horace Greeley's New York Tribune,
to review Arrah-Na-Pogue at Niblo's Theatre.   Ethically
House could not review the play since his name had been advertised with Dion Boucicault's as co-author and he served
as the playwright's agent.[33]   Tribune managing editor, Sidney Howard Gay, evidently approved of the review (which
continued on July 14), or disapproved of the controversy
House's relationship with Boucicault had provoked in the
press.   The next month, Winter replaced House on a permanent basis at a salary of $35.00 per week.   For the next
half-century, he brought a level of scholarship and expertise
to theatre criticism which sets him apart from most of his
contemporaries.   He could converse easily about the major
works of Aristotle; the writings of the English romantics--
Coleridge, Lamb, Hazlitt, and Johnson; and essays by contemporary French, English, and American critics.   He wrote
in a highly artificial style which Stedman compared to the
"heroic swing" of an eighteenth-century dramatic historian.
An invitation to join the Century Club in 1866 suggests that
he was no longer identified with Clapp and his Bohemians but
with the Genteel writers.   In 1875 an obituary for Clapp
noted that only one of the Bohemians was known to have re-
formed.   Winter placed a clipping of this in one of his scrapbooks and wrote beside it, "That's me W. W."[34]

Bohemia had been only a passing phase in his life.
By the mid-sixties, he had embraced standards of taste
which George Santayana in 1911 would label "the Genteel
Tradition."   This term, to Santayana, meant nineteenth-century American idealism which had become lifeless and aca-
demic.   Its decline began in the 1860s (according to its
critics) when the chaos caused by the war and a rapidly
changing American society prompted writers of similar
tastes--Thomas Bailey Aldrich, Richard Henry Stoddard,
Edmund C. Stedman, Bayard Taylor, George William Curtis,
Richard Watson Gilder, Charles Eliot Norton, and William
Winter--to seek refuge in the past rather than to experiment.
They formed a cultural aristocracy which governed official
taste in American arts and letters for the last third of the

nineteenth century. In his Harvests of Change: American
Literature, 1865-1914 (pp. 12-13), Jay Martin suggests that
after the war, writers insisted upon tradition and the past
because "They refused to threaten their culture with the new
in literature, since Americans were, as they believed, too
distracted by the new in life." These writers desperately
looked to the past to find familiar landmarks in a setting
where everything was changing. Aldrich wrote in his last
years:

> Romance beside this unstrung lute
>   Lies stricken mute.
> The oldtime fire, the antique grace,
> You will not find them anywhere.
> Today we breathe a commonplace
> Polemic, scientific air.
> We strip Illusion of her veil;
> We vivisect the nightingale
>   To probe the secret of his note
> The Muse in alien ways remote
>   Goes wandering.

Aldrich and his friends valued cultivation and refinement,
which they associated with travel, good books, and an intellectual atmosphere. They attempted to hold on to a noble
way of life which science and materialism were rapidly des-
troying. In temperament and philosophy, William Winter
belonged more to this tradition than to the Bohemians.

The foundation of William Winter's critical beliefs
was essentially Aristotelian, derived mainly from the English
romantics and American Transcendentalists. He regarded the
theatre as a temple of art and not "merely a workshop for
shrewd and vulgar speculation in popular credulity." He saw
the world as tyrannized by the vulgar and commonplace--"the
countless trivialities that constitute human existence"--with
the artist (or writer) as a lighthouse to inspire, encourage,
ennoble, uplift, educate, and provide an ideal pattern by which
to live. To Winter the artist has a duty to interpret and
champion the ideal. He must choose between the beautiful
and the ugly and guide the tastes of less sensitive men. For
Winter art and literature were held up as a religion to elevate and inspire man.

In his early criticism, he thought it important to explain the difference between genius and talent--a topic popular
with writers of the period. In the Saturday Press of March

24, 1860, he admitted that it was not easy to mark a distinction between the two.

> Genius may be described as creative, sympathetic power. By it, through the emotions, the whole soul is agitated and controlled. Talent is also power, but of a humbler sort. It created nothing. It had no contact with the emotional nature. Talent is special and singular. Genius is comprehensive. The one wins our respect and mercy; the other wins our admiration and love. Talent is given in some measure to all persons, just as memory and conscience are. Genius is possessed by few. It must be voluntary, and cannot be acquired.

To help his readers understand the concept of genius in authorship, Winter turned to "The Literature of Knowledge and the Literature of Power," an essay by Thomas De Quincey which was published originally in the North British Review in 1848, and was reprinted in Volume Nine of De Quincey's collected works in 1858. To De Quincey the function of the literature of knowledge is to teach; the function of the literature of power is to move. He explained: a cookbook can teach us many things but only a masterpiece of literature such as Paradise Lost can touch our soul. Obviously the latter is more important, and genius is necessary to create it. Winter did not fully digest De Quincey's treatise although he discussed it with enthusiasm, agreeing it was "a wise and perfect view" of literature. Where talent might provide literature for most men, genius is necessary to "build nests in aerial attitudes of temples sacred from violation or of forests inaccessible." In other words genius is necessary to interpret the ideal.

In the same essay Winter discussed what impels genius to create and the experience of creating. Literature is the fruit of intellectual labor, he reasoned, "in its highest form, of intellectual labor penetrated with inspiration." But ambition is also important and it comes in two forms: ambition for triumph (worldly power, wealth, and renown), and ambition for truth (a noble life and character). While both forms of ambition have affected men of genius, the greatest men have desired truth more than triumph. A major tenet of his critical philosophy would be that artists and writers seek excellence, not popular applause.

Shakespeare offered Winter the prime example of a man of genius: "He has summoned from the vast realms of imagination, and from the shadowy domain of the past, forms of light and of darkness, of beauty, sublimity, grandeur, horror, that dwell now in all the temples of the mind, that stimulate, and exalt, and, at the same time, satisfy our ideals."[35] Such confectionery reveals much about Winter-- his poetic fancy, his worship of Shakespeare, and his rule for measuring all drama. He would use Shakespeare again and again as a club to subdue any claims to genius among contemporary authors. Such effusive plaudits may seem silly today, but in 1865 they flowed in buckets from the pens of young romantic poets obsessed with the feelings which Shakespeare aroused in their souls. Like many of his contemporaries, Winter thought the poetic nature of Hamlet (of all Shakespearean characters) most nearly attuned to his own. But, with a certain levity, he noted that the Prince of Denmark was so far removed from this "practical, arrogant, ironhanded age--when realism is the dominant philosophy, and the pocket supersedes the soul--such a person would, there is little doubt, be seized wherever found, and promptly consigned to a neighbouring lunatic asylum."[36]

His belief in an idealized art put him in opposition to the new realistic literature of the period, particularly the French sensational plays with their sexual improprieties. He condemned such regular pieces as East Lynne and Camille. His writings express again and again his fundamental beliefs: "The stage is not a place for the analysis of moral ulcers"; "Plays which illustrate the consequences of infidelity to the marriage tie, are, in every respect, a nuisance"; "The sole refuge of this age is art; and that should be kept white, pure, peaceful, and beautiful. What we need on stage is what will cheer, and comfort, and strengthen!" Winter's critical position was not unique; it reflects a world view shared by many of his contemporaries.

In the decade after the Civil War, Winter was given considerable support by men who shared his philosophy and standards. In 1868 Henry Austin Clapp began a thirty-four-year career as theatre critic of The Boston Daily Advertiser, one of the oldest and most conservative newspapers in that city. Like Winter he studied law at Harvard, and sought to combine law and journalism into a career. Unlike Winter, however, he remained in law and never depended upon his pen for his livelihood. While his influence was confined to the Boston area, he was widely read. When his Reminis-

cences were published in 1902, the Critic reported that "with
the possible exception of Mr. William Winter, there is no
drama critic better known outside of his own city than Mr.
Clapp." A staunch moralist, Clapp wanted the theatre to
elevate public taste; he valued Shakespeare above modern
playwrights; he preferred the "grand manner" of nineteenth-
century acting to realistic methods; he considered himself a
guardian of public taste and morals. Like Winter he embraced the major tenets of the Genteel Tradition.

More influential than Henry Austin Clapp, however,
was John Ranken Towse, a brilliant young English journalist
who was appointed theatre critic of the influential New York
Evening Post in 1874. He would hold that position for the
next fifty-four years. While the Post did not have the large
circulation of the Tribune, its readers were that element of
America who frequented the Harvard and Century Clubs--in
other words the intellectual and cultured elite. Well steeped
in the London theatre of the 1850s and 1860s, Towse fought
throughout his career to maintain Victorian tastes in drama
and nineteenth-century standards in the theatre. He believed
that the theatre should "illustrate and enforce the soundest
principles of art, morality, and social law under the seduc-
tive guise of entertainment." This entertainment should be
honest and rational, not necessarily highly intellectual. In
order to be effective, it must amuse or fascinate; however,
if the theatre does nothing but muse, it is "worthless and
probably mischievous." The theatre cannot escape its responsibility as "an elevator of the public mind and morals,"
he concluded. Either it must be "wisely conducted as an
agent of the higher civilization," or cease to be called an
art. Towse's concept reflects the nineteenth-century belief
that art should point a moral or be a significant expression
of man's higher ideals. Such principles have close affinity
to those of William Winter's. Both critics spent the last
years of their lives unsuccessfully challenging realism.

To the generation that followed, William Winter was a
moralist. He always denied such a charge, however, noting
that modern audiences did not wish to deal with immoral
questions in a truthful manner, but wanted to peer into bed-
rooms through the keyhole. In his review of East Lynne he
explained how the theatre had sacrificed truth in order to
tickle the fancy of the public: "A wife and mother is made
to desert her husband, her children, and a happy home, at
the instigation of a villain against whom she has been ex-
pressly warned and because of a suspicious circumstance

which any woman of sense would have seen through immediately. "[37] The plot unwinds in the usual way with the re-
morseful wife breaking from her seducer, then returning in
disguise to her former home, where she dies--"forgiven because she dies. " As a coup de grâce, Winter added,
"Nothing seems to interest the multitude so deeply as a tale
of conjugal infidelity visited in the sequel with the wages of
sin. "

Camille he accused of "sympathetic swindling. " The
play pretended to have an intellectual and moral purpose when
it existed for no other purpose than to make money. You
wipe away your tears, Winter snorted, but your mind retains
nothing: "What is the significance of its pathos? What jus-
tification exists, in the didactic aim and meaning of the drama, for the public illustration of an extremely disagreeable,
not to say a repulsive theme. "[38] For money alone! The
public does not care why they are moved, he believed, as
long as they shed a few tears. There is some truth to Winter's accusations that such plays were produced with purely
commercial interests in mind, but it is not the whole truth.
Both plays expressed moral truths to the audiences of their
day, and this may account in part for their success. Winter
demanded that the theatre offer only an idealized view of
life and shun unpleasant social and moral questions. His
critical position remained unchanged for half a century. He
depended upon the support of the cultured classes and this
support evaporated as his generation--those who thought as
he did--passed away. To accuse Dumas fils, or Sardou
(among others) of exploiting serious themes for sensationalism
in the 1860s, 1870s, and 1880s, was merely to repeat what
his genteel contemporaries were saying. But later, when he
used the same phrases against Ibsen and Shaw, the critical
corps--now younger and better educated--attacked and ridiculed him.

East Lynne and Camille were not the only targets at
this time for Winter's wrath. In the Albion of January 2,
1864, he expressed disgust with Bayard Taylor's new novel,
Hanna Thurston, which dealt with sectarianism, temperance,
anti-slavery, spiritualism, and women's rights--a potpourri
of popular topics of the day. The characters he thought
weak-minded, sensual, and contemptible, "such as might
exist, here and there, in almost any community, but such
as are always the excrescences and never the types of contemporaneous civilization. "

A lack of universal values also prompted his harsh review of J. S. Jones's melodrama, The People's Lawyer, which he viewed in September 1864. Solon Shingle (played by John Owens) was a "coarse, ignorant, sly, inquisitive, loquacious, old Yankee farmer.... The atmosphere of the cattlemarket and the little country grocery store hangs about him. His dress, his walk, his quid of tobacco, his big spectacles, his green umbrella, his creaky voice, his nose flaming with toddy, his habit of expectoration--all are in perfect keeping with his character, and with reality.... Such extreme fidelity to life is not agreeable."[39] John Owens' Solon Shingle attracted the masses because of his realistic characteristics. He did not elevate, cheer, comfort, or strengthen their lives. He did not point to ideals in a commercial age which Winter himself found bankrupt of ideals. "This is one of those cases in which the true artist would sacrifice truth to taste," the critic concluded. In other words, gloss over the raw elements of the old farmer and idealize his nature. Winter believed: "It is not the province of the stage--nor of art, in any form--to photograph the surfaces of actual life.... Art implies selection."[40]

In the 1890s, such standards did not allow Winter to accept the New Drama--the plays of Pinero, Sudermann, Shaw, and Ibsen. He did not think it the province of the theatre to dramatize sociological problems such as divorce, adultery, and the "fallen woman." He refused to consider a depiction of "real" life the proper subject for the artist. Realism to Winter meant disagreeable subjects preached with a moral; and he questioned the wisdom of presenting moral tracts which offered horrible examples of transgressions. Playwrights, he felt, thought they could "exhibit any sort of enormity" if they tell you at the end to avoid evil.

The first American performance of Pinero's The Second Mrs. Tanqueray at the Star Theatre, October 9, 1893, drew his critical wrath. Both the subject (the fallen woman) and the moral it drew (the wages of sin) he regarded as commonplace and in poor taste: "In the name of good-breeding and common sense, let the stage be delivered from that intolerable nuisance, the brother who is always chasing another man's wife, and the sister who cannot take care of her own garters. If we cannot have art of the highest order, at least let us have art that is clean."[41]

His attack later against Sudermann's Magda reiterated some of the same arguments. He (and American audiences) were familiar with the play: Duse had presented it in 1889; Modjeska in 1894; and Mrs. Fiske in 1899. In The Wallet of Time (1913), Winter comments upon the Modjeska engagement: "It is really not necessary for the stage to advise young women that they must not regulate the conduct of their lives according to the dictates of vanity and love of admiration; that they ought not to leave their homes and produce children without having been married. And that they ought not, even by a false avowal of wanton propensity or conduct, to cause their paternal progenitors to explode with fury and expire from apoplexy. "[42] More importantly, the theatre was simply not the place for such subjects to be discussed.

Winter also involved himself in the controversy surrounding the first American performance of George Bernard Shaw's Mrs. Warren's Profession (New Haven, Connecticut, October 27, 1905), and the judicial decision handed down (July 6, 1906) by the Court of Special Sessions. Whether Shaw's play did or did not properly point the moral--that prostitution is evil--Winter thought immaterial; the subject was unfit for presentation in the theatre. "That prostitution exists and flourishes: that prostitutes sometimes suffer terribly: that their existence, and often diseased condition, is a terrible menace to public health: that the regulation and, as far as humanly possible, the extirpation of that dreadful profession is a crying need--all that and much more relative to the subject is known, and widely known. "[43] Then Winter made his usual analogy: "No right-minded, well-bred person introduces an indelicate, not to say foul, subject for conversation in a drawing-room. The introduction of such a subject would be considered--and justly so--an insult. " The critic also took Mary Shaw to task for her willingness to perform the hated role of Mrs. Warren.

It was Ibsen and his "tainted" drama, however, which became the symbol for Winter of all that was wrong with the modern stage. He believed staunchly that "the province of art is the ministry of beauty, and beauty, in art, is inseparable from morality. " The Ibsen drama, on the other hand, had banished beauty and poetry from the stage, Winter believed, and offered in their place "morbid, repulsive plays. " After viewing Mrs. Fiske's Hedda Gabler in November, 1904, he saw little hope that the "degenerate" drama could be stopped:

> The whole world is in an extraordinary commotion; repose seems nowhere to exist; and in all seasons

of extraordinary commotion the scum floats to the top. The community has been afflicted with an epidemic of 'Ghosts'--which is unmitigated filth-- and with an epidemic of 'Candida'--which is reckless, mischievous, conceited, ironical trifling, crazy sentimentalism, and vicious sophistry; and every day the brood of cranks becomes more numerous, the fads more oppressive, the commercial speculators more desperate for novelty, the wild experiments more rife. 'Serious Drama, the consequent morbid stuff is called, or 'The Drama of Ideas, ' but the moment it is examined, it is found to be the drama that illumines the madhouse, rakes in the hospital, or delves in the sewer. Surely there is enough good in human nature, enough romance in human history, enough beauty in the natural world, whereon to base a drama of loveliness and light; and surely a woman of genius, like Mrs. Fiske, has no need to stoop to the drama that is 'baneful'; to drama that banishes poetry and nobility; to the crack-brained devices of Old World charlatans; to 'all that is at enmity with joy. '[44]

In The Wallet of Time, Winter calls Ibsenism a "rank, deadly pessimism ... a disease, injurious alike to the stage and to the public...." The playwright did not point the way towards salvation. He offered no direction or assistance. "A reformer who calls you to crawl with him into a sewer, merely to see and breathe its feculence, is a pest, " the critic concluded. [45]

Since he could neither accept nor stop the New Drama, Winter's voice became shrill, angry, vindictive. The Rochester Post-Express found him the "voice of one crying out in Newspaper Row and not crying very wisely. "[46] The same writer thought that when Winter "writes of the latter day drama every sentence declares him a reactionary. " This also seems the verdict of history.

His principles for evaluating the actor were no less strident. He stated in 1914 (Vagrant Memories) that criticism should be for the "information of the public, not the instruction of the actor. " Therefore, he thought it more important to discuss the "influence and comprehensive effect" of acting rather than deal with "questions of mere

technicality and detail. " Although he could analyze a role
with precision, he usually chose to discuss it in a wider
context. His views on acting place him in the mainstream
of nineteenth-century critical thought.

He considered acting the primary art of the theatre,
and believed that only through great acting could the masterpieces of the drama be adequately represented. Like most
of his contemporaries he thought acting should be more than
an imitation of real life; acting should be life elevated and
made more meaningful. He believed repertory stock company training necessary to develop an actor's voice and body,
and did not favor the new schools of acting. He deplored
the commercial star system which encouraged actors to repeat themselves instead of developing their versatility.
While he advocated a balance between emotional and intellectual acting, he did not believe in impulse, but design:
"No actor was ever successful who did not know before-hand
exactly what he meant to do, exactly why he meant to do it,
exactly when he meant to do it, exactly how he meant to do
it, and who, above all, was not possessed of the ability to
make practical use of that knowledge. " Winter thought the
capability to feel essential for an actor but did not believe
the heart was the "main thing. " It was immaterial, he concluded, whether the actor feels or does not feel while giving
a performance, as "long as he makes his audience feel. "
He considered the actor an artist, and wanted him respected
and honored as one. His most demanding principle for
determining the worth of an actor was personal integrity.
He did not separate an actor's personal and professional
lives. He believed that an actor's stage characters were
but a reflection of his personality.

Like his contemporaries, Winter used terms such as
genius, talent, and culture in discussing acting. In the Albion of January 18, 1862, he referred to E. L. Davenport
as an intelligent and graceful actor but not a genius. What
was lacking in his portrayal of Hamlet? According to Winter, "Intensity of emotion which comes of 'thoughts beyond
the reaches of our soul. ' " Edwin Booth achieved a more
striking success in the same role, Winter thought, --not with
more art, but with more feeling. This might suggest that
Winter was a defender of the emotional school, especially
since he wrote favorably of Matilda Heron in 1862. But he
changed his opinion of Heron after she "pandered to vulgar
tastes" in sensational and adulterous roles. His evaluation
of John Wilkes Booth's acting (March 29, 1862) provides a

clearer definition of several terms. Young Booth had emotional power and personal magnetism--attributes necessary for genius--but his acting was rugged, uncouth, gross. Winter called him an "uncultured genius" who needed training and experience to be seriously regarded as an actor of the first rank.

He contested John S. Clarke's claim to genius in 1862, believing him only an accomplished caricaturist, not an accomplished comedian. Clark possessed neither originality of style nor remarkable "felicity of method."[47] He burlesqued rather than idealized the characters. And while popular comedian John Owens avoided the clichés of the stage Yankee in playing Solon Shingle, yet he imitated life rather than idealized it. To be fair to Owens, however, one should note that Winter hated the stage Yankee.

His reaction to Charles Kean's visit to New York in April 1865 suggests that he considered virtue a requirement for genius. Kean was scheduled to open on April 17 as Cardinal Wolsey in Henry VIII. The assassination of President Lincoln, however, postponed this event until April 26. Winter was at the opening. While finding some elocution problems in Kean's delivery, Winter thought him a well-trained and brilliant actor: "If genius be the power to awaken all the emotions of the heart, and to sway our soul, as the storm wind sways the sombre pines, ... Mr. Kean possesses it, beyond a doubt."[48] He disagreed with other critics--Towse for one--who claimed that Kean had talent and culture but not genius. In his finest roles--King John, Louis XI, and Cardinal Wolsey--Winter felt he evinced "comprehensiveness of conception, and ... fidelity to details in the execution of his ideal." But then Winter equivocated. The actor's genius may not be equal to that of his father, or of George Frederick Cooke, or of Junius Brutus Booth. In total, however, his career "has been purer than theirs, in his conscientious devotion to the dramatic art, and with their will his name be remembered." Winter had shifted his critical stance from five years earlier. In defending the good name of Rufus Choate in 1860, he had advocated that "no man is good unless he is great."

Winter judged harshly the personal character of Edwin Forrest in determining his worth as an actor. He thought the actor possessed great talent, manly beauty, and physical strength.[49] He praised his hard work in the face of failure and disappointments. He was aware of the actor's triumphs at the Park Theatre in 1826, and ten years later at Drury Lane Theatre, which brought him wealth, popularity, and respect from his peers. But Winter believed that weakness of character tainted his art. His hissing of Macready at Edinburgh; his alleged involvement in the Astor Place Riot; the divorce suit; his cruel treatment of his fellow actors "alienated from him, at once and forever, the sympathy of the better classes of the people." Winter made it very clear that he should be numbered among these people.

Much of the time he simply ignored Forrest. When the actor opened for a month of repertory in New York on November 13, 1865, not a word appeared in the Tribune until November 27, 1865. [50] Such rudeness of Winter's part is not adequately explained by noting his dislike of the actor's style. Charlotte Cushman, an actress often compared with Forrest, he lauded as late as 1871 for her majesty and intellect when fellow critics were describing her as melodramatic and excessively masculine. Winter's silence seems to have been prompted more by Forrest's offstage antics than by his muscular style.

But Winter was too shrewd early in his career to become seriously involved in the "old and ever-recurring controversy" over the merits of Forrest. "He has been for many years active and successful in the dramatic profession. He has received, in large measure, both approval and abuse.... It is not worthwhile, however, to meddle in the dispute.... As a materialist, in the dramatic art, Mr. Forrest is foremost and alone--without a model, but not without a great many shadows." [51] Yet, Winter could not resist calling Forrest's acting "clumsy capers" in the Albion of December 23, 1865.

Forrest represented to Winter the "lower" physical element in art. He was selfish: "He did not love dramatic art of its own sake, but because it was tributary to himself. The motives of his conduct were vanity, pride, self-assertion, and avarice of power, praise, and wealth." [52] In youth he had "revolted against discipline." In manhood "he revolted against culture." Winter found him "constitutionally a savage and always in rebellion." Instead of discussing Forrest's acting techniques, the critic frequently ridiculed his style, describing it as: "snorts," "grunts," "brays," "belches," "gaspings," and "gurglings," "protracted pauses," "lolling tongue and stentorian roar." [53] Winter compared such acting to the poetry of Walt Whitman, where too much emphasis was placed on the flesh. Forrest could not achieve greatness, then, because he lacked "harmonious and symmetrical blending of the spiritual and physical."

Edwin Booth most clearly typified Winter's idea of genius in acting. He first viewed Booth at the Boston Theatre on April 20, 1857, as Sir Giles Overreach in Massinger's A New Way to Pay Old Debts. In October 1862, with their personal friendship still several years in the future, 54 Winter could chide the actor for then sacrificing art to popular applause ("something of the clap-trap still adhered to his style of acting"). 55 Booth had lacked independent taste and experience although he showed promise. His natural advantages were "a mobile and expressive face, an elegant figure, a sympathetic and pleasing voice, a temperament of great sensibility, a strong intellect, based in a torrid zone of passion ... an actor of more than ordinary power." Now (October 1862) after Booth had spent a year in London and Paris, Winter detected a marked improvement in his acting: "Time, foreign travel, experience and study have matured his judgment and polished his style." Winter noticed: "From first to last, he not only does not make points where points are usually made, but he does not make a point at all. He is natural, simple, impressive--winning the honest and earnest admiration of all who honor the dramatic art." In the following month, the critic viewed Booth's Romeo, Hamlet, Shylock, and Richard III. While the actor was guilty of ranting in the latter role, Winter thought the other roles were presented with delicacy, consistency, and finish: "In all, he exhibits the genius to comprehend and the intellect to embody."

Booth made theatrical history during the 1864-65 season by playing Hamlet for 100 performances at the Winter Garden Theatre in New York. Winter viewed this Hamlet on several occasions. In the Albion of December 3, 1864, he suggested that the requirements of the role were identical to Booth's gifts: "Intellectual spirituality, blending masculine strength with feminine softness; imagination, preponderant over reason, and groping in shuddering audacity upon the fearful confines of the other world...." Charles Shattuck in his The Hamlet of Edwin Booth suggests that "Winter presumes to see Booth's insides, to identify with Booth's mind, to become Booth, to play the Hamlet role with his pen."56 Since Winter believed an actor's stage characters were but a reflection of his personal character, he did presume to see the insides of the actors he reviewed. He chose not to ana-

lyze the performance in technical terms because he wanted
to discuss Booth's interpretation of the philosophical and
spiritual dimensions. He suggests this in a letter to Booth,
written in the fall of 1872:

> One of the most effective, perhaps the most ef-
> fective of all the attributes of your Hamlet is its
> direct applicability to general experience. All hu-
> man creatures, save those cursed with an indurated
> insensibility to suffering, perceive and feel the
> misery which makes a burden of so much of life.
> That is a matter of emotion, not intellect; there-
> fore it is very general. We all feel at times that
> there should be--almost that there must be--some-
> thing after death, something so much better and
> greater than our little life here that we cannot even
> picture it in imagination. Yet there comes to most
> a revulsion to doubt and despair. If we only knew!
> But whatever falls upon us; however heart-rendering
> and mind-wrecking our experience of affliction may
> be; however much we may wish 'that the fever
> called living were over at last,' still we must en-
> dure and strive and go on living out our lives until
> the natural end and doing our duty as well as we
> can until that end, even though the rest be silence.
> It is your perception of this common experience;
> the clarity with which this common experience is
> felt by your audience to be perceived and understood
> by you; the exquisite sympathy and beauty with which
> you interpret it, more perhaps than anything else,
> that endears your performance to the people. That
> is what I was trying to convey in my recent no-
> tice. [57]

Edwin Booth was the acknowledged leader of his profession during the last third of the nineteenth-century; William
Winter was the foremost dramatic critic. These men maintained a close, personal friendship which must have affected
the objectivity of Winter's reviews. [58] But Booth fulfilled all
the critic's criteria for great acting: he interpreted the great
masterpieces of the theatre; he was versatile, able to successfully perform a wide range of characters--Shylock as well
as Hamlet; he possessed a beautiful voice and a poetic temperament; and most important, his acting onstage was but an
extension of his sensitive, refined, intellectual, honest nature.

Winter also established personal relationships with a

number of other actors and actresses during his career, including John McCullough, Joseph Jefferson, Lawrence Barrett, Richard Mansfield, Ada Rehan, and Adelaide Neilson. While contemporary and modern historians have judged him harshly for allowing these friendships to affect his critical judgment, Winter considered himself a fair man. He believed that familiarity with actors gave him insight into their personalities, and thus into the characters they portrayed. And he saw nothing wrong with encouraging actors who sought the ideal in their characters. Friend or foe, he judged each by an exacting set of standards. He believed no man could rise above himself: his character determined his worth, both as an artist and as a man. John McCullough was "a direct man in his art" because he was "a direct man in his nature."[59] To Winter, McCullough's acting was "the flower of his character." Charlotte Cushman, thought old-fashioned by most of his contemporaries, he called "not a great actress merely, but she was a great woman."[60] Lawrence Barrett was a "man of high principle and perfect integrity. He never spoke a false word nor knowingly harmed a human being."[61] Henry Irving "was greater than anything he ever did." Winter called him a "vibrant, unconquerable spirit and a ceaseless exemplar of beneficent purpose and noble endurance."[62] On the other hand, Charles Fechter did not measure up to greatness because he was intensely selfish, "conscious of no moral purpose to be served by his art."[63] Sarah Bernhardt, while possessing "ample and exact control of the instruments of her vocation," presented stage characters in whom "vanity, cruelty, selfishness, and animal propensity are supreme."[64] To Winter, "no person was benefited, cheered, encouraged, ennobled, instructed, or even rationally entertained by the prospect of those embodiments, or any one of them...." Because of his devotion to the theatre, William Winter sought the friendship of those actors who aimed to express its highest ideals. This could not include those actors who performed in the New Drama or other sensational plays of the period.

Winter maintained a personal and professional relationship with Augustin Daly in the 1880s and 1890s--a relationship which, to many, compromised his critical integrity and earned him the nickname of "Daly's house poet." They were contemporaries. Daly, like Winter, had launched his career as a dramatic critic in the early 1860s, but he had been interested more in writing plays and producing. The two men had a falling-out in the early 1870s. Perhaps Daly's sensational French plays offended Winter's ideals; or perhaps Winter's harsh remarks against these plays--Frou-Frou and Madelein Morel--prompted the rift.[65] Not until

Daly's failure at the New Fifth Avenue Theatre in 1877 and his opening of the renovated Woods Museum in September 1879 did he seek for a reconciliation with Winter--a reconciliation which was materially to benefit both men for the next twenty years. Daly hired Winter to write introductions to revivals of Shakespearean and old English comedies, and to prepare acting versions of Shakespearean plays. Winter, in turn, could read new plays in advance of performance. He accompanied Daly to Europe in April 1883--at the manager's expense. [66] He wrote A Daughter of Comedy, about actress Ada Rehan, at Daly's insistence. Contemporaries accused him of defending the manager's policies and praising his plays as part of his job.

Certainly Winter compromised his reputation by accepting favors and employment from Daly. But he approved of Daly's artistic policy after 1879 and needed little encouragement to give him support. In The Wallet of Time, Winter describes Daly with his finest superlatives:

> Daly was animated by the highest ambition, in his relations with the stage he was conscious of a solemn responsibility and he acted from conscientious and noble motives. The early part of his career as a manager was, naturally, marked by some wildness of experiment, but he soon obtained a firm control of the business and of his resources, and he then shaped the policy of aiming at the best, and from that purpose he never deviated. [67]

A year later, in Vagrant Memories, Winter further eulogized Daly: "He neither boasted in prosperity nor complained in adversity. He never broke faith with the public." [68] Winter valued Daly's friendship. To offer Shakespeare and the classics for refined and sensitive tastes seemed to him the very essence of theatre.

William Winter defended his critical position in 1889 by answering accusations made by Dion Boucicault in the North American Review that newspaper critics were both corrupt and detrimental to the stage. Boucicault's position was that "the newspaper press had practically displaced the public in the exercise of judgment; that press advertisements allowed actors to occupy high places; that journalists were incompetent to judge dramatic events; and that as a result, there could be no great drama or actors. [69] Debating Boucicault before the Goethe Society on January 28, 1889, Winter answered these charges, to his own satisfaction at least. He admitted that the press was not perfect, but pointed out that "newspapers would not exist if the people did not like them and want them, and the people would not like them and want them if their own minds were not reflected in them."[70] He did not believe either the press or the public possessed much literary judgment--and play reviewing was an extension of audience opinion. In his opinion, an actor wins the public's favor--"not so much by the merit of what he does as by the virtue of what he is." He concluded that newspaper criticism settles very little: "[It] establishes no man's rank, fixes no man's opinion, dissuades no man from the bent of his humor. The actor whom it praises may nevertheless pass away and no place be found for him." In Winter's judgment, newspaper criticism "accomplishes all that should be expected of it when it arouses and pleases and benefits the reader, clarifying his views, and helping him to look with a sympathetic and serene vision upon the pleasures and pains, joys and sorrows, the ennobling splendors and the solemn admirations of the realm of art." A. M. Palmer, manager of the Madison Square Theatre, thought the address "the best thing ever given before the Goethe Society."[71]

William Winter established his reputation in the twelve years from 1865 until his first trip to England in 1877. In 1868 the Spirit of the Times (May 30) described him as New York's first and foremost critic, whose "kindliness of nature" made it difficult for him to censure an actor or manager. Yet the same writer noted that his conscientiousness "holds his gentle disposition in tolerable check, and his severity is the more dreaded when the axe does fall." In 1865 he had hoped to play a major role in shaping the future of the theatre. "We have simply to tell the truth as to plays and players, as to the principles of dramatic art and the fruit of dramatic labour," he preached somewhat naively.[72] "By thus disseminating true ideas, we shall continually affect and gradually elevate the standard of popular taste, until at last that taste, which is now content with merely vulgar farce and gaudy commonplace, shall suddenly find itself disgusted with these trivial matters." As he grew older Winter's gentle disposition was strained to the utmost by the avalanche of commonplace, vulgar, realistic plays; a horde of self-seeking, untrained actors; and mercenary speculators draining the theatre of its energy and life in the name of profits. The more he sought his ideal art, the more it eluded him. His carping against the new order froze his image in the minds of posterity.

Harsh attacks against Winter began in the 1870s, questioning his impartiality and openmindedness. Perhaps the most vicious appeared in the scandal-mongering New York Dramatic News on July 21, 1877: "Like all little things, Willie is rather a pet with his little coterie. Little in mind, he suited Booth. Little in body, he amused Mc-Cullough. Little in morals, he suited Rip Van Winkle [Joseph Jefferson]. Little in scholarship, he suited every American star actor who lacks ability to fill a first-class stock position." The Dramatic News concluded that a "bad poet was spoiled when he was made a critic." Nym Crinkle (Andrew C. Wheeler), in the Dramatic Mirror of April 6, 1889, also found Winter more poet than critic: "Mr. Winter does not appear to have heard of the disagreeable side of life. He has concentrated his faculties on the disagreeable side of Mr. Winter.... He is avowedly not a journalist, but a poet. He is not winning; he is warbling. He is reading Charles Lamb in a dim, agnostic seclusion while the fray goes on outside and his window is closed." Neither the Dramatic News nor Nym Crinkle could muster the forces to challenge Winter seriously in the 1870s and 1880s, but they did reflect the opinion of a growing number of writers who found his critical position too narrow.

By 1900 his day was over; those who demanded a closer relationship between art and "real life" had won the fray. The editor of the Dramatic Mirror, Harrison Grey Fiske, expressed a majority opinion on November 23, 1907, when he accused Winter of "hopelessly confusing the duties of the reviewer with those of the moralist." In the editor's opinion, Winter's views "are the views of the past and his horizon is circumscribed by that which entered it during youth and middle age.... The emasculated, the obvious, the artificial, and the obsolete are preferable to the virile, the subtle, the true, and the modern."

Dramatic tastes as well as Winter's reputation had undergone a rapid change. Only nine years earlier (July 10, 1898), Fiske had encouraged Winter not to retire: "There has never been a time when the influence of your virile pen was felt so much and when it was needed so much, as now. You give comfort and courage to those that are struggling to preserve the stage as a decent and beneficial institution in this country, and you help to make the public discriminating and wholesome in its tastes--at least, that part of the public to whom the earnest and the ambitious must appeal and on whose support they must depend."[73]

Winter at that time had just written favorably about Mrs. Fiske's forthcoming performance of Becky Sharp, and Fiske no doubt felt some obligation to return this favor. But now the critic's harsh attacks against Mrs. Fiske's acting of Ibsen, and his savage denouncing of Harrison Grey Fiske's production of Percy MacKaye's Sappho and Phaon (October 1907) for immorality prompted Fiske's response. For three years they sparred bitterly in the press and through private correspondence on the subject of a critic's ethical responsibilities.

Winter's departure from the Tribune might have been predicted as early as 1905 when Hart Lyman replaced Whitelaw Reid as editor. The latter had allowed his dramatic critic free rein to do as he pleased. Lyman began excising from Winter's copy some of his harshest remarks. Winter complained to managerial editor Roscoe Brown, who replied that Winter's copy did injury to "some of our advertisers." Lyman supported Brown and informed Winter that for the Sunday Tribune he must not criticize but merely report. The debate continued into the summer of 1909, when about five hundred words were cut from Winter's essay, "Dirty drama," and several reviews were rejected completely. In August, Lyman refused to publish, among several items, a poem with anti-semitic overtones. Winter resigned on August 8. Since the Tribune made no mention of his departure, he was forced to take out an advertisement in the paper to announce his retirement. In 1918, after his death, his son Jefferson privately printed In the Matter of William Winter and the New York Tribune to give the family side of the argument. 74

During the eight years remaining of his life, Winter lived as an independent man of letters, writing books and contributing to various periodicals. Old Friends, published in 1909, chronicles his early career including his fling with Bohemia. He wrote several biographies, including lengthy volumes on Richard Mansfield and David Belasco. Studies of Shakespeare, stage reminiscences and a volume of poetry attest to his constant labor. All told, he published more than fifty books in his lifetime.

After his retirement from the Tribune, he received tributes from his many friends across the country. On December 15, 1909, at a dinner held in his honor at the National Arts Club of New York City, John Ranken Towse of the Evening Post broke his forty-year moratorium against giving dinner speeches. He praised Winter's "great abilities and influence ... steadily exerted in the support of all that is best and most beneficial in dramatic art."[75] Detroit critic George P. Goodale wrote him in 1911 to praise his book, Gray Days and Gold. "Your industry is amazing; your intellectual nimbleness, your ready erudition and your matchless literary style are a constant spur to me in my work."[76] Such sincere personal tributes must have been gratifying to the old critic in his last years. Both Towse and Goodale were respected contemporaries--men who shared his critical philosophy and world view.

William Winter died on June 30, 1917, from uremic poisoning. A secular service was held on July 3, after which his body was cremated and the ashes interred in the family plot at Silver Mount Cemetery, Staten Island. His critical principles, however, like those of the Genteel Tradition, had long been in decline. And his style--serious, effusive, florid--had come to seem old-fashioned beside the lively prose which Clapp and Wilkens had first popularized in the Saturday Press. Henry Clapp, Jr. had taught him the necessity for wit and satire to enliven weighty matters, but Winter turned his back upon the French methods and followed older models. Clapp had not been wrong, only ahead of his time. By 1917 George Jean Nathan and H. L. Mencken had aptly demonstrated that in criticism, wit and satire are preferable to poesy and sentiment.

CHAPTER FIVE

STEPHEN RYDER FISKE
"ariel"

Born on November 22, 1840, in New Brunswick, New Jersey, Stephen Fiske had all the advantages which wealth, education, and political influence could bring to his career. [1] His father, William Henry Fiske, was a partner in a large iron foundry in New Brunswick. His grandfather, Haley Fiske, a judge and prominent leader of the Whig Party, was a close personal friend of Horace Greeley. [2] Stephen grew up in a religious, church-going home where attending the theatre was not allowed. His mother permitted him, however, to visit the pious lecture room at Barnum's Museum. Here he viewed old favorites such as Faint Heart Never Won Fair Lady and pantomimes by the Ravels. "I remember to this day how delighted I was, how eagerly I watched every part of the pantomime," he recalled in 1865; "how I marvelled when one of the Ravels was cut to pieces and put together again, and how I lingered behind when the green curtain fell and the audience was dismissed, with an inchoate idea of hiding under one of the seats and seeing the Ravels play all the rest of my life. "[3]

His interest in journalism developed at Rutgers College where he edited the school paper and contributed to the college magazine. His literary efforts created considerable controversy. In one article he caricatured his professors and their methods of teaching; in another he imitated the style of Charles Dickens and was accused of plagiarism. While he had talent as a writer, he studied law and later passed the New York bar examination. There is no evidence, however, that he ever practiced as an attorney. Instead he turned to journalism: first as local editor for the Brooklyn Transcript (probably in 1859), and a year later as special correspondent for James Gordon Bennett's New York Herald. He attracted Bennett's attention while reporting on the Prince of Wales'

visit to this country in 1860. While at Niagara Falls, he al-
legedly ordered the telegraph line held open. When it was
claimed by another reporter, he sent the first chapter of
Matthew and the twenty-first chapter of Revelations to tie up
the wire and prevent an important story from getting through
to another newspaper. [4] Fiske was among the first journalists
to protest against the policy of anonymous reporting; in Harper's New Monthly Magazine for February 1863, he published
a well written article on the modern newspaper and the new
role played by reporters. He aimed to show modern journalism as an honored and respected profession.

Stephen Fiske's opportunity to advance from reporter
to theatre critic came directly as a result of Ned Wilkins'
death. He had known Wilkins both professionally and perso-
nally; later, he would acknowledge the critic's influence upon
his own career. Comparison of the two writers is unavoid-
able. Like his predecessor, Fiske wrote for both the Herald
and Leader. As "Ariel" in the Leader he attempted to be
clever and witty, writing in a terse, lively style. Henry
Clapp accused him of using French words and phrases with
no clear idea of their meaning. Fiske represented the new
breed of reporter-critic. Well schooled in Bennett's techniques of sensational journalism, he believed news could be
created as well as merely reported. Round Table accusations in 1864, which depicted Bohemians as back-scratching,
corrupt, and self-serving hacks, seem pointedly directed
against him. William Winter held him responsible for the
anti-Booth editorials in the Herald after the assassination
of President Lincoln. Labeled as opportunist by friend and
foe alike, Stephen Ryder Fiske made a bid for success in
the early 1860s as a dramatic critic and a playwright.

He was handsome, well-educated, and shrewd. His
career was patterned after those of a number of his contemporaries. The success of Dion Boucicault in the 1850s and
1860s served as a model for an aspiring young dramatist.
Tailoring plays for popular actors from French, German, and
English sources seemed to offer an opportunity for fame and
fortune in a theatre dominated by the star system. In the
1850s Wilkins had followed (and paralleled) Boucicault's example; and in the 1860s Augustin Daly would establish his
reputation with borrowed plumes--Leah the Forsaken, Grif-
fith Gaunt, and Under the Gaslight. Like these men, Fiske
saw that theatre managers were eager to produce the dramatic works of prominent critics. The reason is obvious--it
assured them of a favorable press. On the other hand,

critics could earn up to ten times the amount of their weekly salary by adapting or translating a play. An ambitious young man need only combine these two professions to gain a measure of success.

Fiske made his debut as a playwright with My Noble Son-in-Law at Wallack's Theatre on the evening of April 7, 1863. Adapted from Le Gendre de M. Poirier by Emile Augier, the piece was carefully tailored for the Wallack company and for an audience accustomed to elegant comedies without vulgar jokes or buffoonery. According to a reviewer for Spirit of the Times, [5] the plot offered well-worn dramatic materials. A snobbish, nouveau-riche merchant marries his daughter to a spendthrift nobleman who lacks self-respect, independence of character, delicacy of feeling, and "even a good tailor." The son-in-law quickly tires of his marriage and of his in-laws. His flirtation with a countess is discovered by his father-in-law through a letter. The wife then demands a separation. Everything is in a state of confusion. Hearing that the son-in-law is about to fight a duel for the countess, however, the wife forgives him. He gives up the duel and the countess and "proposes to be a good boy, eschew frivolities, adhere closely to Parliament, attend to the interests of the public, and be in deed, what he is in name, a Noble Son-in-Law."

Critical reaction to the production was mixed. The reviewer for the Spirit thought it successful. He described the dialogue as pleasing, two or three characters well developed, the acting superb--especially that of Lester Wallack, Mrs. Hoey, and John Gilbert--and the scenery elegant. The Herald reviewer (probably Fiske) was lavish in his praise: "It is refreshing for once to meet with an adaptation which neither attempts to appropriate untranslatable French witticisms nor to introduce into a foreign piece our local slang. In giving full play to his own independent judgment and taste, the author has succeeded in producing a piece which may serve as a model to some of our popular playwrights. "[6] Figaro (Henry Clapp) disagreed. In the Leader of April 11 he termed My Noble Son-in-Law "the worst constructed and most incongruous play" that Wallack's "ever consented to put on the boards." Clapp clearly disliked Fiske. He accused him of attempting to imitate Wilkins' style of writing without knowing anything about the French language. A schoolboy would be ashamed of his blunders, Clapp judged. Odell describes My Noble Son-in-Law as a free rendering of Le Gendre de M. Poirier, which "made something of a hit. "[7]

Fiske's next dramatic effort followed in about eighteen months. He adapted Charles Dickens' Martin Chuzzlewit for Mrs. John Wood and the Olympic Theatre. The production opened on September 25, 1864, for a five-week run with J. H. Stoddard as Pecksniff and Mrs. Wood as Bailey the waiter. Mercutio (William Winter), in the Albion of October 1, discussed both the novel and Fiske's dramatic version. Dickens, he thought, was a false artist because he exaggerates excessively. It was only his "undertone of truth that lifts his novels above the level of mere caricature." On the other hand, Fiske's adaptation was "well enough done" although everything was in excess: "The stage is literally crowded with eccentricities--odd people, astounding wigs, raiment of crazy rainbows, queer bonnets and shirt collars. And, in short, a miscellaneous assortment of improbable paraphernalia." Very little of this was sufficient, Winter concluded, "in excess it cloys and wearies."

Other critics found more merit in the production. Touchstone (John Darcie), in the Spirit of the Times for October 15, described Martin Chuzzlewit as a good adaptation-- "as good an adaptation as can well be made of a book so profuse in incidents and characters." Augustin Daly favored the piece in the Evening Express although the circumstances surrounding his review were unusual. Daly was out of New York managing a tour for actress Miss Avonia Jones; his brother Joseph substituted for him, as he normally did on such occasions. In a letter dated September 15, 1864, Augustin instructed Joseph to "speak as flatteringly as you can" of Martin Chuzzlewit in order to court the favor of Fiske and his fellow Bohemians.[8] The Bohemians had not treated Daly's early plays kindly--especially his Leah the Forsaken in 1863. Fiske had called it "dramatic hash" and "wretched" (Herald, January 20, 1863). Augustin asked his brother to "try the effects of soft words now, on these gentlemen." Joseph complied by mentioning Fiske and predicting success for the play.[9] Pleased, Fiske wrote Augustin to thank him for a favorable notice.

A strong rivalry developed between Daly and Fiske.[10] They wrote in a similar style. Aided by the ghost writing of his brother, Joseph, Daly contributed to five papers over a nine-year period (1860-1869), including the Sunday Courier, Evening Express, Sun, Citizen, and the Times. But his career in journalism was a means to an end. In 1869 he severed his relationship with the New York Times to follow a career in the theatre as a playwright and manager.

Within six months of his Dickens' dramatization,
Stephen Ryder Fiske brought out Corporal Cartouche or the
Forlorn Hope, adapted from a popular French melodrama,
Le Vieux Caporal. With Henry Placide in the title role,
the play opened at the Winter Garden Theatre in late March
1865. The plot, as told by Mercutio in the Albion of April
1, is set in France at the time of Napoleon. A soldier is
entrusted with the care of a baby girl--General Roquebert's
daughter by a secret marriage. When the General is killed,
the soldier leaves her in the village of St. Laurent. He is
captured. After sixteen years at hard labor in the Russian
mines he escapes and returns to the village. The girl, now
grown into a beautiful woman, has fallen into the hands of a
villain. When the soldier tries to assist her, he is falsely
charged with robbery. In his fury he suffers a paroxysm
and is left unable to speak, write, or read. He cannot tell
the daughter about her father and her claim to a fortune.
The play ends happily, however, when a pistol discharge
shocks him and restores his senses.

Critical reaction was favorable. William Winter
called Corporal Cartouche a masterful play: "It is one more
stroke upon those harpstrings of the heart, which will never
cease to vibrate, as long as any goodness remains in human
nature. Its burden is the grief of an old man, suffering under cruel calamity and injustice; and by this it absorbs our
interest and wins our tears." Winter was especially pleased
that the play suggested a high ideal of honor and love. Delighted with this response, Fiske wrote Winter on April 3 to
thank him for the "beautiful article" and his candor in "speak-
ing the truth."[11] The assassination of President Lincoln
closed the production on April 14 but it re-opened April 26
and ran until May 1, a modest success by standards of the
day.

Fiske would later question whether a critic who writes
plays can judge other plays fairly: "Dramatists who do not
pay tribute to him must interfere with his business," he wrote
in the Dramatic Mirror for March 1, 1890. "Managers who
decline to produce his pieces cannot be as dear to him as
those who have made them successful." He concluded that a
man cannot serve two masters. If he plans to be a dramatist he should resign from his paper before producing his
first play. If he plans to be a critic he must not listen to
the advice of managers and actors. But Fiske did not blame
too severely those critics who "fall into temptation." He did
blame proprietors of newspapers: "They profess to require

intelligence and integrity, and they will not pay the salaries which these qualities are worth. "

After establishing himself as a playwright and dramatic critic, Fiske suspended what seemed like a promising career and sailed with James Gordon Bennett, Jr. on the first trans-ocean yacht race to England, December 11, 1866. He may have had several reasons for making the trip. First, gossip had him romantically involved with Mrs. John Wood. She had finished her third season at the Olympic Theatre and departed for England on July 11. Secondly a quarrel between Bennett, Sr. and major theatre managers in 1965-66 resulted in advertisements being withdrawn from the paper and coverage of theatrical events curtailed (Odell reviews the controversy in Annals of the New York Stage, Vol. VIII, p. 1-2). And thirdly, perhaps the challenge of sailing the Atlantic on the first ocean yacht race appealed to his love of adventure. Young Bennett was a boyhood friend. Their yacht, the Henrietta, outdistanced the Vesta and the Fleetwing to arrive at Cowes on Christmas day.

Fiske was given assignments by the Herald which took him to Ireland, Paris, Austria, Naples, Spain, and finally back to London. Here he pursued an active career in journalism, writing for Tinsley's Magazine a series of papers on English life as seen by an American. The series later appeared in a book entitled English Photographs. With the profits from his writings, Fiske purchased The Hornet, a "satirical and serio-comic journal" devoted to literature, criticism, and theatrical news. He was determined to become a prominent figure in London Bohemian society and used the editorial pages of The Hornet to stir up controversy. He attacked the Lord Chamberlain's right to censor plays and the poor quality of English acting. He accused London critic Clement Scott of duplicity and lack of integrity. He thought Scott had reviewed Les Cent Vierges, at the St. James's Theatre in July 1873, for both the Telegraph and the Observer. The practice was common enough at that time, but in this case opinions expressed in the two papers had differed. The former damned the play as "stuff which leaves a disagreeable taste in the mouth and threatens to poison the blood. ... The original notion is nasty, and the details of it are even nastier still. "12 The Observer review noted the suggestive nature of the plot, calling it "funny" and "free" from vulgarity. Clearly this seemed a breach of professional ethics, a point which Fiske exploited in The Hornet. Clement Scott was the regular reviewer for both newspapers but he had

not written the Observer review and he sued Fiske for libel.
Fiske exploited the situation by printing, verbatim, tran-
scripts of the trial. He had learned well the practices of
Bennett's Herald. In the face of extensive name-calling, the
staid Scott became sufficiently scandalized to withdraw his
complaint. Fiske then claimed victory and turned to other
activities: London correspondent for Wilkes Spirit of the
Times, agent for Augustin Daly's plays, and manager of the
St. James's Theatre. The combination of The Hornet and
theatre managing would prove disastrous in 1874.

No information has been uncovered about Fiske's work
as a correspondent for the Spirit. His career as Daly's
agent in London, however, was brief and undistinguished.
From their correspondence, twenty-eight letters remain (the
Folger Shakespeare Library, Y. C. 3092), written by Fiske
during the 1873-74 season. The letters provide a rare
glimpse of the duties and practices of a theatrical agent.
Fiske wrote to Daly describing available actors and their
desired salaries; new plays and "hot" playwrights; good buys
in costumes; and general theatre gossip. He repeatedly asked
Daly for large sums of money to enable him to wheel and
deal in the London theatre market. "It is not because people
distrust you that they want advances," Fiske explained in a
letter, August 21, 1873. "It is because they are too poor to
leave [London]."

Stephen Fiske's association with St. James's Theatre
began in October 1869, when he managed a production of She
Stoops to Conquer for Mrs. John Wood, who had leased the
theatre. He had been associated with Mrs. Wood in New
York when she produced his Martin Chuzzlewit in 1864. Always generous in praising her work, he abandoned all pretense of objectivity when reviewing her Pocahontas
(Brougham's Pocahontas, or the Gentle Savage) in September
1865: "Were I a super and such a Pocahontas were at the
stake, I should ... completely change the denouement of the
play by eloping with the heroine, in the first act. "[13]

At St. James's Theatre, Mrs. Wood hired a number
of American actors--Barton Hill, Mark Smith, A. W.
Young--and entertained visiting American theatrical dignita-
ries. During her engagements abroad, she sub-leased it to
various managers. In September 1871, while she was on tour
in New York, Fiske helped organize an opera company and
sent it to play the provinces. In February 1873, he managed
and provided financial backing for Richard Mansell, who had

subleased the theatre from Mrs. Wood. Fiske's adaptation
of Sardou's Rabagas, re-titled Robert Rabagas, opened there
on February 25 with Charles Wyndham in the title role. According to the Era, London's leading theatrical paper, "Mr.
Fiske has given us something to laugh at--and, indeed we in
common with the whole house, did laugh, and that very
heartily."[14] The play aimed to satirize some of the dema-
gogue tendencies of the day. Although it was not rewarding
financially, Fiske was encouraged to manage the theatre on
his own for the 1874 fall season. He produced only one
operetta, The Black Prince, which failed miserably. The
production was ill-advised from the beginning. Advertised as
a new comedy-bouffe with music by Charles LeCocq and libretto by H. B. Farnie, The Black Prince in reality was
several minor works of LeCocq purchased from his publishers and arranged for Farnie's libretto. Such shoddy work
angered London critics, as did Fiske's puffery of the production. The Era noted with scorn his hints about the "extraordinary demand for seats," the extravagant costumes, pretty
girls, the naughtiness of bare legs, and the excitement of a
yacht race.[15] The production closed on December 15. In
his history of St. James's Theatre, Barry Duncan notes that
a sensational scene involving the sinking of an iron-clad war-
ship was so poorly done that the audience roared with laughter.[16] Meanwhile, Stephen Fiske had departed quietly for
New York, leaving behind debts from both his theatrical and
journalistic ventures. But this youthful American journalist
had made an impact. Joseph Hatton, his successor on The
Hornet, praised him for introducing to London journalism
"bright and chatty personal items and gossip."

His return to New York in December 1874 lacked the
glamour of his departure eight years earlier. Now without
a job, he turned to his old rival, Augustin Daly, who had
been suffering through his second season at the Fifth Avenue
Theatre. Odell explains that Daly had experienced "the most
troubled autumn of all his experience as manager."[17] After
four months he had offered thirteen productions with little
success except for a superb revival of School for Scandal.
Daly hired Fiske as his business manager. In six weeks,
the new executive predicted, the theatre would be turning
people away. "He is the right man in the right place," the
Spirit of the Times prophesied on January 30, 1875, and
events quickly supported such optimism. The Big Bonanza,
adapted by Daly from Gustav von Moser's Ultimo, opened
February 17 and ran until June 28, for a total of 137 performances. On the evening of the 100th performance, Fiske

gave to the ladies a souvenir of silver miniature bricks and a program with a gilt hornet in relief on one side of the cover. [18] The Pittsburgh Evening Leader of April 10, 1876 credited Fiske with promoting the piece to its long run, noting that Daly never expected it to run more than two or three weeks. The Chicago Inter-Ocean thought the play's success illustrated the value of a "judicious display of advertising fireworks. "[19]

The success of Pique (again an adaptation by Daly) in December 1875 also depended upon Fiske's publicity campaign, which included a barrage of letters to the Herald denouncing charges that Daly had stolen the manuscript. He believed in staying in the public eye, announcing in the Arcadian that the Dramatic News had apologized to Daly for accusing him of stealing Pique. That publication had done no such thing and called the Arcadian a "disreputable and fast declining sheet. "[20] The Dramatic News protested that Fiske was allowed to write "puffs" in the Herald and other papers under the pretense of "arguing the case about the author of Pique." Such comments, of course, added to his growing reputation as a promoter. Again he offered souvenirs to each lady on the 100th and 150th nights of the run. The Brooklyn Sunday Sun, on July 16, 1876, called Fiske "brilliant, quick-witted, and industrious." The paper concluded that "what he does not know about advertising may safely be included among the lost arts."

Little is known about Fiske's private life. In the early 1860s, gossip linked him romantically with Olive Logan and Mrs. John Wood. Following his return from England, he married Mrs. Mary Hewins Burnham, formerly Mary Fox from his Bohemian days at Pfaff's, after an affair which created considerable scandal. Mr. Burnham attempted to shoot and stab Fiske. [21] A humorous lecturer and writer, Mary Hewins Fiske wrote under the initials M. H. B. for the St. Louis Republican and as "Giddy Gusher" for the New York Dramatic Mirror. She was a feminist who fought actively to improve the role of women.

Much of her life with Stephen remains obscure. The Spirit of the Times of April 7, 1877 announced that a son had been born to the Fiskes but no further information has been uncovered. Evidence suggests that for several years prior to her death in 1889, Mary Fiske maintained a separate apartment and her own circle of friends. Augustin Daly, in a letter to his brother Joseph on July 8, 1879, refers to

Fiske as "the late spouse of M. H. B. "[22] While her obituary
in the Dramatic Mirror (February 9, 1889) notes her marriage to Fiske, an article about her death in the Spirit of the
Times of the same date makes no mention of it. Instead,
the writer reveals an intimate knowledge both of the deceased and of possible causes of her marital difficulties:
"Under a manly, independent manner she concealed a kindly,
womanly heart. No case of distress, disease or persecution
ever appealed to her in vain. Like all true humorists, she
could be as pathetic as she was laughable.... The main-
spring of her life was a constant craving of good fellowship,
in which she included as many women as men. For many
years no theatrical festivity has been complete without her
bright, inspiring presence. Her affection for her blood relations was beyond description. " Harrison Grey Fiske made
the funeral arrangements while Robert G. Ingersoll, a personal friend, delivered the funeral eulogy. Stephen Fiske was
not listed among the mourners.

His association with Augustin Daly ended on a bitter
note in September 1877. Poor financial conditions, excessive
rent on the Fifth Avenue Theatre, and a heavy debt of
$45,000 forced Daly to post closing notices on September 10
after his production of The Dark City failed. A letter dated
September 10, from Joseph Daly to Augustin, indicates that
Fiske would represent their interests in the bankruptcy pro-
ceedings in estimating the value of "things before & behind
the curtain. "[23] No specifics are available but the Dalys
were surprised and embittered when Fiske took over the
management from the Gilsey Estate which owned the theatre.
After redecorating the house, Fiske re-opened it on October
15 with a resident company to support visiting stars. Mary
Anderson made her New York debut on November 12 as
Pauline in The Lady of Lyons and followed this with Juliet
and Meg Merrilies--old warhorses selected to demonstrate
her versatility. Helena Modjeska began an engagement on
December 22 as Adrienne LeCouvreur. Fiske then filled in
with opera and pantomime until he closed for the summer on
June 15. In Odell's assessment, the season was unsuccessful.

D. H. Harkins joined Fiske as co-manager for the
1878-1879 season. Formerly a leading actor and stage manager in Daly's company, Harkins had become involved in a
dispute with Charles Coghlan over assignment of roles in
1877; he broke his contract and was dismissed. His new responsibilities were to hire and organize the supporting com-

pany while Fiske managed the front of house operation.
Mary Anderson returned on August 29, followed by Modjeska
on September 30, Edwin Booth on November 11, and Joseph
Jefferson in his well-worn role of Rip Van Winkle on December 16. Mary Anderson made the managers a $4500 profit,
which they lost on the other engagements. According to
Nym Crinkle (A. C. Wheeler), Booth was not brilliant; Jefferson's Rip Van Winkle failed to attract much excitement,
and the acting company was weak. Expenses were excessive.
Fiske accused Harkins of poor judgment in hiring which
forced him to employ additional actors for each production.
During the Jefferson engagement, on January 4, 1879, the
company refused to perform unless they were paid a week's
salary. The theatre was closed. Joseph Daly, in a letter
to his brother (January 17, 1879), suggested that both Fiske
and Harkins had been paying private bills out of the box office, leaving the theatre insolvent. 24 And while each had
tried to get rid of the other, Harkins had allowed Fiske to
spend his own money in running the theatre while saving his
finances to settle debts with the owners and gain control.
If this was true the plan worked; Harkins sued Fiske to dis-
solve the partnership and emerged as the sole manager.
But one must read with caution the letters relating to this
matter between Joseph and Augustin. They now hated both
Fiske and Harkins.

On January 4, 1879, Nym Crinkle predicted in the
Spirit of the Times that "Fiske does not care for the white
elephant [Fifth Avenue Theatre] and will gravitate into journalism where, indeed, he belongs." No doubt he had inside
information. On the same date Fiske and a young reporter
for the Sun, Ernest Havier, founded the New York Mirror
(later the Dramatic Mirror) to combat the blackmailing practices of the New York Dramatic News. Founded by Charles
A. Byrne in October 1875, the Dramatic News sought to
build a large readership through sensationalism and scandal-
mongering--much like Bennett's Herald. An editorial in the
New York Mirror of January 11, 1879 accused the publication
of a multitude of sins: "Assaults were ... begun on the professions themselves. Actors, managers and dramatists were
not free from the wanton and sweeping attacks of their new
found organ. Their most private affairs began to be the subject of articles, their business relations were given coarse
publicity, and an era of vituperation was speedily begun. If
the editor had a quarrel over some household furniture with
a manager, the paper was full of assaults on the stars whom
the manager was playing. If an attache of the company

wished to sell a play, the censure of the paper was
threatened to the manager who would not come to terms. "

Such an aggressive editorial policy caused Byrne to
be involved in numerous libel suits and physical attacks.
Augustin Daly sued him for libel in 1876 and won; Byrne
could not pay and was placed "on limits" by the court--in
other words he could not leave New York. Such goings-on
offended traditional critics accustomed to judging the theatre
by well-established principles. They supported the Mirror's
anti-Byrne campaign even though its methods differed little
from those of the Dramatic News. In a letter to Augustin
on February 12, 1879, Joseph Daly praised the Mirror for
calling Byrne a "felon" and a "convict, " and noted that the
"dramatic profession rejoices accordingly. "[25] Despite such
efforts, Byrne would remain a force in theatre journalism
for another decade.

After establishing a new dramatic weekly, it is not
clear what role Fiske continued to play. Because of financial difficulties, it is unlikely that he invested any sizable
amount of money in its operation. Havier served, at least
publicly, as editor until November 8, 1879, when eighteen-
year-old Harrison Grey Fiske took charge. During the next
thirty-one years, the younger Fiske (only distantly related
to Stephen) made the Mirror (later Dramatic Mirror) respected and read by the theatrical profession. He worked to
eliminate corrupt practices and to raise standards of production. Stephen Fiske always held a paternal attitude towards
the paper, contributing articles and much praise even when
he disagreed with the opinions of its editor.

Events were to prove that Nym Crinkle had another
position in mind for him. After a two-year term writing a
dramatic column, "Causerie, " for the Spirit of the Times,
Nym wanted to take a similar post on the New York Star, a
Democratic paper of considerable influence. On February
22, 1879, Fiske took over Nym's Spirit duties; for the next
twenty-three years, he described the American theatre in a
popular column, "Spirit of the Stage. "

Stephen Ryder Fiske was well qualified to fill this
position. His readers did not demand the kind of scholarly
essays that magazines such as Harper's Monthly and Weekly,
or Atlantic might require. They wanted bright and readable
reviews, exactly what he could provide. He brought to the
Spirit of the Times extensive journalistic experience--both

in New York and London--and a first-hand knowledge of the
European stage. When he compared native fare with what
was offered in London or Paris, he spoke with authority.

Fiske never discussed explicitly the principles upon
which he based his criticism. In the early 1860s when he
was writing for the Herald and the Leader, his style and
critical ideas were drawn from his predecessor, Ned Wilkins: he praised Jules Janin as the most brilliant of Parisian critics; touted entertainment for the masses as more
important than high art for the elite; and tried to write in
a clever manner. By 1879 he had few illusions about the
profession, having worked in both New York and London.
Theatre was a business, and like any other business it must
be run efficiently and effectively. He had no tolerance of
shoddy work whether by playwright, manager, scene painter,
or actor. Undoubtedly his importance as a critic lies in his
efforts to raise professional standards in the American theatre.

Fiske was well acquainted with the dramatic carpentry
and outright plagiarism which infected much of American
playwriting in the late nineteenth century. He had done such
hack work himself--a scene from one play, an act from
another, an amusing situation from a third, and a sensational
effect from a fourth. If a play had been successful in Paris,
it could with a change of locale, title, and names, make
money in New York. If a novel had attracted attention, some
writer stood ready to convert it into a profitable play. Dion
Boucicault boasted that he took what he thought best for art,
"whether it be a story from a book, a play from the French,
an actor from a rival company." Augustin Daly ransacked
the theatres and libraries of Europe and America for materials to dramatize. "When have we had in modern plays,
anything that can be truly called literature?" Fiske asked in
1888. "There are exceptions, but they are few enough to
prove the rule that the modern drama is not literary. On the
contrary, it is turned out, as if by machinery, in partnership
with the stage carpenters and scenic artists, and nobody ...
thinks of the words except as accessories to fill up the time
till the great scene is ready or to be cut out to make room
for a ballet or procession."[26] Fiske later quipped: "Playwriting is a profession of thieves. The French stole from
the Spanish; the Italian and Germans from the French; the
English from the Italians, French, and Germans; and the
Americans from everybody."[27]

Boucicault's (and later Daly's) methods of pirating and adapting plays, Fiske thought, were ingenious from a business point of view. In spite of his campaign in North American Review against the evil influence of the press, Boucicault had involved theatre critics pecuniarily in his plays by forming the Star Club of Critics and with them adapting The Poor of New York from the French. The piece made considerable profits for all concerned, not only as The Poor of New York, but also The Poor of Philadelphia, The Poor of Boston, the poor of any city in which it was acted. Boucicault also allowed a critic to write a line or two in one of his manuscripts and would then copyright the play under both their names. He knew from experience that the critic usually found a play worth seeing if he stood to benefit financially from its success. Fiske warned about the consequences of such practices: not only did the critic suffer in lost reputation, so also did the playwright. While Boucicault assembled the best comedies since Sheridan and the best Irish melodramas ever, his claim as the "Shakespeare of Ireland" rested on pirated plays and his fame disappeared even before his death.

Boucicault's Rescued, or a Girl's Romance, at Booth's Theatre on September 13, 1879, demonstrated to Fiske what was wrong with the playwright's stitched-together adaptations. The so-called sensational scene, by now obligatory, was the passage of a railway train over a swinging bridge which the villain has left open and the heroine closes. For legal reasons the scene could not duplicate exactly Daly's famous train scene from Under the Gaslight; nevertheless, it was a borrowed effect with no purpose other than to be sensational. "There is no reason why the bridge should swing," Fiske noted; "No dramatic reason why the heroine should be on hand to foil the villain. All the characters are moved, like puppets to secure certain situations."[28] Because the materials were familiar and the ingredients trite, the audience soon lost interest in the outcome.

Fiske came to demand original plays rather than the stitched-together adaptations. He thought Edward Harrigan the most imaginative of late nineteenth-century American playwrights--the American Molière--who provided a "genuine abstract and brief chronicle of the time." His Mulligan Guard plays provided a glimpse of New York life of the 1880s with the Irish, German, and Negro immigrants crowded together in the slums. In The O'Reagans (1886) he ridiculed aldermen, civil service examinations, street preachers, and Irish fund-raising campaigns. When Harrigan announced the opening of his new theatre in December 1890, Fiske was delighted: "Unquestionably, he is the best, most original and most popular of American dramatists. "29

A few other native dramas gained his endorsement. William Gillette's Held by the Enemy, presented at the Madison Square Theatre in August 1886, Fiske praised as the best war play ever written and not surpassed until twelve years later when the same author wrote Secret Service. He thought both pieces superior to David Belasco's The Heart of Maryland (1895), which also dealt with the North-South conflict. Belasco borrowed much of his play from various sources: the idea of the title from Ross Whytal's drama, For Fair Virginia; the sensational lighthouse scene from Shore Acres; the attempt to arouse Northern patriotism without offending Southern prejudices from the common ragbag of Civil War dramas. 30

Fiske championed Bartley Campbell for a time after My Partners was successful at the Union Square Theatre in October 1879. While the piece needed revision (the seduction of the heroine left her without sympathy and offended Fiske), it contained original ideas and suggested that Campbell had talent. Two months later, however, he found The Gallery Slave deficient in plot and warned the young playwright to take his own time and not be hurried back into mediocrity. With The White Slave (1882) Fiske turned against Campbell, denouncing it as "unworthy of serious consideration." Instead of an original drama of American life, Campbell had simply re-written Uncle Tom's Cabin. A "most promising" young native playwright had been spoiled by sudden fame, Fiske concluded: "He makes no secret that his ambition in carpentering up this stupid plagiarism is catch-penny, not artistic. "31

Charles Hoyt, like Campbell, impressed Fiske with his artistic promise before sudden fame spoiled him. When Hoyt's A Texas Steer opened in November 1890, Fiske objected to his naiveté about Washington, D. C., and to his loud and vulgar language: "Mr. Hoyt ... has done better, can do better and must do better than A Texas Steer. "32 Fortunately A Trip to Chinatown, Hoyt's next offering, introduced a new character, Welland Strong, whom Fiske thought "quaint and original." The play would run for 650 performances, the longest consecutive run of any play given at that time in the United States. Hoyt's A Temperance Town

(1893), however, Fiske thoroughly disliked: "It is not true
in Vermont or anywhere else, that all the respectable people
are cranks, perjurors, conspirators, and spies; that all
drunkards are noble, generous, and heroic, and that all the
illicit rumsellers are Union veterans, with one arm and two
motherless children. "[33] After dismissing the plot as
"trash, " he attacked the play's didacticism. "The theatre
is a place of amusement, not of argument for or against
prohibition nor of scenes which shock and wound the feelings
of respectable persons. " To Fiske, thesis dramas and
plagiarized adaptations were to be avoided.

The Old Homestead by Denman Thompson and The Henrietta by Bronson Howard, he regarded as the two finest
plays yet written on American life. Both were first presented in 1887, the former at the Fourteenth Street Theatre
and the latter at Union Square. The Old Homestead reminded
the critic of Harrigan's vaudeville sketches: "It keeps the
audience in alternate tears and laughter, and achieves a
genuine popular success. "[34] The charm of the piece was its
naturalness: "Anybody who has ever lived in the country has
encountered just such people and heard just such talk. As
most city folk were born and bred in the rural districts, the
familiar scenes go right home to the hearts of the audience. . . .
It is like an old cradle song, heard again in late life. " While
Fiske found The Henrietta a brilliantly written satire on
American capitalist life, he objected to a clergyman being
caricatured. The minister turned away from a dying man
when he should have fallen on his knees to "redeem the
character, now very repulsive, and point the moral more
keenly. "[35] In other words the behavior of the minister
should have been idealized.

Fiske did not approve of the New Drama. Zola's
Thérèse Raquin he considered false both to art and nature.
"American girls will not go to a theatre to see a hussy and
her paramour murder her husband and then undress themselves and sit by the fire and talk about it. No father will
take his daughters, no lover will escort his sweetheart to
look at this sort of unveiled vileness and there is no use arguing about it. "[36] He accused the taint of Ibsenism of
poisoning the drama on both sides of the Atlantic: "Every
playwright has to be more nasty than his rivals. " James A.
Herne's Margaret Fleming he found "commonplace, abortive,
immoral . . . a play of seduction, adultery, and delirium
tremens. "[37] Sounding much like William Winter, he asked,
"When is this Ibsenish nonsense to stop and how many more

otherwise respectable people are to be infected with it. " In
May 1891 he viewed <u>Hedda Gabler</u> with alarm: "The des-
picable heroine has no redeeming quality. For the sake of a
comfortable home, she marries a man whom she despises,
and she begins to betray him before the honeymoon is
over. "[38] An incident which occurred at the first American
production of <u>John Gabriel Borkman</u> in 1897 appealed to his
sense of the absurd: "After the rascally hero had seduced
his wife's sister, and his son had been seduced by another
man's wife, there was an odor of fire and brimstone in the
auditorium, and the audience, conscience-stricken by the
thought that the infernal regions had opened to engulf them,
the actors, and the play, hurried out of the theatre" (November 27, 1897). A burning calcium light made the odor. Obviously delighted with the course of events, Fiske quipped:
"It came most opportunely as a warning of the fate of those
that gloat over Ibsen's plays. " Like his better-known con-
temporaries--Winter and Towse--Fiske wanted nothing to do
with realistic drama; he viewed Ibsen as obscene and dull.
But while he adhered to romantic idealism--the mainstream
of nineteenth-century critical thought--he considered theatre
a form of entertainment and amusement, not an ideal art.
It is his low regard of theatre which separates him from
highbrow critics Winter and Towse.

In August 1893, Beerbohm Tree, actor-manager of
the Haymarket Theatre in London, sent Fiske a printed copy
of his lecture, "The Imaginative Faculty, " which he had delivered before the Royal Institution of Philosophers. His
thesis--that acting is purely an affair of the imagination--
Fiske rejected: "The dramatist instructs the stage manager
as to what he wants done and the stage manager instructs
the actor what to do. Any professional who should give free
rein to his imagination and suppose himself to be the character he impersonates would be fined for altering the stage
business or discharged for varying the words of his part. "[39]
To Fiske acting was make-believe: "If an actor identified
himself emotionally with his various parts and felt by turns
like a prince, a peasant, a thief, a murderer--if an actress
really mourned for her dead lover or father or child--no
constitution could long stand the strain of such emotions, nor
would the natural representation of them be effective upon
the stage. "[40] Acting appears true to nature because the artist makes the necessary artistic allowances, he believed,
"just as panorama, painted coarsely and broadly, accurately
represents nature when seen at the proper distance under the

proper lights. " Fiske had joined a sometimes heated and long-standing debate about whether actors should feel the emotion they portray. An English translation of Denis Diderot's The Paradox of Acting in 1883 renewed the argument. Diderot had argued that the actor should remain unmoved. William Archer's Masks or Faces? A Study in the Psychology of Acting (1888) provided a new defense for the emotional school. [41]

Fiske did not have a high opinion of actors or acting because he found nothing in acting that resembled art. "It originates nothing ... creates nothing ... preserves nothing. At its very best it is mere imitation." While admitting that the greatest actor is the one who best expresses the sentiments of the dramatist, Fiske explained that "he is only a medium through which the dramatist speaks." Brilliant actors--Siddons, Rachel, the Keans, the Kembles, Garrick, Macready, Forrest, the elder Booth, Talma, and Cushman-- have left nothing but a memory. "Had they been poets, " the critic continued, "we should have had their books; had they been musicians, we should have had their works expressing every emotion.... But as they were only actors--imitators of other people, make believers of a night--nothing of them is left but a splendid memory, some out-of-date stage business, and a portrait at the Garrick Club or Brown's Chop Shop. "[42] Fiske's insistence upon a tangible, verifiable product as the criterion for determining art seemed quaintly old-fashioned beside the enlightened views of Constant Coquelin and Henry Irving. These actors demanded that acting be as highly regarded as the other arts despite its ephemeral quality.

He preferred to see Americans engaged in other activity than acting. "It is a profession which reaches its highest development after a country has finished more serious matters and is more or less worn out, " he wrote in 1888. "We like to think of Americans as too individual to pretend to be other people; too original to repeat other people's lines; too independent to redden their noses to amuse the gallery for twenty-five dollars a week. "[43] When we need no more workers, Fiske concluded, we will have plenty of time to produce players. His views directly conflicted with those of Winter and Towse, who considered acting the highest theatrical art, and reflect his obsession with materialism, and the philosophy of individualism and free enterprise which dominated American life at the turn of the century. He admired managerial success more than great acting.

Fiske blamed the actor for the deplorable reputation of the acting profession. His arguments were: the actor does not vote, professes no interest in politics, cares nothing for patriotism, escapes jury duty, pays little taxes, seldom attends church, and behaves as if he had no responsibility except to himself; he wants to be accepted as an equal in society while violating social and religious proprieties. Consequently society rejects him. As a result no father wants his daughter or son to pursue a career on the stage.

Because of his low regard for acting, Fiske seldom praised an actor for his talent alone. Instead he asked whether the actor had taken an active interest in his art? Elevated his profession? Encouraged other artists? Commissioned new plays? Created new roles? Revived old plays? Or, had he made plenty of money easily? Appeared in the same roles? Taken whatever company was available? Never concerned himself with the scenery or costumes? Writing in 1886, he accused Edwin Booth and Joseph Jefferson of neglecting their profession:

> They come to New York, year after year, and expect people to go to see them without ever presenting anything to attract the public. No dramatist writes new plays for Edwin Booth. He sticks to Shakespeare, not only because it is great, but because it is cheap. The Theatre, the company and the accessories are furnished for him and he never seems to care whether they are good, bad, or indifferent. He goes through his part, well or ill, according to the whim of the night or the state of his health, pockets his cheque and disappears until the stage is ready for the next performance. No playwright devises new comedies for Mr. Jefferson. He bought up Boucicault's dramatizations of Rip Van Winkle and The Cricket on the Hearth years ago, and for such old farces as Lend Me Five Shillings he pays no royalties. [44]

Fiske believed that Jefferson and Booth, as leaders of their profession, should have worked to establish an American school of acting or to develop the native drama. He credited Edwin Forrest with working more to develop an American drama by offering prizes, writing suggestions, and producing the best native plays available. And Lawrence Barrett, while not nearly as great an actor as Booth, worked harder to improve the state of his art. Fiske concluded that Booth had

limited himself to the "old legitimate round" and would be
remembered only as the ideal Hamlet.

On the other hand, he thought that Henry Irving and
J. L. Toole--English actor/managers--had assumed a greater
responsibility for the advancement of their country's theatre.
They purchased and produced new plays; revived old plays
with tasteful scenery; took an active interest in art, literature, and drama; and worked to improve the social position
of actors. While New York managers had presented elaborate scenery before the Irving tours, Fiske explained in
1896, they did not understand the simplicity and artistry of
scenery, properties, and supernumeraries. "As the curtain
rises in an American theatre now," he noted by way of contrast, "you see at once the influence of Irving, for the auditorium is darkened to throw up the picture on the stage.
The American system was to keep the auditorium bright, so
as to show off the house and the costumes of the ladies of
the audience, as at the Italian Opera."[45]

Until the Irving visits, the critic thought, the management of the supernumeraries was a hopeless task:

> In tragedy, melodrama, or spectacle, in the
> middle ages or the classic ages, or the anytime
> at all of fairyland, the supers marched on two by
> two, and ranged themselves in lines on each side
> of the stage, and marched off two by two, no mat-
> ter what happened in their sight and hearing--a
> murder, a trial, a duel, an earthquake, or a
> miracle. Irving changed all that. When the sol-
> diers in Faust came straggling across the scene in
> picturesque groups, the American managers nodded
> each other and said, 'of course: that is the way
> the ancient warriors marched when not in battle.'
> The groupings in Faust, the searches in Louis XI
> and later the marches in Macbeth, further instructed
> them.

American managers learned how to use supernumeraries because Irving taught them.

And music was never employed dramatically in this
country, Fiske believed, until after Irving's first American
tour in 1883. "We had the theory of dramatic music, but it
was ludicrously practiced. There was the 'hurry' in the orchestra for melodrama.... Mostly the music was used to

drown the noise of shifting the scenes.... But the continuous music of the Irving plays, now suggesting the emotions of the situation, now intensifying the effects of the acting, now dominating the scene, now almost unheard in the excitement of the dramatic incident, was unknown. People said of Irving's first productions, 'Why, they are like grand opera.'"

Irving contributed more to the American stage than any native actor, Fiske concluded, giving dignity and importance to theatrical art and teaching the public to respect and value it. Other critics agreed, particularly John Ranken Towse of the Evening Post. Looking back on the actor's career, Towse wrote in 1916: "He reawakened popular interest in the legitimate drama, showed managers once more how Shakespeare could be made to pay, demonstrated by financial success the efficiency of the artistic theatre as a commercial enterprise and the superiority of the stock over the star system, and gave a permanent uplift to the social status of the actor."[46] Although Augustin Daly had accomplished several of these ends prior to Irving's first visit in 1883, neither Fiske nor Towse had apparently noticed.

Stephen Ryder Fiske was keenly aware of the business side of theatre. His "Spirit of the Stage" kept managers aware of fads and trends in the entertainment industry, warning them about any competition for the amusement dollar. In September 1879 he found the theatres empty because everyone had attended the Astley Belt Walk at Madison Square Garden. On March 21, 1885, he explained why everyone was rushing to the dime museum at the Park Theatre: "The juvenile tragedian N. S. Wood may be seen in 'The Boy Detective' for only 10¢." And the theatre promised that a larger entertainment for a dime would be offered the following week with popular star Little Corinna. "These entertainments are experimental," he warned, "but the dime show is a success everywhere." In 1885 he alerted managers to the popularity of roller skating: "At least 15,000 persons are disporting themselves on roller skates and 10,000 looking at the skaters each night." "The audience have not drifted away from the theatre," he teased, "they are rolling away." In 1895 he warned about the baseball craze and thought ingenious the automatic baseball game set up at Palmer's Theatre. A replica of the Polo Grounds was placed onstage with two-feet-high figures, and each day's games reproduced by information relayed by wire.

Fiske offered advice on how to lure customers into the

theatre. Managers should exploit national sentiments in choosing and advertising their attractions. Patriotic Americans respond with enthusiasm to flags and banners hung up in front of the theatre and in private boxes. They enjoy hearing the theatre orchestra play national airs. And at all theatres, he thought, "There must be an actress capable of attiring herself as the Goddess of Liberty and reciting 'Hail Columbia' or 'The Star-Spangled Banner.'" Dewey's victory at Manila Bay in May 1895 created such an outpouring of patriotic fervor that Fiske wanted managers who had closed for the season to reopen their theatres and not miss out on the money. [47]

Any public disturbance affected theatre business. Reports of rioting, firing upon the police, and calling out the militia in the cab-drivers' strike of February 1889 frightened the audience from the theatre. Ladies were the real theatre patrons, he explained, and with news of violence would keep the family home. He made the same point on February 13, 1892, explaining that the recent fire at the Hotel Royal had reminded women of theatre fires and kept "nervous people at home." The political activities preceding an American election always affected theatre business. "How can anybody be expected to pay a dollar and a half to see a dramatic spectacle when he can see a parade of plumed knights or a torchlight procession gratis."[48] And Fiske warned that ladies would not venture into the overcrowded streets during such festivities, nor would they go near the playhouses during election day. It was the custom during the 1880s to read election returns from the stage between acts--a custom which usually sparked off disturbances. Fiske noted one such incident on election day (1888) at the Bijou Theatre, where Republicans took offense at a party of Democrats who waved bandannas when the returns were read. The Democrats took offense because the bandannas were hissed. Fights broke out. Chaos reigned. No reliable returns were received during theatre hours and Fiske wanted the practice stopped. [49] The theatres also suffered during any public calamity. They closed for almost two weeks after the assassination of President Lincoln in 1865. President Garfield's death in September 1881 closed numerous theatres and Fiske estimated the loss in revenue to be $15,000 in New York alone and $250,000 throughout the country.

Of all the events which siphoned off the audience, however, nothing could match the circus and Lent. Each spring, Barnum's Circus emptied the theatres. Fiske would

lecture about the fickleness of the audience but found no way
to keep them from deserting the theatre en masse. The circus made more noise, had more glitter, and appealed more
directly to crowds than the theatre. Even those who extolled
the virtues of aesthetic and intellectual entertainment would
end up going to the circus and taking their children.

During Lent the theatre was off-limits for several religious denominations including the Episcopalians and the
Catholics. The opera, however, was considered an acceptable form of entertainment. "Fashion--not religion--has de-
creed that for forty days and forty nights 400 persons may go
to the opera to hear how Wagner's heroes married their own
sisters, but must not go to the wicked theatres. "[50] Fiske
looked for ways to reconcile the church and stage. As a
reasonable concession to religious sentiments, he proposed
that theatres close on Ash Wednesday and Good Friday. On
April 2, 1886, he announced that the theatres in New York,
with only a few exceptions, would close on Good Friday:
"This is a great step towards the complete reconciliation of
the church and stage. " Now he hoped that the "most fanati-
cal clergyman can no longer stigmatize the theatres, as the
Devil's church and identify playhouses and perdition. " On
March 8, 1890, he pleaded with managers to close on Good
Friday, explaining that "deference to religious sentiment pays
in this world--to say nothing of the next. " When business
remained good during the 1897 Lenten season, Fiske concluded that the church had lost the battle to keep members
away from the theatre. Fashion and respectability--not religious beliefs--kept people away from the theatre; thus, the
theatre must become a fashionable and respectable place of
amusement like the opera.

The centralization of the American theatre was inevitable, in Fiske's view. Business and government were becoming highly centralized in the last two decades of the nineteenth century and for the professional stage to expand and
grow it must be reorganized on big business principles. Consequently Fiske approved of the Theatrical Syndicate's attempt
to gain control of the American stage in 1896. By 1903
seventy first-class theatres had fallen into their hands; and
by gaining control of booking, they indirectly controlled over
seven hundred theatres by contracts which gave them exclusive rights to supply entertainment. [51] While they did
eliminate much of the general disorganization which had been
common in the 1880s--double bookings, broken engagements,
cancelling of attractions, abandoning of bankrupt companies

on the road--they appraised a play by its value in dollars
and by no other standard.

Between 1900 and 1905 a number of critics savagely
attacked this monopoly. Towse charged in The Nation that
the Syndicate's only ambition was to gratify, not to direct or
improve the public taste. [52] Winter, Walter Prichard Eaton,
Norman Hapgood, Brander Matthews, and James S. Metcalfe
joined Towse in denouncing the purely commercial policy of
the Syndicate. Stephen Fiske, however, pointed out in 1903
that the Syndicate offered the public "more theatres and better theatres; more new plays, more new stars, more performances, and in some respects better performances than
we ever had before. "[53] He defended the Syndicate from
charges made by Harrison Grey Fiske of the Dramatic Mirror that they did not send complete New York companies (as
agreed) on the road and shifted bookings which had been
previously contracted. Stephen Fiske reminded his colleague
on the Dramatic Mirror that the original casts of Broadway
productions were seldom or never sent into the provinces:
"When a play is successful, two, three, sometimes half-a-
dozen companies are sent out to reap the immediate benefit
of the success. "[54] This employed actors and thus benefited
the theatre. Also, the provincial managers were not de-
ceived into thinking that they were booking every member of
the original cast. And since the public was only interested
in seeing stars, it was of no consequence to them whether
every member of the cast was from the original production.
The public was not interested in how an attraction was
booked, he added, or in what terms were agreed upon.
Their only interest was whether an attraction was worth seeing when it was placed before them on the stage. Fiske defended the practices of the Syndicate, reminding his readers
that the organization was concerned only with operating the
theatre on business principles: "Managers and actors who
find its methods more profitable and more convenient than
the old hap-hazard system will join it and support it. Others
will not. "

Writing about the theatre was not Stephen Fiske's only
activity. In 1881 he edited the New York Star and in 1893,
with Ernest Havier, founded a new comic weekly, Hallo.
With his customary wit Fiske suggested that in Hallo, managers were to review their own productions in order to ensure
that they received fair value for their advertising dollar. [55]
Other of his literary achievements include numerous short
stories and articles contributed to popular magazines, then

collected and republished in three volumes: Paddy from Cork, and Other Stories (1891); Holiday Stories (1891); and Jack's Partner and Other Stories (1894). In the early 1880s he also wrote a series of articles for Knickerbocker Magazine on prominent New Yorkers including James Gordon Bennett, George William Curtis, Charles Dana, and the tragedian John McCullough. Under the title Off-Hand Portraits of Prominent New Yorkers, he published the series as a book in 1884. None of his stories are significant literary works. Like much of the popular writing of the period, they are clever, amusing, and shallow.

The Spirit of the Times was incorporated into the Chicago Horseman in December 1902 when it could no longer compete with the daily papers in reporting sporting events, nor with the theatrical trade papers in covering the professional stage. Fiske, together with several of his colleagues from the now defunct Spirit, then organized a new weekly, Sports of the Times, which began publication on December 20, 1902. His "Spirit of the Stage" was re-titled "Footlights" and became little more than a theatrical gossip column. Later, as the publication stressed outdoor sports, space allotted for "Footlights" steadily decreased. But although his career was in decline, he was called the "Dean" of newspaper critics in 1908. [56]

Further changes in the publishing market continued to relegate him to the background. After its April 25, 1912 issue, Sports of the Times was incorporated into The Field Illustrated, a journal devoted to outdoor America. Fiske contributed a column entitled "Play and Players" until May 1, 1914, when the publication became a monthly agricultural journal. The change left no space for news about the theatre. Fiske retired. Two years later, on April 27, 1916, he died in New York at age 76.

His worth as a critic has been discussed by his colleagues. Ali Baba (Arthur Hornblow), in the Dramatic Mirror of June 13, 1891, described Fiske as a "brilliant writer ... gifted with a remarkably facile and, at times a caustic pen, and he possesses a wonderful memory in which is stored away a fund of information on all conceivable topics. He, moreover, enjoys the distinction of being a reliable prophet concerning the fate of a new play." Lewis Rosenthal of the New York Telegram in 1893 found his critical thoughts "acute, crisp, and trenchant." Fiske, in his opinion, "strives to do the right thing by managers, players, and payers. "[57] And Joseph Hatton praised him in 1895 for writing the "brightest page of stage criticism and gossip in New York journalism. "[58] Thus, in his day, Stephen Fiske was recognized as a critic of ability and influence.

In a "gilded age" where ruthless men such as Jay Cooke, Jay Gould, Andrew Carnegie, J. Pierpont Morgan, and John D. Rockefeller were admired and respected, Stephen Ryder Fiske offered a commonsense, practical view of the theatre--not as an art but as a form of mass entertainment. He was a shrewd judge of public taste. His criticism reflects an acute awareness of the public's needs, wants, and fears. Unlike most of his colleagues, he believed that the centralization of theatre in this country--like the centralization of all economic life--was desirable and inevitable. And he recognized that this change diminished the importance of individual effort and emphasized activities essentially cooperative in nature. Theatrical companies (e. g., Henry Irving's), not individual star performers, gained his unqualified support.

Fiske was firmly grounded in the principles and practices of the nineteenth-century theatre. In his early career, he borrowed from French critical methods. Unlike Winter, he did not believe that the stage was an elevator of civilization; he also would not admit the necessity of viewing "real" life there. To Fiske, the purpose of theatre was to amuse and entertain in a professional manner. It was his insistence that the theatre be run in a thoroughly professional manner which separates him from most popular critics of the period.

CHAPTER SIX

ANDREW C. WHEELER
"nym crinkle"

Death continued to stalk the Pfaffian group in the decade following the Civil War. Artemus Ward died in 1866, followed by Charles B. Seymour in 1869, Ada Clare in 1874, and Henry Clapp, "the oldest Bohemian, " in 1875. No critical movement could withstand such loss of talent. Clapp and Wilkins' attack upon the cultural standards of the Boston Brahmins seemed forgotten in the war's aftermath. Stephen Fiske and William Winter had fled Pfaff's--Fiske to London and Winter to more respectable surroundings. Fiske would return in late 1874; in 1879 he would energize the dramatic columns of the Spirit of the Times. But his Bohemian days were in the past. He had little interest in opposing the cult of high art which permeated American art and letters in the "gilded age. " Winter, of course, had no wish to challenge elitism; he wanted to join it. Together with Thomas Bailey Aldrich, Richard H. Stoddard, Bayard Taylor, and Edmund C. Stedman, he served as an arbiter of art and letters in this country during the reign of the Genteel Tradition.

A hot-tempered young journalist, completing an assignment as a war correspondent, found the Bohemian style of personal, aggressive, and witty dramatic criticism suited to his tastes. Andrew C. Wheeler, better known as Nym Crinkle, began haunting Pfaff's shortly after his arrival in New York, sometime in 1864-1865. He was to write for numerous New York daily and weekly publications but established his reputation mainly as dramatic and musical critic for the World. For thirty years he shocked, delighted, and infuriated his readers with a combination of wit, verve, devastating sarcasm, and keen insight into the professional stage. Called by James Huneker "more brilliant than reliable, "[1] Wheeler followed closely in the footsteps of Clapp.

128

The New York Telegram of March 10, 1903 noted that at
Clapp's death, "his mantle was offered to Mr. Wheeler."

Andrew Carpenter Wheeler was born at No. 19 John
St., in New York City, to Eliphalet and Anna (Brown)
Wheeler. The exact date of his birth is disputed, although
either June 4 or July 4, 1832 seems most likely from available information. [2] He was the second of three children and
the only son. His father, a state legislator for two terms
(1834 and 1835) came from an established family which had
resided in New York for four generations. Andrew grew up
in what seems a typical middle-class environment. In 1835,
when he was three years old, the family moved to Terre
Haute, Indiana. Four years later they returned to New York
where he attended public schools and probably enrolled for
two years at College of the City of New York. [3] As a child
he had access to his father's library. His later writings re-
veal a wide knowledge of literature and art--a knowledge
which suggests that, lacking the advantages of a formal education, he gained one on his own.

Available sources indicate that he married Ann Mulligan, daughter of a Brooklyn shopkeeper, in 1853. They
had four children: Grace, Minnie, Frank, and Eliphalet.
He began his career in journalism in the New York Times
in 1857. Founded by Henry J. Raymond, the Times aimed
to set the pace in New York journalism as a quality newspaper rather than aim for mass circulation like Bennett's
Herald. Mott notes that "It had strong opinions, and it was
fond of controversy but it never descended as Greeley sometimes did, to Billingsgate."[4] Raymond wanted a paper which
took a higher moral tone than the Herald or the Sun, but he
did not want it identified with the various causes (e.g.,
Fourierism) which Greeley and the Tribune supported.
Wheeler worked for Raymond for about six months, but quickly made a reputation as an aggressive reporter. He resigned to travel across the frontier regions of this country--
the Great Plains--at that time "the scene of bitter political
struggles, frequent encounters between the settlers and the
Indians, and the home of lawlessness."[5] For two years he
lived and worked in Kansas, Iowa, and Colorado. The experience made a deep impression upon him. In his short
novel, The Iron Trail (1876), he vividly recalled the region:

There's something peculiar in the beauty of a
cultivated prairie that baffles description. The
level lines and low down horizon have a charm that

is unexpected. In the first place, the colors are
brighter and deeper than in any other picture.
The earth shows long rich patches of blue-black
earth, against which the emerald green of the
young wheatfields gleams with a rare brilliancy,
and over which the blue sky--a deep unruffled ul-
tra marine--arches itself in unobstructed splendor.
Then the broad unbroken sunshine. No massed
shadows; everything in a bath of brightness. The
sense of space, the freedom of vision and the constant impression that one is in an illimitable mead,
and that motion is unaccompanied by exertion,--an
illusion due in great measure to the stimulating
air--all serve to make the charm an entirely new
one, and one that appeals to all the impulses no
less than the senses.[6]

There is no record of what happened at this time to
his wife and children. Much of the time Wheeler was penni-
less. In 1859 his uncle, pastor of the First Presbyterian
Church in Milwaukee, helped set him up as a reporter for
the Milwaukee Daily Sentinel under Rufus King, the editor.
Later he served as city editor and published "The Chronicles
of Milwaukee," a rambling account of the history and development of the city. When the Civil War broke out, he served
as war correspondent for several papers including the Daily
Sentinel. His reports, "vivid and vigorous" in style, attracted wide attention.

During the war he began submitting articles to New
York weekly papers under the signature of Trinculo, a pen-
name apparently inspired by Stephano's speech from The
Tempest: "Come on, Trinculo, Let us sing: Flout 'em,
and skout 'em; and skout 'em and flout 'em; Thought is free."
Trinculo's stories for the Leader, such as "Out at Night"
(February 24, 1866) and "The Cholera Comedy" (July 14,
1866), are gossipy tales of little or no worth. But his
style--amusing and witty--appealed to the new mass readership of periodical literature. His epigrams--Wildean in na-
ture--reveal a wry sense of humor; for example "The highest
duty of mankind in a French play is to marry the woman that
somebody else loves."[7] Beginning in 1870 he took over the
dramatic desk of the Leader, replacing Henry Clapp. Under
the Trinculo label he described the New York amusement
scene in a manner reminiscent of Clapp ten years earlier.
Later, O. W. Riggs of the Brooklyn Times attempted to
characterize his Leader work: "His criticisms were French

only in their lightness of touch, their brilliancy of expression. There was a saxon solidity at the bottom, a recognition of broad, homely truths. "[8] In this respect, Wheeler resembles Wilkins.

It is not certain when Wheeler became a dramatic critic for the Sunday New York World. The first article positively identified as written by him appeared on October 31, 1869, under a new pseudonym, Nym Crinkle. The origins of this name are disputed. Wheeler noted in his diary that he invented it. [9] His obituary in the Dramatic Mirror credits it to Alpha Child, a reporter for the Milwaukee Daily Sentinel, who tired of the name and gave it to Wheeler. [10] No further evidence on the subject has been uncovered. It was as Nym Crinkle that Wheeler became known and feared for his devastating attacks upon plays and actors.

He continued writing for the World until the paper was sold in 1876 by Manton Marble to Thomas A. Scott; then he moved his column to the Sun, succeeding Joseph Howard, Jr. as dramatic critic. Under the editorship of Charles A. Dana, the Sun boasted the largest circulation of any daily newspaper in New York--131,000 in 1877-1878. [11] It held the reputation of being a colorful paper which emphasized the human interest story. Nym Crinkle's style and that of the Sun seemed to mesh well; yet he remained with Dana for only about one year. During that time, however, he resurrected Trinculo to write an amusement column, "Causerie, " for the Spirit of the Times, beginning on February 3, 1877. For about two years Causerie offered a combination of stage gossip and specific comments about actors and plays. In January 1879, wheeler left this post to begin editing the New York Star, a newspaper supported by organized labor and the New York Democratic Party, and owned by John Kelly. Several ill-advised ventures in journalism followed. In six months he tired of the Star and founded the Sunnyside Press in Tarrytown, New York. This paper failed after one year. Apparently he founded Nym Crinkle's Feuilleton, which also failed, but positive evidence about this affair is lacking. When Joseph Pulitzer purchased the World in 1883, Wheeler returned as dramatic critic and editorial writer at a salary reportedly equaled only by the sports writer.

Wheeler's aggressive and belligerent personality created many enemies for him. Perhaps no one hated him as much as Charles A. Byrne, editor of the notorious Dramatic

News. During February 1876, Wheeler became involved in
a lawsuit between Augustin Daly and Byrne over the former's
new play Pique. 12 Byrne claimed that Wheeler told him that
he had read a similar piece entitled Flirtation by a Miss
Eleanor Kirk Ames; later, when attending a performance of
Pique he recognized it as identical with Flirtation. Byrne
printed the accusation that Daly had stolen Pique from Miss
Ames; Daly brought a lawsuit for $10,000 against Byrne.
The Dramatic News editor had obtained a signed affadavit
from Wheeler, but on the day of the trial the critic failed to
show up in court; he was "hid under a friend's bed in a private house on 18th Street." Byrne lost the suit and Daly was
awarded damages of $2363.63. "When a fellow-journalist
who has been considered a close friend for eleven years,
pledges his honor to perform his plain duty in an emergency,"
Byrne wrote in an editorial, "a duty of importance to you and
of no material effect to himself, and when, we say, this man
at the last hour deserts you, and makes you responsible for
what he should bear, would it be too strong language to call
him coward, cur and snake."13 References to "A. Cur.
Wheeler" filled the pages of the Dramatic News for the next
few months. In days of personal journalism, powerful editors played rough.

In the 1880s Wheeler challenged William Winter as
the most able critic in New York. There is little doubt that
he was more popular. The circulation of the World in 1887
was 189,000 for the daily edition and 244,850 for the Sunday
version, compared to 70,000 and 85,000 for the Tribune. 14
But each paper attracted a different audience. The World
did not interest the intellectual elite, as did the Tribune, but
appealed to the working classes and small businessmen.
Consequently Nym Crinkle aimed his remarks to the latter
groups. Like Walt Whitman he extolled the virtues of the
American working man. "Labor is worship, and there is
no labor so acceptable and so ennobling as that which seeks
to make the earth produce," he wrote in the World on May
5, 1872. "To believe this is the first step to manliness and
virtue, and independence."

Nym Crinkle acquired such wide-spread popularity that
he was asked to write for leading dramatic weeklies. From
August 1886 to November 1889, "Nym Crinkle's Feuilleton"
graced the front page of Harrison Grey Fiske's New York
Mirror (Dramatic Mirror), the best dramatic paper in the
city. Beginning on October 19, 1889, he added a regular
column for Deshler Welch's The Theatre magazine, a publi-

cation of quality which solicited articles from leading critics and working professionals. At this time Wheeler was at the zenith of his career; if not the most respected stage critic in this country, he was at least the best known. In 1895 he worked briefly for the New York Journal when William Randolph Hearst hired the entire staff of the Sunday World including the editor, Morrill Goddard. And in the late 1890s he wrote a series of articles on the theatre for the Saturday Evening Post and for New York's liveliest magazine, the Criterion, joining James Huneker, Vance Thompson, and Charles Henry Meltzer.

Nym Crinkle briefly took to the stage himself during the mid-eighties, but as a lecturer, not an actor. Incensed by Robert Ingersoll's attack upon Christianity, he followed Ingersoll around the country on the lecture circuit to rebut Ingersoll's atheistic views in a talk entitled "Skylarks and Daisies. " A writer for the Minneapolis Mercury of February 28, 1886 found him an accomplished speaker:

> Mr. Wheeler's manner of speech is a quiet one. He never allows himself to be carried away into extravagance of tone or gesture, but there is something in the voice, in the eyes as they rest on his audience, an almost irresistible evidence that the man firmly believes what he says. [15]

This same writer found the combination of Wheeler's sarcasm and appeal to the audience's sentiments devastating. When Ingersoll stated that he could write a better book than the Bible, Wheeler advised Christians that if they could beat "that sentence into the heads of the people they will never bother much with what Mr. Ingersoll thinks of the Bible. They will be too completely overwhelmed with what he thinks of himself. " Wheeler seemed less an evangelist than a man defending the foundations of nineteenth-century civilization.

Like most of his contemporaries, Wheeler sought success as a playwright. He claimed to have written a play for $100 in Des Moines, Iowa, during his sojourn West when, penniless, he discovered a traveling tent show in need of a new melodrama. He wrote one "within a remarkably short time, "[16] collected his money, and departed to Milwaukee. His first dramatic effort of historical record, however, he penned in collaboration with Steele MacKaye in 1876. Entitled Twins, the play offers a plot situation dependent upon mistaken identity--similar to Twelfth Night, A Comedy of

Errors, or The Menaechmi. In his diary Wheeler sketched
out the plot of the play, which pits an effeminate brother
against a masculine one:

> ... the first one marries a termagant who rules
> the establishment for a certain time. Then ensues
> Taming the Shrew business. But at the expiration
> of the time, everybody having been deceived by the
> change, No. 2 refuses to give up his place....
> The termagant rather likes best the man who shows
> himself capable of ruling. In this dilemma No. 1
> resorts to ... involving no. 2 in financial difficul-
> ties in order to regain his place. [17]

His obsession with masculinity and femininity characterized
most of his writing. He had little use for masculine women
or feminine men.

With Lester Wallack in the dual leading roles of the
twin brothers, Chester and Mark Delafield, Twins opened at
Wallack's Theatre on the evening of April 12, 1876. The
New York Times praised the work and described Wheeler's
dialogue as "brisk and bright."[18] But much of the critical
reaction was unfavorable. The Spirit of the Times complained that the first act offered nothing but talk.[19] Percy
MacKaye later blamed the play's failure on critics hostile
to Wheeler. Reviews of the production suggest that Twins
lacked dramatic action and possessed a hackneyed plot.

Eleven years later Wheeler wrote the libretto for a
comic opera, Big Pony, or The Gentlemanly Savage, for
which composer Edward J. Darling provided the music.
Called by most critics a musical extravaganza, Big Pony as
conceived by Wheeler aimed to satirize conventional social
customs, the Indian question, and numerous other current
topics of interest. With comedian Nat Goodwin in the leading
role of Big Pony, Chief of the Umbilicas, the extravaganza
opened at the Bijou Opera House in New York on March 31,
1887. Possessing little literary merit, Big Pony, as one
critic pointed out, served as a vehicle for "a shower of puns,
quips, topical songs and allusions, all passable and many of
them very apt, funny and telling."[20] Goodwin appeared onstage in a full dress suit, black wig, gold earrings, a row
of diamonds in his shirt front, moccasins, pocket-tomahawk,
and eagle's feather. The Mirror reported that he "intervenes
in the marriage of a Mexican hidalgo, fascinates the bride,
abducts the feminine half of the wedding party--all too willing

to be abducted--marries the fair one to her U.S. Lieutenant
lover, saddles himself with the duenna, and in general con-
ducts himself like a beneficent copper-colored deus ex ma-
china, in a manner to warm the heart of the Indian Educational Bureau or a Boston Philanthropist. "21 The first and
third acts of this foolishness were well received but a poor
second act ruined the production. Goodwin made disparaging
comments about the play during the performance, which both
delighted the audience and angered Wheeler.

Big Pony was not well received by critics. A reviewer for the morning Herald found it rather ordinary:
"To be entirely candid, Mr. Wheeler's lyrics and his dialogue and Mr. Darling's music are all of the most commonplace quality. There are no tuneful numbers, no bright
lines, and the topical verses are entirely devoid of wit or
sparkle. Not a laugh greeted any of the efforts to be funny,
and had it not been for the fun and frolic introduced by Mr.
Goodwin and the members of the company, the 'Big Pony'
would have been a flat failure. "22 Wheeler never forgave
Goodwin's impromptu remarks, which he blamed for the
play's failure. In the Mirror of May 28, 1887, he suggested
that a syndicate of capitalists was planning to send the actor
abroad to enable him to learn how to act. A year at the
Paris Conservatoire, he said, should teach him the difference
between impersonation and mimicry; the Berlin School of
Plastic Art might help him learn the difference between de-
clamation and gagging; a year at Vienna or Baden would be
spent developing his memory; and a few months at St. Petersburg could be devoted to teaching him how to avoid guying the
other actors. "It is confidently predicted that by a rigid
course of study Mr. Goodwin will be enabled in two years to
act, " Nym Crinkle quipped. The actor presented his side of
the incident in his own Nat Goodwin's Book.

Wheeler's next dramatic effort, Jack Royal of the
92nd, failed to catch the attention of the public in 1891 despite some well placed puffs in the daily press. Written as a
vehicle for popular actor Harry Lacy, the play was completed
in May 1891, received an October production at the Park
Theatre in Philadelphia, and opened in New York at the Bowery Theatre in November. Set during the draft riots of 1862,
Jack Royal was little different from the countless action-
packed melodramas which played the Bowery. A hero in the
person of Lieutenant Jack Royal of the U.S. Engineers de-
feats Confederate plans to disrupt production of steel plates
needed for Union iron-clad ships. During the excitement he

falls in love with Kate Delaplaine, daughter of the Steel
Works proprietor. At the end of the play he prepares to
ride away to fight the rebs without knowing whether Kate
loves him. The following obligatory scene, however, brings
events to their desired conclusion:

Kate

Some day you will know all, but I must tell you
now that my hope, my heart, my very safety goes
with the departing sound of your drums.

Royal

(tenderly) Miss Delaplaine----Kate----

Kate

Try and understand me.

Royal

You are agitated. What is the matter.

Kate

(Hurriedly) This is no place and there is no time
for explanations, but you once professed to love me.

Royal

It was not a profession---it was a confession.
It may have been hopeless----

Kate

It was not hopeless. [23]

Such tender scenes were the stock-in-trade of nineteenth-
century melodrama. The play survived only one season and
was not revived. The majority of critics thought it old-
fashioned and weak.

Wheeler next collaborated with Edward M. Alfriend in
1895 on The Great Diamond Robbery, a murder-mystery
which featured super-sleuth, Dick Brummage. It was to be
Wheeler's most successful play. The plot offers all the

twists and turns of a good detective story. The theft of
valuable jewels in Europe is linked to politics and crime in
New York. Clinton Bulford, an American banker, has un-
knowingly married a Russian adventuress who is involved in
the theft. At the opening of the play, she poisons her husband to hide her identity and blames the murder upon Frank
Bennett, an honest clerk at her husband's bank. Bennett
becomes a fugitive from justice; to clear his good name he
seeks the help of his sweetheart, Mary Lavelot. Dick Brummage, the master of disguises, now enters the case. He
links the Russian jewel theft with Frau Rosenbaum, an old
hag who runs a den of thieves in New York. And he discovers that she is protected by a New York senator. Allusions to politics and city low life give the play a touch of
local color. For example, "You must have been in politics
yourself, " the Senator states in Act III in reference to Mrs.
Bulford's diamond ring. "I've carried the district attorney's
office in one pocket and the Central Office in the other, but
I never had a stone like that on my finger." Justice triumphs. Dick Brummage solves all the crimes and proves
Frank's innocence. Mrs. Bulford takes poison. "The God
of Justice reigns even in New York, " Mary Lavelot cries in
the final scene. [24]

A classical actress, Fanny Janauschek, shocked elit-
ist critics by playing the role of villainous Frau Rosenbaum;
W. H. Thompson acted Dick Brummage. The Great Diamond
Robbery opened on the evening of September 4, 1895, at the
American Theatre, to mixed critical reaction. The Dramatic
Mirror saw nothing new in the plot and disliked such sensational ingredients as murder and sudden death. [25] The New
York Times, while more favorable, thought the tender sympathies of the audience "not sufficiently appealed to." Instead, the spectator "is oftener shocked and horrified than
compelled to sympathize with afflicted virtue. "[26] Stephen
Fiske in the Spirit of the Times found the piece "merely a
rehash of other dramas and the only talent employed upon it
was in picking out effective scenes to imitate. "[27] The play
does resemble a number of other melodramas of the period.
Dick Brummage seems modeled on Conan Doyle's Sherlock
Holmes--a character around which William Gillette would
build a play in 1899. Wheeler used the term "scenewright"
to describe writers who adapted and fitted the material of
others to their own use. The term could well be used to
describe his own dramatic efforts.

A. C. Wheeler wrote or co-authored a number of

other plays including The Oil Syndicate: An Original, Spectacular, International Drama in five acts and nine tableaux (with his second wife, Jennie P. M. Wheeler); The Heart of Fire, a melodrama (with Edward M. Alfriend); The Pulque Girl, a musical fantasy; The Scarlet Plume; and The Master of the Household. He was responsible for parts of The Still Alarm and Blue Jeans, plays credited to Joseph Arthur. None of his dramatic works survived their day. Even the most popular--The Great Diamond Robbery--did not rise to the level of such successful melodramas of the period as The Ticket-of-Leave Man, Sherlock Holmes, and Secret Service.

By the time Wheeler began his career as a theatre critic in the late 1860s, his style and critical beliefs were well established. Like his Bohemian predecessors, he wrote in a lively epigrammatic manner, employing Latin and French phrases as well as a generous supply of multi-syllabic English words. He thought his vocation a worthy one which demanded some ability. "A dramatic critic ought to have intelligence, culture, and experience enough to go to a play and reason rationally about it afterwards," he wrote in 1884.[28] "He ought to be able to point out what is false in sentiment, defective in logic, vulgar in action and immoral in tone." Other attributes which he thought important were a clear vision and the quality of human sympathy. His major "besetting sin," he confessed, was indecision--perhaps a normal "sin" for any critic who relied on his impressions rather than on well defined critical principles. Often Wheeler would argue the unpopular side of an issue; then, he would change views when public opinion shifted. He hated with an intensity which left him many enemies. According to Deshler Welch, "Generous with his friends, and too bitter in his dislikes, my special criticism upon him is that his power has been carelessly dissipated."[29]

Where Clapp and Wilkins had turned to Jules Janin for inspiration, Wheeler sought out French heavyweights, Madame de Staël, Sainte-Beuve, and Hippolyte Taine.[30] At a time when William Winter was defending aesthetics inherited from English romantics, Wheeler followed the French in postulating race, moment, and milieu as determining agents in cultural advancement. A literary work, he argued, could not be separated from its social, economic, or political roots, or even from its cultural and moral sources. He drew largely upon the ideas of Taine. In the introduction to his influential three-volume History of English Literature (1863),

Taine describes a literary work as "not a mere individual
play of imagination, the isolated caprice of an excited brain,
but a transcript of contemporary manners, a manifestation
of a certain kind of mind. "[31] And Taine theorized that "we
might recover, from the monuments of literature, a knowledge
of the manner in which men thought and felt centuries ago. "
He analyzed English literature from historical, geographical,
and sociological standpoints. To Taine belongs the credit for
a style of literary criticism we call "sociocultural. "

Wheeler considered himself a critic in the Taine tradition, and others agreed. Deshler Welch felt that he was
not "an aesthetic critic" after the style of Hazlitt or Lamb,
but rather was like Taine, abreast of the age "in tone and
style. "[32] Wheeler strove for precision in his analysis,
rather than offering only "rhapsody" in the manner of the
"Charles Lamb and William Hazlitt" school of criticism.
He called his method "scientific" and the English school
"aesthetic. "

The difference between the two schools he explained
in a Dramatic Mirror (February 25, 1888) critique of English
actress Ellen Terry. Where the traditional critic (referring
no doubt to William Winter) would call Miss Terry a "charming woman, " the phrase is not precise and can be said about
a number of actresses: "It is a verbal mantle used to cover
up the poverty of judgment in the critic, and the poverty of
achievement in the actress. It means only that the personality of the performer pleases the eye. " Instead of making
general statements, the critic ought to provide specific physical and biographical information. For example, Wheeler
described Miss Terry's nervous mannerisms: "The tension
of muscle under nervous strenuousness is continuous. This
betrays itself to the eye in the constant endeavor of the
organism to retrieve itself in some kind of motion. Her
involuntary starts, her little darting actions without other
meaning than the effort of the nervous energy to expend itself
along the muscles, the unpremeditated strides, the curiously
irrelevant use of her arms: the freedom when she gets into
rapid motion--all these show unmistakably ... her condition. "
Wheeler considered such remarks precise or scientific.

His critical method is evident in a November 9, 1889,
Dramatic Mirror review of actor Robert Mantell. "Looked
at in a dress coat he is manly, elegant, refined, graceful
and intelligent to the eye. His figure is a tall and handsome
one. His carriage is erect. His limbs are Apollo-like--

long, round and sinewy, without being massive. His head is small and symmetrical, and his face, while not being handsome in the fashion place sense, nor yet quite effective always in the melodramatic sense ... is yet capable of great dignity of mien and tenderness of emotion." To Wheeler this precisely described Mantell's physical and mental characteristics. Not content merely to describe the actor as "charming" or "dignified," he presented instead a detailed list of those characteristics which some persons might call "charming" or "dignified."

He believed that a scientific critic judged an artistic work on its artistic intentions rather than on some vague theory held by intellectual circles. "Does the play, the picture, the book, the music, do the work it promises to do, and does it do it well?" he wrote in 1872. "That is the height and depth and breadth of criticism."[33] Mantell, for example, should not be compared to Edwin Booth or to Henry Irving but must be considered on his own terms, including his limitations, intentions, physical endowments, and intellect. With a touch of sarcasm, Wheeler suggested that actors who invited attention to their looks, physique, health, limbs, and clothes must be measured accordingly. Consequently, when Clara Morris "obtrudes her invalidism into art, we may meet it with pathological acumen. When Mrs. Potter exhibits her clothes, we may bring the technique of the loom and the haberdasher. When Miss Terry parades her temperament we may study her temperament."[34] To do this, of course, a critic must acquaint himself with all aspects of the professional stage. He must attend rehearsals, socialize with members of the profession, and attempt to learn everything about the inter-workings of the theatre. Wheeler thought it important that he know actors as human beings and not as art abstractions.

As a scientific critic Wheeler attempted to answer one of the most controversial aesthetic questions of the Victorian era: does art have any obligation to conventional morality? To look at art with the disinterestedness of a scientist implies no concern with morality. But Wheeler did not satisfactorily reconcile this issue in his own mind. On one hand he chided "sensitive dilettantes" for demanding that the stage function as a Sunday School; on the other, he demanded moral plays. This paradox can be explained only by noting that Wheeler was a man of many contradictions, much like the age itself. In 1871 he found such excessive virtue in The Man o'Airlie that after the second act he yearned for a "hari-kari"

or the "braining of a few babies. "[35] Seven years later he
ridiculed the Reverend Dewitt Talmage's moral crusade
against the theatre, calling him an "ignorant swashbuckler"
from the 16th century who "believes that might makes right,
and that an army of police, if you make it large, can ex-
tirpate sin from the world by main force. "[36] Any urchin
from the public school has more sense, he suggested. "Art
does not seek a moral purpose. Its end is beauty. " A
decade later he thought that the mission of the stage was not
to teach morality "any more than it is the mission of por-
trait-painting to teach ethics. "[37]

Immorality, he tried to convince himself, was determined by the playwright's treatment of his subject, not by
the subject itself. Thus he differed with William Winter on
the question, "Is Camille an immoral play?" Because a
courtesan's degenerate life came to a pitiable death, he
thought it "one of the most moral of plays. "[38] On the other
hand he called Rip Van Winkle an immoral play because it
shows a drunken and lazy man rewarded and his good industrious wife punished: "It upsets all my preconceived notions
of morality, duty, manliness, and aesthetic integrity, to
perceive that he is not only a privileged but an honored
scapegrace. "[39] Science or not, Wheeler subscribed to the
doctrine of poetic justice--evil must be punished and good
rewarded.

Despite his avowed claims to be a scientific critic,
he was too much a product of his age to accept gross violations of conventional morality. "Men who seek nastiness of
any kind, either as a means or as an end, " he wrote in
1872, "are enemies of mankind. " And two years later he
added, "After all, I care not so much whether the theatre be
classic or romantic, so long as it is kept wholesome. " Artists should hold the mirror up to life in general, he believed, not to private affairs of individuals nor to specific
crimes. Instead of presenting "stale and puerile incidents
of a bawdy-house brawl, " they might reflect upon the heroism
of the working man or the intensity of city life. Or they
might interpret the actions of the wealthy or of those in politics. In 1866 Wheeler denounced The Black Crook for its
nudity, or semi-nudity--and this was a musical extravaganza
which even the staid Winter enjoyed. In spite of statements
to the contrary, he remained a romantic at heart, wanting
not the worst but the best of human activity dramatized.

His opposition to the Genteel Tradition affected all of

his writings. With nostalgia he looked backwards to an earlier America where strength and heroism were prized rather than cultivation and elegance. He wanted literature and drama to depict masculine heroes. He deplored the effeminacy and affection which permeated the art and letters of his day. "When Howells [William Dean Howells] and his scholars made decoration and not character the test in art," he complained in 1889, "they invited the whole phalanx of incompetent gentility into the arena of hard work. They have been at it with their crochet needles ever since." Charles Shattuck likens Wheeler to a "minor Aristophanes": "... he hurled blows and roars against the genteel ivory-towerism, the false estheticism, the romantic nostalgia, the cult of prettiness and preciosity which governed 'official' art in America during the last third of the nineteenth century."40 Wheeler accused the Genteel writers of substituting sentimentalism for passion, charm for vigor, cool intellectuality for emotion, and ladies and gentlemen for men and women. In the drama, blood and iron were abandoned for "sweetness and light." Edwin Forrest was pushed aside for Edwin Booth. The critic's belligerence against this cultural change in America increased as he grew older.

He especially hated those artists and writers who attempted to make Shakespeare more palatable to refined and sensitive tastes. While he was not a Shakespearean scholar--like Richard Grant White, William Winter, or John Ranken Towse--he had definite ideas on how Shakespeare should not be produced. For example, he objected to dressing up Shakespeare in coat and tails, and resisted any attempt to exorcise the vulgarity and brutality from Elizabethan drama. Such scenes, he thought, were conceived in a barbaric age when "men went to the theatre because they could no longer go to the witch burning or the bear baiting."41 He admitted that it takes courage to call Othello a cruel play, "but so it is." And Antony and Cleopatra is a "sensual play. It does not mince matters in dealing with the effects of voluptuous passion on a brave man's character." Shakespeare knew what kind of morality Cleopatra represented and did not deodorize it. 42

If we are going to produce Elizabethan dramas, Wheeler advised, we should preserve the spirit as well as the color of them. When Edwin Booth attempted to reduce the violence in Othello, the critic's temper was aroused. Booth (as Othello) killed Desdemona with a dagger rather than strangling her: "He put Desdemona's bed on the stage.

He crawled to it with a dagger in his hand, and with his face to the audience tried to picture all the emotions that raced through his aching soul as he slowly brought his dagger up to her young sweet body. "[43] Where the actor saw Othello (at least in Wheeler's mind) as a "spiritual and sacrificial priest, smothering Desdemona from some high, abstract, transcendental, Brahminical motive," Wheeler, with Forrest and the Italian actor Tommasso Salvini in mind, saw Othello as a barbarian who could not control his passions. He regarded Booth's interpretation as a nineteenth-century attempt to tone down sixteenth-century cruelty.

And he harshly criticized Booth's attempt to relieve Gloucester in Richard III of coarseness and make him a sympathetic character. In his opinion Gloucester came from a warlike race of butchers "who kill without compunction and die without fear. He has the intrepidity of a bulldog and the sagacity of a fox."[44] He was a villain and deserved to die like one. "He has no sensibility," Wheeler noted. "He is impervious to kindness, deaf to warnings, callous to love. He disregards the curses and the prayers alike of his mother and of his victims; he scoffs at the parental blessing, and mocks the sacred character of the office he is straining every nerve to attain." Because Richard was a man without a conscience, it was false to civilize such a character.

In an age which sought to remove the excesses of vulgarity and violence from Shakespeare's plays, Wheeler found himself out of step with contemporary fashion. He could not tolerate the emasculation of the playwright's language by William Winter, editor of stage versions used by Edwin Booth and Augustin Daly. Marvin Felheim has noted that Winter substituted "villain" for "lecher"; "stomach" for "belly"; and "sup" for "to lie with a woman" in The Merry Wives of Windsor produced by Daly in January 1886.[45] Wheeler opposed the sentimental and prudish tastes of the Genteel School, particularly their attempt to turn Shakespeare's characters into Victorian ladies and gentlemen.

Unlike his elitist contemporaries--Winter and Towse-- Wheeler did not regard drama as a serious art that would elevate and inspire mankind; rather, he saw it as something like the newspaper, dependent upon the moods and tastes of the hour. "What we want is more nowness in the serious drama," he wrote in 1886. Like the newspaper the drama must provide the public with the best and freshest of everything. In 1874 he had admitted liking French plays, Alixe

and Led Astray, because they were about contemporary life:
"After all our Anglo-Saxon spleen has been expended on the
French dramatists let us acknowledge that the French stage
is the only stage that reflects life about it. The very im-
moralities of that stage are a reflex of the life which feeds
it. Vital and urgent questions concerning the relative duties
of the sexes agitate French society, and something of the
philosophy, the poetic justice, and the social injustice of the
reality are caught and dealt with cleverly by the dramatists. "46 And if the French drama can reflect French society, he preached in his best Taine manner, American
drama can reflect traits of American society--the dignity of
labor, heroism of duty, equality of men. This did not mean
that he approved of realistic plays; he simply wanted democratic principles reflected on the stage. He preferred romantic works which "tugged at the heart strings, " not treatises
on social problems. "Don't prate of intellectuality, " he wrote
in the World, May 31, 1874. "By no possible human effort
or conceivable superhuman miracle can you make the intellectuality of the stage keep pace with the intellectuality around
it. " His favorite subject was pure love triumphing over evil.

Wheeler was a patriotic man who spent much of his
career advocating a distinctly American drama. He believed
native writers were not devoid of dramatic instinct but that
they were without ideas, able only to "puddle what has already been invented. " A five-minute analysis of original
American drama, he quipped in 1871, will produce "two nig-
gers, one English fop, an American belle, four miles of
honest paint, and a jumble of Indians, gamblers, vagrants,
and villains who yell, swindle, steal, and murder as if there
was but one rule governing all those things known to humanity. "47 He rejected the theory that this country lacked suit-
able material for the drama: "I am of the opinion that men
in America have the same inscrutable hearts, prone to love
and hate and lie and venerate, that beat in the jungles of Af-
rica or the saloons of London; they are swayed by pretty
much the same vices and animated by the same virtues;
swollen with vanity or collapsed with humiliation; roaring, de-
fying, praying, suffering, achieving, and dying--everywhere
with the same desperation or devoutness. "48 He wanted a
drama for the tradesmen and working classes--the "most
valuable portion of the community"--not for the upper elite.
Perhaps that is why he preferred melodrama to other kinds
of theatrical offerings.

He twice sat through Davy Crockett at Niblo's Garden

in 1874, delighted with the naive simplicity of the story and the noble heroics of Davy Crockett as portrayed by Frank Mayo. [49] His passions were aroused when Davy held shut the door of the hut to keep out the baying wolves. And his sense of justice was rewarded when the hero rescued Eleanor Vaughn from a bad marriage and married her himself. Despite Davy Crockett's social deficiencies, Eleanor came to realize that he was a gentleman, "and more than that, a man." Wheeler approved of making the frontiersman a hero as he did the basic theme of the play--Western vitality and virtue triumphing over Eastern weakness and corruption.

Wheeler lauded Steele MacKaye's masculine characters in Paul Kauvar, a romantic melodrama which premiered at the Standard Theatre in New York on December 24, 1887. "There is a sinewy purpose to his drama," the critic wrote, "and he has tried the audacious experiment of substituting blood and iron for sweetness and light.... I admire one thing in Steele MacKaye. He hasn't let down the pegs of his romanticism to please this fad. It has a lusty blare in it that is not of our hour, and the hero has got to be masculine or he will not fit the work."[50] Set in the midst of the French Revolution, the play reveals the heroism of Paul Kauvar and his romance with the daughter of the Duke de Beaumont. There is much action: Paul risks his life to save the Duke and his daughter, offering at one time to die on the guillotine in place of the Duke. Wheeler faulted the play's improbabilities and sentimentalism, but excused its weaknesses and praised its romantic qualities.

His comments about two Civil War melodramas reflect similar tastes--his love of action, romance, and human situations. In 1888 he described William Gillette's Held by the Enemy as a "drama of original material, with a symmetry, a purpose and a human interest that stand as excellent models of stage work."[51] Set in a Southern city occupied by Northern forces, the play centers on the efforts of three men-- Lieutenant Gordon Hayne of the Confederate Army, Colonel Harvey Brant and Brigade Surgeon Fielding of the Union Army--to win the hand of Eunice McCreerys. The abundance of heroics was certain to please an old romantic like Wheeler.

Bronson Howard's romantic comedy, Shenandoah, attracted his attention in 1889 for many of the same reasons. The play is set in Charleston on the eve of the war. A New Yorker, Kirchival West, and a Virginian, Robert Ellingham,

are friends. With the firing on Fort Sumter, they end up on
different sides of the conflict. Complications are compounded
when each falls in love with the other's sister. To Wheeler
the merits of the play lay not in the treatment of the war,
but in its effect upon humans: "It is not the motion and
noise of armed hosts, but the calm agony of human hearts,
the strained relationship of old friends, the wreck of hopes,
and the break down of loves in the tempest of passion that
hold attention until the atmosphere clears and the cruel war
is over."[52] He especially approved of Howard's strong, masculine characters presented in a romantic setting.

Wheeler encouraged a number of other American playwrights, including Bartley Campbell, Edward Harrigan, and
Clyde Fitch. What excited him about Campbell's western
plays (My Partner, The White Slave, The Galley Slave) was
the playwright's thoroughly native flavor. "There are
touches in 'My Partner' that might have been written by Walt
Whitman or Beecher [Henry Ward Beecher]," he wrote in
1884. "They never could have been written by Tennyson or
Matthew Arnold."[53] In many ways, Edward Harrigan's
sketches of urban and ethnic problems satisfied his demand
for nowness in the theatre. "He went down to the dock and
into the garrets and cellars," Wheeler wrote of Harrigan's
Mulligan Guard's plays in 1888; "he climbed up among the
squatters and strode into the shipyards. There wasn't anything so poor and lowly that it escaped him, whatever its
color or birth or condition."[54] At that time, Harrigan's city
low-life plays reminded him of the novels of Charles Dickens.
And he compared Clyde Fitch to Richard B. Sheridan after
viewing his first play, Beau Brummel, in 1890. According
to Wheeler, it was "a genuine comedy depending for its interest wholly upon its picture of manners and its play of
character...."[55] He thought the piece an "admirable departure from the morbid school just now so popular." Delighted with the review, Clyde Fitch wrote Wheeler, May 21,
1890, to thank him for the "immense encouragement and wel-
come comfort yr brilliant and kind criticism of 'Beau Brummel' has given its author."[56]

His penchant for American plays and his romantic bent
led him to ignore or reject the New Drama. His arguments
against Ibsen differ little from those of Winter and Towse.
In The Theatre of January 4, 1890, he directed an angry
diatribe against A Doll's House.

'A Doll's House,' as presented to us on the

stage, proved to be one of the most exasperatingly
tedious narratives that ever called itself drama.
It ignored all the canons of dramatic art that by
long experiment have been accepted by the world.
It violated the simplest principles of stage con-
struction and stage representation.
    It consumed a whole act in explaining its postu-
late. It employed superfluous people, and employed
them offensively and tiresomely. It assumed to
deal with character instead of events, and it dealt
almost exclusively with a characterless woman.
It ostentatiously set out to give us an ethical treatment of life, and it left the commonest duties of
life in an inextricable muddle. It was heralded as
a play that went straight to human nature and
treated it with the honesty of realism; and it presented us with a weak monstrosity that does not
belong to normal life, and who violated in her conduct the plainest and commonest laws of human development.

Wheeler could not tolerate the didactic qualities, the lack of
overt action, and the pessimistic nature of the Ibsen drama.
He wanted love and romance on the stage, not "cant and
scholastic sputter and high art gabble."

    In his views on acting, Wheeler placed his trust in
emotional inspiration and mistrusted the intellectual approach
to acting which William Macready had popularized in the
1840s and 1850s. He believed genius essential for great
acting and defined the term as a product of both hereditary
gifts and inspiration which allows the actor to transcend himself. "Doctors may disagree as the genesis of genius," he
explained in the Dramatic Mirror of July 9, 1887, "and no
student of acting will dispute the statement that its distinguishing peculiarity is unconsciousness of means." He noted
that Clara Morris, Tommasso Salvini, Fanny Janauschek,
J. B. Booth, and Edwin Forrest all admitted to being swept
away by emotion or inspiration during a performance. "I
remember Forrest's last performance of Lear," he recalled,
"and who that saw it can ever forget it? It was the strongest
physical exhibition I had ever witnessed. By some weird
power he became Lear: he no longer acted but was acted on.
The sorrows of the old king were at last not imaginary but
real. The great, obdurate heart of the tragic king was
melted in his own grief and the tears ran down his furrowed

cheeks and he groaned and traveled in spirit under a terrible load. "57

To Wheeler, Edwin Forrest exemplified rugged in-dividualism, heroism, moral courage, and masculinity--character traits which he identified with Jacksonian America. In 1871 Forrest appeared to him as a "sort of histrionic Niagara or Mississippi. " His wrath "burned like a prairie fire, and he wore the natural imperiousness of Black Hawk or Red Jacket. " He was "nobly virile in impulse, in con-formation, in function, and in projected purpose. " And of utmost importance, he was "destitute of any of the later feminization that has decorated the stage hero with sexless complaisance. "58 Wheeler concluded that "In physical en-dowment and natural instinct he stood head and shoulders ... above any man who walked the boards. " There is no question but that he considered Forrest a pioneer in the de-velopment of this nation's theatre, and thus deserving of re-spect and honor.

The actor had been badly wounded, however, by those who accused him of coarseness, muscularity, roaring and ranting, an imperious manner with associates, disregard of the amenities of public life, defiance of public opinion, and contempt for criticism. Wheeler expressed sadness over the actor's loss of reputation in his old age, and suggested in 1871 that he should have retired earlier and spared the pub-lic the spectacle of a declining career. When the two men met for the first time in Boston at the Peace Jubilee of 1872, Forrest remembered those remarks. Wheeler recalled the occasion of their meeting some twenty-seven years later in the Criterion of September 23, 1899:

> Passion congested his dark, seamed face to a
> sudden purple, and tied the veins in his gladiato-
> rial neck into knots. Some kind of premonitory
> hissing, as of coming lava, issued from his lips,
> followed by volcanic rumblings, deep down.
> The first articulate phrase that fell upon my
> ears was: 'You dam-ned whippersnapper, have you
> come here to bark at my heels or to lick my
> boots. ' Then followed a violent and blasphemous
> explosion of denunciation and contempt, so utterly
> out of proportion to the cause that he must have
> felt, and, in fact, I happen to know that he did so
> feel, was quite unworthy of him or the occasion.

Fellow critic Edward H. House, who accompanied Wheeler on this occasion, fled at this outburst.

Rather than resenting the abusive language and conduct, the critic remembered thinking that it was the actor's prerogative to be violent and unreasonable in gusts: "I tried to explain to him that it was not possible for me to write of him vindictively, and that what I have said had proceeded from a boundless admiration of him." Forrest's wrath, however, was not so easily abated. Looking fiercely at Wheeler, he shouted, "Who are you, sir, to order me off the stage? Have you set the limits to my career and fixed the boundaries of it? I can't leave the stage. Damn it, sir, it is leaving me. When you understand me you will respect me." Evidently Forrest did not harbor ill-will towards the critic for very long. A few months later in Philadelphia, he sent for Wheeler and apologized. "'Harkee,' he said, 'I may have done you some injustice unwittingly, but you can understand that a bruised man forgets the dam-ned amenities at times!'" While this account may be colored by nostalgia--an old man's version of an incident which happened twenty-seven years earlier--it does suggest a reason for his continued and strong support of Edwin Forrest.

He defended the reputation of the actor in July 1877, when the Reverend W. R. Alger's Life of Forrest was reviewed harshly in the New York Times. In a lengthy "Causerie" essay in the Spirit of the Times for July 14, Wheeler explained the importance of Forrest's style.

> The truth is that Mr. Forrest embodied and represented in himself unconsciously the vital, burly, aggressive Americanism of his age. It was as directly opposed to the creamy smoothness and prancing propriety of Macready's art as Walt Whitman's virile lines are opposed to the dainty and supersensuous dialectics of Mr. Tennyson. That it was a better art or a nobler nature was not and never has been claimed. That it was an honest, vigorous, natural expression of genius, and moved the world as genius only can, ought to have been acknowledged by those who were placed to scrutinize it officially.

To charges that Forrest could not play Shakespeare, Wheeler replied that such accusations meant he could not play it according to the Kemble or Macready standard. And with

pointed reference to William Winter, the critic noted how
John McCullough had been touted by both the New York
Times and the Tribune as the "greatest actor that the country has produced," when in reality McCullough had been a
pupil of Forrest's. "In Richelieu, Othello, and Metamora
he reproduces the exact stage business, the walk, gesticulation emphasis, and accent of his master, and Mr. Winter
praises to nausea the copied peculiarities which he condemned
in the original." Modern historians have pointed out that by
1877, McCullough had refined somewhat the excesses of the
Forrest style. [59] Wheeler apparently did not notice such al-
terations, however, until the following year.

He concluded that the old actor was being maligned
for his personal rather than his professional life. "I am
well aware that the rage for 'staying away from his performance came in with the 'genteel folk' just after the Macready difficulty," he wrote in the World of February 19,
1871, "and that Mr. Forrest threw down the gauntlet to the
press after offending the fashionable world, and that the circumstances attending the famous divorce suit were distorted
to his injury." He repeated such charges throughout his
career, and much of what he wrote was true. Polite society, as well as many critics, ignored Forrest after his divorce hearings. His appearances in New York during the
1860s were scarcely noticed by the majority of the press.
Referring to the genteel writers as the "mush and milk"
school, Wheeler charged them with refusing to consider the
actor's talent separate from his divorce and the Astor Place
Riot of 1849. He blamed "dilettanti pens" on one side and
rivals on the other for undermining the actor's reputation.

He spoke of Charlotte Cushman's talent as also being
"distinctively American." [60] "As we all remember it," he
wrote in 1871, "there is the breadth of the prairie and the
surge of Niagara in it. The gothic grandeur of Walt Whitman
and the rhythmic cadence of Whittier. Something that wasn't
built like the pyramids, but grand, like the Sierra Nevadas."
He found her most effective in strong roles such as Lady
Macbeth, Queen Katherine in Henry VIII, and Meg Merrilies
in Guy Mannering. During October 1871, he viewed one of
her last performances as Meg Merrilies. Both the play and
the role were considered unfashionable at the time, and he
cautioned against the performance. Although captivated by
her power, he admitted that she had not touched his heart:
"Hers was to me a physical excellence that wounded as often
as it healed.... I recall her Meg Merrilies even now with a

shudder, and while the elf locks and ghastly face remain im-
perishable in my memory I cannot for the life of me recall
anything else more worthy of preservation. "[61] Charlotte
Cushman had disappointed him. She had lacked a light
touch--unstudied humor and gentle pathos--as well as grace
and dignity. Wheeler now admitted that he had always felt
her acting was flawed: "She was always too terribly in
earnest to do more than move you, and to delight you it was
necessary to be something less. I really believe that the
remembrance of her genius was that of slightly painful admiration. "

He was never captivated by the emotional school. He
did not enjoy watching actresses like Matilda Heron or Clara
Morris give way to uncontrollable histrionics on the stage.
After the death of Heron on March 7, 1877, Wheeler reviewed her career in the Spirit of the Times: "She had no
patience, no remorse, no wait in her. It was all impulse,
mood, fever or chill. To-day she was the actress of the
world, tomorrow she became the abject wreck. "[62] But Matilda Heron had suffered a mental breakdown before her
death, and Wheeler was not unsympathetic: "We seldom stop
to think how close the best of the great emotional players
come to insanity when they give full reign to their sensibili-
ties. " Other actresses of the same school, specifically Clara Morris, he found crude and coarse, able to portray only
strong passions, not light and "more joyous" ones. While
he thought Morris effective in suffering French heroine roles,
he was simply not interested in such morbid dramatic fare.

Wheeler suggested in 1874 that John McCullough's robust physique and strong voice made him the appropriate artistic heir to Forrest and Cushman. The actor had spent
eight years in California, somewhat isolated from the cultural
change which was transforming the East. Now he arrived in
New York with his "portfolio of melodramas under his arm"
and appealed to the same crowd that had cheered Forrest.
"There is nothing about John that your dilettante and technical
scrutinizer will admire, " the critic warned. "He could have
issued from no other portal than that in the Rocky Mountains
with all that breezy out-door puissance, that clear open face,
and that broad western romanticism. "[63] The actor hoped for
success by offering old war horses from the Forrest arena--
Spartacus and Damon--to refined Eastern audiences. "Does
wholesome John clearly understand that this is all wrong?"
Wheeler bantered. "That he has no right to move people?
That we don't want to be moved? That the vigorous, manly

sort of thing is exploded? That wholesomeness is as much
out of place in a theatre as brimstone is in the pulpit?"
And yet, the critic noted with sarcasm, the audience seems
not to have noticed. "There is thunder in the gallery. Yea,
believe me, there are flashes in the parquette and drops
patter out of the dress circle."[64] Critical response in general was favorable for McCullough. William Winter in the
Tribune praised him for avoiding the worst faults of the Forrest school.

      Wheeler did notice technical deficiencies in McCul-
lough's acting, despite his honest ruggedness. For instance,
the actor was "deficient in rhetorical grace." He demonstrated monotonous reading of lines, lacked subtlety, and did
not always understand what was dramatic. These problems
were apparently alleviated when he studied for three months
in 1877 with Steele MacKaye. By May 1878, Wheeler
noticed remarkable improvement: "The native vigour, reso-
nance, and fire were there, but they were disciplined and
controlled. A nicer balance of faculty was apparent. The
intelligibility of the subtler emotions had been made sharper
and clearer. There were noble climaxes of passion, less
waste of energy in making himself felt, a cleaner adaptation
of tone and gesture to the exigent thought--more repose, more
dignity, more grace."[65] McCullough's talent, he concluded,
lay somewhere between Forrest's and Edwin Booth's, "with
something of the fervor and majesty of one, and more than
the culture of the other."

      Edwin Booth's lack of emotional power disturbed the
critic much more than McCullough's technical deficiencies.
While he described Booth as the greatest artist upon the
American stage, he limited such praise to those of the actor's
roles which demanded intellectual rather than physical or emotional force. Wheeler thought that to see Edwin Booth de-
lineate Richard III and Iago was to see the best acting of
which our stage was capable. His Richard III, for example,
was a "consistent, unmistakable individuality that announces
itself by the unvarying expression of a malign will in action,
carriage, and speech. Once seen, it is never forgotten."
And Booth's Iago was "the most profound and startling picture
of essential evil--that mysterious, subtle element of malign
power whose existence in nature furnishes the shadow of religion and the outline of superstition--that, I believe, it is possible for histrionism to produce."[66] This characterization
reminded Wheeler of Edwin Booth's father.

His opinion of the actor's Hamlet varied. In the Sunday World for January 9, 1870, he accused Booth of borrowing bits and pieces from other Hamlets, thus assembling a "most splendid mosaic." Also he thought Booth catered to contemporary fashion: "Mr. Booth's Hamlet is the perfect expression of the artistic taste of our times. That taste is characterized ... by the substitution of finish for feeling, elaborateness for earnestness, accuracy for emotion." In his attempt to make Hamlet "a model of historical accuracy, elocutionary perfection, and pictorial beauty," Booth attained a technical perfection which sacrificed emotion to form. In the Spirit of the Times, February 7, 1870, Wheeler accused him of ornamenting Hamlet with the refinements of contemporary stage culture. The result was not a sixteenth-century courtier, but a nineteenth-century gentleman.

Within two years Wheeler had softened his criticism. "The Hamlet of Edwin Booth, both as regards the chief character and the play, is a more consummate work of art than any Hamlet that preceded it--more exactly incarnating and illustrating the author, and with more of the spirit and knowledge of the age in it than any contemporaneous theatric exhibition."[67] Booth's impersonation had offered mental discipline, culture, repose, and excellence throughout, the author noted, "that the father's with all its magnificent and volcanic power, was utterly deficient in." And in rhetoric and elocution, "No actor on the English stage speaks a purer English with a better delivery than Mr. Booth. "I have stood in the corner of his theatre farthest from the stage and heard every syllable of his whisper when there were 2,000 people in the house." On this occasion at least, Wheeler applauded Booth's "exquisite toning of emotional manifestation which is in accord with the temper of our civilization." He concluded, somewhat surprisingly, that we are not less passionate or less sensitive than our ancestors but express our feelings with a more subdued manner. This does not mean that Wheeler had joined Winter and Aldrich at the Century Club to sing the praises of Edwin Booth. He had many opinions about the actor--and some were favorable.

In 1900, some seven years after Booth's death, Wheeler sought to determine his place in history.

> Mr. Booth ... was gifted in an extraordinary
> degree with the elocutionary faculty. He inherited
> from his father a grace of utterance, the most incisive and the most euphonious. This quality gave

a new gloss to his Hamlet. Besides all others that
were contemporaneous, it was Ciceronean. But we
know, now that our blood is cool, that it was in no
sense a creation. On the contrary, it was an ex-
purgated synthesis of Kemble, Kean, Macready, and
the actor's own father, the unlike traditions of each
appearing at times in a wonderful compromise that
leaned now to this and now to that predecessor, until it became worn down to a discreet uniformity.
No one could see then, what was sure to be seen in
the later retrospect, that Mr. Edwin Booth was, in
great measure, the result of a reaction from Gothic
conditions of acting that had been carried to the
farthest extent by Edwin Forrest. Mr. Booth's appearance was not so much a renaissance as a relief. His Hamlet, quite aside from its princely
grace and mimetic fervor, chanted itself into our
ideal empyrean, and we measured every virile attempt at originality in others by this exquisite
transcription. 68

The tradition which Booth inherited died with him, Wheeler
believed, when ensemble replaced individualism. The critic
blamed Richard Wagner for this shift in aesthetics. The
brilliant German had enlarged the scope of the stage-manager,
made an amalgam of all the arts, reduced the actor's personal aura in favor of the ensemble, and suppressed histrionism
for a material realism. But while in principle opposed to re-
ducing the status of the individual actor, Wheeler in 1900
praised Henry Irving's attempts to improve the state of theatrical art by attention to all phases of production. He agreed
with Stephen Fiske that Irving was successful in demonstrating
to this country the "practical and aesthetic value of the theatre as a worthy instrument of culture and morals. "69

Wheeler's eclectic tastes allowed him to enjoy the natural, human, and feminine style of Eleanora Duse in 1893.
He praised her Camille for its lack of theatrical effect and
for the absence of the clichés associated with the role:
"Her farewell to Armand is a new revelation of tenderness
and sincerity, unaccompanied by traditional stage business.
The uniqueness of the exhibit is in the artist's showing of
her own convictions in her own way. They flow easily into
emotion and utterly repudiate the trademarks of stage symbo-
lism. "70 And Duse's portrayal of Francine in Dumas fils'
Francillon drew similar comments: "Her acting ... was
most beautiful in all its details, wonderful in its consistency

and fidelity, in the certainty of its touch and in the spirit
which infused it.... it is one of the most remarkable attributes of this remarkable player that she seems completely
to identify herself with the character which she is for the
time being representing. She seems to feel it, even to live
it; the stage appears never to be in her mind, and it is
scarcely in the minds of her auditors. In relief, of course,
the seeming simplicity is most complex, and the artlessness
elaborate art; but the impression conveyed never fails to be
that of a living experience."[71] The actress's femininity together with her natural and untheatrical style appealed to
Wheeler, and he considered her the greatest tragedienne he
had ever seen.

In his last years he changed his opinion about the accomplishments of Augustin Daly. For years he had attacked
Daly for catering to the genteel public. In The Theatre of
November 30, 1889, Wheeler admitted that he had misjudged
the talented playwright and manager. "I look back now with
a curious feeling of wonder at my own virtuous indignation
poured out, column after column, upon 'Moorcroft, ' 'The
Flash of Lightning, ' 'Saratoga, ' 'Fernande, ' and 'Madelein
Morel. ' I recall the bitter quarrel over 'Pique' and ask myself what it was all about. " Wheeler now admired Daly's
accomplishments: building up "character for his theatre instead of buying cheap reputation"; introducing new people--
Clara Morris, Sara Jewett, Kate Claxton; and offering new
ideas, new stage settings, and new costumes. Daly had
built up a reliable stock company which offered continuous
good work to the better class of patrons. He did not care
what the mob said, Wheeler asserted, but what "the discreet
public knew. " As a result of his efforts to make the theatre a respectable place of amusement, opening night changed
from "black night" (fathers and brothers attended without
daughters and wives) to one to which the entire family would
come without enquiring what was on the bill, "confident that
whatever it was, it would be unexceptionable and well done. "
For the critic to praise Daly's efforts towards making the
theatre a respectable institution, after years of condemning
him for that very act, shows a remarkable change in attitude.
But Wheeler changed many of his views during his final
years.

In the 1890s he turned his back upon the professional
stage to pursue other ends. The reasons for this sudden
change in his career are not clear. In 1970 Paul Wheeler
suggested that his father had become disgusted by actresses

who sold their virtue in return for a role.[72]   But other
events may have contributed more to influence his thinking.
In 1889 his wife Ann died.   Three years later, in 1892, he
remarried.

The new Mrs. Wheeler was a young actress thirty
years his junior--Jennie Pearl Mowbray, the daughter of a
flour manufacturer from Winona, Minnesota.   Educated at a
Methodist college before pursuing a career as an actress,
she became a protégé of Mrs. James Brown Potter, a society woman trained by David Belasco for the stage.   In
March 1889, she played Olympe to Mrs. Potter's Camille in
a production which Nym Crinkle reviewed in the World.
"Miss Mowbray," he wrote, "played Olympe with unusual
naturalness, gayety and self possession, giving it indeed much
more color and meaning than is usually accorded to it."[73]
She enjoyed some success in 1890 as Nellie Carr in George
H. Jessop and Ben Teal's The Great Metropolis.   Apparently
she left the stage shortly after her marriage to Andrew, and
within the year, in December 1892, gave birth to a son,
Paul Mowbray Wheeler.   The Christian Advocate of March
20, 1903 suggested that Jennie had exercised a "strong and
molding influence" over the religious life of her husband.

Wheeler took his wife's maiden name for a new pseudonym and changed his literary personality during the last
years of his life.   Until after his death in 1903, few persons
knew the true identity of J. P. M. or J. P. Mowbray.   Joseph
B. Gilder, editor of the Critic and literary adviser to the
Century Company, wrote him on January 10, 1902:   "Few
things that have happened of late years has interested me so
much as the rumor that JPM & ACW are twins & that there's
only one of them, who is both.   If it be a fact, it is one of
the most extraordinary psychological phenomena that have
ever come to the notice of the undersigned."[74]   Mowbray
wrote about life out-of-doors, farming, and animals.   He removed himself as far as possible from the theatre and
seemed a different man with different interests.   His books
about nature--The Making of a Country Home, A Journey to
Nature, Tangled up in Beulah Land--were widely praised.
His diary attests to his obsession with Christianity, death,
the Bible, and his own spiritual needs.

More and more he retreated to his farm outside of
Monsey.   He loved animals and kept a sow whom he called
Clara Morris, a fox-terrier given to him by Lily Langtry,
and at least thirty other dogs.   Writing in the Mirror of

July 2, 1887, Wheeler had admitted that his proper avocation was agriculture, with criticism an incidental pastime. "Art trembles at my sweet, unsophisticated nature," he mused. With the proliferation of materialism and science, Wheeler, like Thoreau, withdrew from this world in protest against its vulgarity, lack of passion, and lack of spiritual values.

Wheeler attained momentary popularity as a novelist at the end of his life. His published novels include The Toltec Cup: A Romance of Immediate Life in New York City (1890); The Primrose Path of Dalliance: A Story of the Stage (1892); and The Conquering of Kate (1903). The latter novel he may have written with his wife. Leander Richardson, a friend of Wheeler's and editor of the New York Dramatic News and Times, reviewed The Primrose Path of Dalliance on June 25, 1892: "In very many respects I have always regarded Wheeler as one of the most remarkable writers it has ever been my good fortune to read. He adds to a wonderfully clear and analytical mind a style that is not alone attractive, but so much his own that no man has successfully imitated it." Despite such kind words, Wheeler's powers of observation and ability of expression were not keen and he failed to establish a reputation as a novelist.

Wheeler sought to regenerate the late Victorian society by warning repeatedly that the sacrifice of spiritual values to science and materialism would end in personal and national tragedy. "The new idolatry is Brains," he scribbled in his diary, "but what has become of the Peace that passeth understanding."[75] We gather facts, thinking that we are pursuing truth, but "truth is just beyond our impressions. It hides in the superdepths of the soul, to disclose itself at times suddenly mysteriously and authoritatively."[76] He sadly deplored the loss of simple faith and hope which allowed civilization as well as individual man to enjoy life more. "No gain in knowledge can compensate this loss," he mused, turning to Matthew Arnold for words to express the melancholy of his own soul:

> But that serene, that earnest air,
> I saw, I felt it once--but where?

Wheeler, no less than William Winter, longed for a serenity and earnestness of living that had passed forever.[77]

He died of apoplexy on March 10, 1903. Three days later, on March 13, his funeral was held in the Methodist

Church in Spring Valley, a short distance from Monsey, and
he was buried in an unmarked grave in Sleepy Hollow Cemetery at Tarrytown, New York. The Dramatic Mirror of
March 21 reported his passing:

> For many years he was one of the foremost
> representatives of a class of American newspaper
> men that is fast disappearing. In the school of
> letters to which he belonged, individuality of
> thought, aggressiveness and vigor of expression
> were the qualities most cultivated and most ad-
> mired. Mr. Wheeler possessed these qualities
> in the highest degree. He was a writer of extra-
> ordinary versatility and whatsoever subject he
> elected to discuss became in his hands the most
> important and fascinating subject imaginable for
> the moment to his readers. He wrote with the
> wit of an Irishman, the sturdy assurance of an
> Englishman, and the grace of a Frenchman. His
> command of the language was superb.... He had
> the power to conjure word melodies on every
> theme--now thundering denunciation, now flashing
> epigrammatic darts of criticism, now singing
> tenderly in a minor strain, perhaps, and lending
> fresh beauty to some world-old thought of emotion.

Before he died, Wheeler came to deplore newspaper
criticism. In his opinion, the newspaper press wanted the
event not the truth; thus, the theatre journalist writes about
everything that is "current and conspicuous and charming and
ephemeral, and ignores everything that is not."[78] Years of
such "superficial and trivial chronicling" had devalued theatrical art in the eyes of intelligent playgoers, he concluded.
As a result theatre is considered a social event, and actors
and actresses playthings of the public, unlike music, which
is treated as a serious art by public and critic alike. Thus
offended by the trivial and ephemeral nature of both the late
Victorian stage and popular journalism, Wheeler turned from
them to find salvation in religion and mysticism.

EPILOGUE

Theatre criticism in the New York press changed significantly during the last quarter of the nineteenth century, reflecting changes in both theatre and press. The death of one theatrical era and the beginning of another was evident with the demise of the resident repertory stock company and its replacement by the combination company, single play, typecasting, and long run. Actors who had set standards for over a generation disappeared with the old system. The deaths of John McCullough, Lawrence Barrett, and Edwin Booth signalled an end to the grand style of nineteenth-century acting. Realistic acting, as represented by Mrs. Fiske, required a closer adherence to the patterns of everyday life. The New Drama of Ibsen and Shaw began to find an audience among intelligent playgoers despite the protests of major critics. Themes previously avoided or treated superficially in early Victorian drama--adultery, divorce, illegitimacy, venereal disease--were discussed frankly in realistic plays.

The increased demands of mass journalism for circulation and advertising revenue altered the purpose and function of stage criticism. Newspapers, now becoming Big Business, were intent on making a huge profit rather than serving traditional interests. Theatrical managers brought increased pressure to bear upon editors and critics, threatening to remove advertising if one of their productions was harshly reviewed. Since they also were expanding their empires--buying and leasing theatres from coast to coast--publishers listened to their threats. While much was written about the need for independent criticism--especially in relationship to advertising pressures--in practice money usually affected policy.

In the September 1877 North American Review, Dion Boucicault took aim at the professional theatre critic in an article entitled "The Decline of the Drama." While this playwright, manager, and actor aired his personal gripes against the "mischievous influence of the press," he drew the public's attention to the growing power of newspaper criticism.

The modern day critic, he advocated, provides the audience with "ready made opinions"; this relieves the public from the responsibility of forming their own. The critic is "urged to be racy, and so learns to cover with pertness of style his baldness of treatment, and to put a satin face upon a shoddy argument. " In his new role as the spokesman of the drama, the critic has displaced that group of "refined and educated playgoers" who formerly stood guard over the theatre. Finally, said Boucicault, the critic is governed by the editor, who regards the drama as "a popular and trivial resort. " The critic must "be kind and say everything pleasant. " And he must not offend those who buy space in the advertising columns. Boucicault's article aroused much controversy, and rebuttals from leading dramatic critics. The New York Mirror (Dramatic Mirror) of February 8, 1879, however, agreed with several of Boucicault's points and stressed the worthlessness of professional criticism.

Heated discussion in the press continued for over a decade. In chapter four we noted that William Winter attempted to refute these charges in a debate with Boucicault before the Goethe Society in New York on January 28, 1889. To add to his former arguments, Boucicault reviewed the conditions under which the critic wrote his review: "The performance of a new play or a new opera terminates at or about eleven o'clock. The journalist must have his copy in the hands of the compositor by half-past twelve! Now, within these ninety minutes he should deliver himself of a thoughtful, well-digested essay on what may be an important addition to the literature of the age. It is contended that, whatever practice and experience he may have, it is impossible that he can accomplish the task with justice to the dramatist, to the actors, or to himself. "[1] These charges were difficult for Winter to answer, and have been debated ever since. They suggest that the newspaper had begun to play a somewhat different role in matters regulating the theatre.

Boucicault had reason for his concern. The growing importance of the newspaper was obvious by 1879. In 1870 there were about 4500 daily papers in this country; by 1880 this number had grown to 7000. [2] The British Quarterly Review of January 1871 called America, "The classic soil of newspapers; everybody is reading; literature is permeating everywhere; publicity is sought for every interest and every order. "[3] Circulation climbed to new records in the 1880s and 1890s. The New York Herald claimed 77,000 readers daily in 1860--the highest in America; this reached 95,000

by 1872; and ranged between 130,000 and 150,000 in the early
1880s. Joseph Pulitzer's purchase of the New York World in
1883, and his New Journalism, boosted that paper to the top
with an amazing circulation of 189,000 in 1887. The World
became the most profitable newspaper ever--at least until
William Randolph Hearst entered the New York newspaper
market in 1895. Hearst purchased the Morning Journal, re-
named it the Journal, and immediately challenged Pulitzer
for the lead in circulation. His new formula of sex and
crime sensationalism drew angry denunciations from both
press and pulpit. Traditionalists were offended by this vul-
garization of the American press, and called Hearst's tactics
"Yellow Journalism." But profits and circulation were the
only words that Pulitzer and Hearst understood. Their intense competition resulted in a proliferation of newspapers.
The Sun, the World, and the Herald--among major New York
newspapers--added a separate afternoon edition. They also
added a separate theatre critic to satisfy public interest in
the affairs of the stage. The New York Mirror Annual of
1888 lists twenty dramatic critics in New York. By the turn
of the century, this number had grown to twenty-five, including both daily and weekly writers. [4]

Due to increased interest in speculator sports and in
touring theatrical companies, sporting and theatrical weeklies multiplied in the post-Civil War Period. Critics for
these papers wrote not only for the general public, but for
the profession. There were 138 combination companies on
the road during the 1881-82 season; by 1894-95 this number
had increased to 234. [5] It was essential for an increasingly
mobile theatre profession to have some means of keeping informed about playing dates, availability of jobs, and where-
abouts of associates. Founded in 1852 as a sporting paper,
the New York Clipper added theatrical news in the early
1860s and became recognized as the "Bible of the profession"
until first challenged in 1905 and finally incorporated into
Variety in 1924. The Spirit of the Times and the Dramatic
Mirror both offered theatrical news and reviews besides
working to eliminate corrupt practices in the profession.
Byrne's Dramatic Times (1881), a carbon copy of the New
York Dramatic News, offered stage gossip and trade information. The Theatre, begun by Deshler Welch in 1886,
sought a culturally elite audience but despite financial support from Augustin Daly, died in the early 1890s. Arthur
Hornblow was more successful with a journal by the same
title in 1901.

By the 1890s, the theatre critic had become an important part of the American cultural scene. His views were printed in books and on billboards. From his lowly beginnings as either a reporter or dilettante, he was at last recognized as providing a crucial service to the theatre. He wrote lively prose, kept his readers abreast of what was happening currently in the theatre, and became a personality in his own right. The influx of French critical methods together with the practices of the New Journalism had brought a lighter tone to his reviews. The term "American Theatre Criticism" now suggested a style distinctly different from the English.

Without overstating the accomplishments of these five Victorians, it is clear that they laid the groundwork for American theatre criticism to develop into a profession. When they came on the scene, reporters were assigned to cover a theatre opening as a newsworthy event. When they departed, newspapers had established dramatic departments staffed with qualified critics. During their career, both the press and the theatre were undergoing rapid expansion. They served as pioneers, establishing standards and practices which continued into the present century. They provided a valuable service to society, debating in public forum the vital aesthetic issues of the day: the proper relationship of art to reality and to conventional morality.

While each of these critics launched his career in rebellion against entrenched critical dogma, he came to represent an established school: Winter, an elitest, abandoned his Bohemian days and embraced the Genteel Tradition; Fiske, a pragmatist, came to regard the theatre as little more than show business; Clapp and Wheeler, both populists, opposed the Genteel School and wanted a theatre which appealed more to Democratic tastes; Wilkins, a brilliant stylist, died before he could establish fully his reputation. But despite their differences, none of these critics strayed too far from the mainstream of nineteenth-century critical thought. All were shaped by a society which valued a romantic and idealized art.

The latter Victorians including John Ranken Towse, Harrison Grey Fiske, James Huneker, Edward Dithmar, Brander Mathews, Norman Hapgood, and Alan Dale examined with renewed interest the vital questions regarding morality and reality in art, and the proper role and function of the theatre. They will be studied in a later book.

NOTES

INTRODUCTION

[1]Francis C. Wemyss, Theatrical Biography of Eminent Actors and
Authors, Compiled from the Standard and Minor Drama (New
York, n. d.), p. 4. Archie Binns, Mrs. Fiske and the American Theatre (New York: Crown Publishers, Inc., 1955), p.
81. Binns discusses Fiske's fight against the Theatrical Syndicate, pp. 77-84.
[2]Monthly Anthology, 4 (February, 1807), 85. Quoted in David
Grimsted, Melodrama Unveiled: American Theatre and Culture, 1800-1850 (Chicago: Univ. of Chicago Press, 1968),
pp. 35-36.

CHAPTER ONE

[1]See Vincent L. Angotti, "American Dramatic Criticism, 1800-1830, "
Diss., Univ. of Kansas, 1967, p. 28.
[2]Quoted in Harold C. Shiffer, "The Opposition of the Presbyterian
Church in the United States of America to the Theatre in
America, 1750-1891, " Diss. Univ. of Iowa, 1953.
[3]"Introduction to the Dramatic Censor, " The Mirror of Taste, and
Dramatic Censor, I, (January, 1810), p. 51. Quoted in
Angotti, pp. 26-27.
[4]Arthur Hobson Quinn, A History of the American Drama, I (New
York: F. S. Crofts and Co., 1944), p. 14.
[5]William Dunlap, History of the American Theatre, I. (1833; rpt.
New York: Burt Franklin, 1963), p. 373.
[6]Bruce I. Granger and Martha Hartzog, eds., Letters of Jonathan
Oldstyle, Gent., Vol. VI of The Complete Works of Washington Irving (Boston: Twayne Publishers, 1977).
[7]Letter of July 10, 1819. The Letters of Washington Irving to
Henry Brevoort, II, ed. George S. Hellman (New York:
G. P. Putnam's Sons, 1915), p. 99.
[8]American theatre historians draw our attention to the contribution
of Washington Irving as a theatre critic. See Barnard Hewitt, Theatre U. S. A. ; Garff Wilson, Three Hundred Years
of American Drama and Theatre; Montrose J. Moses, The
American Dramatist, and others.
[9]"Edmund Kean's Richard III, " rpt. in The American Theatre as
Seen by Its Critics, 1752-1934, eds. Montrose J. Moses
and John Mason Brown (New York: W. W. Norton & Company, Inc. 1934), p. 50.

[10]"Charles Kemble's Hamlet," rpt. in Moses and Brown, p. 58.

[11]Alfred Van Rensselaer Westfall, American Shakespearean Criticism, 1607-1865 (New York: H. W. Wilson Company, 1939), p. 153.

[12]New York Courier Enquirer, March 30, 1847.

[13]Westfall, p. 147.

[14]Eric Wollencott Barnes, The Lady of Fashion (New York: Charles Scribner's Sons, 1954), p. 153.

[15]Grimsted, p. 43.

[16]Arranged and illust. by Thompson Westcott, 1868, Vol. III, p. 244; on Reel 7, "Source Materials in the Field of Theatre," Univ. Microfilms.

[17]Nathaniel Parker Willis, Memoranda of Jenny Lind (Philadelphia, 1851). Lloyd Morris, Curtain Time (New York: Random House, Inc., 1953), p. 140.

[18]New York in Slices by An Experienced Carver (New York: 1849), p. 89. Quoted in Joseph Jay Rubin, "Whitman as a Drama Critic," The Quarterly Journal of Speech, XXVIII (February 1942), 47.

[19]Southern Literary Messenger (May 1836), rpt. in Vol. VIII of The Complete Works of Edgar Allan Poe, Virginia Edition, ed. James A. Harrison (New York: Thomas Y. Crowell & Co., 1902), p. 322.

[20]The Histrionic Mr. Poe (Baltimore: Johns Hopkins Press, 1949), p. 103.

[21]The Broadway Journal (March 29, 1845), rpt. in Vol. V of The Complete Works of Edgar Allan Poe, pp. 118-119.

[22]Rpt. in Vol. VI of The Complete Works of Edgar Allen Poe, p. 36.

[23]Vol. VI of The Complete Works of Edgar Allan Poe, p. 112.

[24]Most of Whitman's dramatic writings are published in The Gathering of the Forces, eds. Cleveland Rodgers and John Black, 2 vols. (New York: G. P. Putnam's and Sons, 1920); and The Uncollected Poetry and Prose of Walt Whitman, ed. Emory Holloway, 2 vols. (New York: Doubleday and Company, Inc., 1921).

[25]Black, II, 327-330.

[26]Holloway, I, 153.

[27]Brooklyn Daily Eagle (August 25, 1847), Black, II, 339.

[28]Black, II, 338.

[29]Eagle (October 7, 1846), Black, II, 341.

[30]See Garff Wilson, A History of American Acting (Bloomington: Indiana Univ. Press, 1966), pp. 122-124.

[31]Morris, Curtain Time, p. 181.

[32]Marvin Felheim, The Theatre of Augustin Daly (Cambridge: Harvard University Press, 1956), p. 191.

[33]See Alfred L. Bernheim, The Business of the Theatre: An Economic History of the American Theatre, 1750-1932 (New York, 1932), p. 30.

[34]Frank Luther Mott, American Journalism, rev. ed. (New York: Macmillan Company, 1950), pp. 229-238.

[35]April 26, 1862, p. 267.

[36]William Winter, Old Friends (New York: Moffat, Yard and Company, 1914), pp. 80-82.

[37](Metuchen, N. J.: The Scarecrow Press, Inc., 1972), p. 23.

[38]"How Jules Janin Became a Journalist," Temple Bar: A London
Magazine for Town and Country Readers (September 1875),
p. 74.

[39]"The Last of the Bohemians," The Galaxy (January 1875), p. 214.

[40]Old Friends, p. 309.

[41]C. T. Congdon, Reminiscences of a Journalist (Boston: James
R. Osgood & Company, 1880), pp. 22-23.

CHAPTER TWO

[1]Old Friends, p. 58.

[2]For biographical information on Clapp see: Ebenezer Clapp,
compil., The Clapp Memorial: Record of the Clapp Family
in America (Boston: David Clapp & Son, 1876), pp. 39-40,
341-342; also C. T. Congdon, Reminiscences of a Journalist,
pp. 338-340; Winter, Old Friends, pp. 57-63; Albert Parry,
Garrets and Pretenders: A History of Bohemianism in
America (New York: Covici Friede Publishers, 1933), pp.
20-48; John J. Mangan, "The Newspapers of Lynn," The
Register of the Lynn Historical Society for the year 1909
(Lynn, Mass.: Frank S. Whitten, 1910), at Lynn Historical
Society; Alonzo Lewis and James R. Newhall, History of
Lynn, Essex County, Mass., 1629-1864 (Lynn: George C.
Herbert, 1883 and 1890), Lynn Public Library; The Pioneer
(newspaper published in Lynn), copies at Lynn Historical So-
ciety.

[3]The New York Leader, June 25, 1864, p. 5.

[4]Clapp dedicated his The Pioneer: or Leaves from an Editor's
Portfolio (Lynn, Mass.: J. B. Tolman, 1846) to Rogers for
opening his eyes "to the infinite beauty and entire practica-
bility of the distinctive principles of the New Testament."
Preface, v.

[5]Frank E. Manuel, The Prophets of Paris (Cambridge: Harvard
University Press, 1962), pp. 212-213. The book provides an
excellent summary of the ideas of Charles Fourier. For a
discussion about Fourierism in America see Redelia Brisbane,
Albert Brisbane: A Mental Biography (1893; rpt. New York:
Burt Franklin, 1969).

[6]The Pioneer, p. iii.

[7]The Pioneer, p. 12.

[8]New York Saturday Press, April 9, 1859, p. 2. Cited hereafter
as Sat. Press.

[9]Henry Clapp, Jr., Letter to the Reverend John Pierpont, April 27,
1946, p. 2, Pierpont Morgan Library, New York, N.Y.

[10]Clapp, Letter to William T. Hamilton, Orthodox Clergyman, September 25, 1844, rpt. in The Pioneer, p. 64.

[11]April 27, 1846, pp. 8-9.

[12]See Mangun, "The Newspapers of Lynn."

[13]While no hard evidence on the length of his stay in each country
has been uncovered, Clapp mentions in "Portrait of Paris"
that he lived three years in London and three in Paris. See
Sat. Press, November 13, 1858, p. 1.

[14]Sat. Press, November 13, 1858, p. 1.

[15]Sat. Press, January 8, 1859, p. 1.

[16]"Un Prince de la Boheme," Pleiade, vol. 6, pp. 823-824, as quoted in Malcolm Easton, Artists and Writers in Paris: The Bohemian Idea, 1803-1867 (New York: St. Martin's Press, 1964), pp. 134-135. I am indebted to Easton for information about Murger and the French Bohemians.

[17]Easton, p. 127.

[18]Parry, Garrets and Pretenders, pp. 110-111.

[19]Old Friends, p. 58.

[20]Figaro's letter of October 8, 1954 (published in the New York Herald on October 29) suggests Clapp's witty and sarcastic style.

[21](New York: Robert M. Dewitt. Calvin Blanchard, 1857), Columbia University Library.

[22](New York: Rudd & Carleton, 1857), Library of Congress.

[23]William Dean Howells, Literary Friends and Acquaintances, eds. David F. Hiatt and Edwin H. Cady (Bloomington: Indiana Press, 1968), p. 63.

[24]Horace Traubel, With Walt Whitman in Camden, II (New York: Rowman and Littlefield, Inc., 1961), p. 375.

[25]Ferris Greenslet, The Life of Thomas Bailey Aldrich (Boston: Houghton Mifflin Company, 1908), p. 43.

[26]Laura Stedman and G. M. Gould, Life and Letters of Edmund Clarence Stedman, I (New York: Moffat Yard and Company, 1910), p. 208.

[27](New York: G. W. Carleton and Company, 1884), p. 232.

[28]Howells, pp. 63-64.

[29]Sat. Press, October 23, 1858, p. 2.

[30]Sat. Press, November 6, 1858, p. 2.

[31]Sat. Press, June 9, 1860, p. 2.

[32]Sat. Press, December 31, 1859, p. 2.

[33]Howells, p. 62.

[34]Parry, Garrets and Pretenders, pp. 16-17; Winter, Brief Chronicles (New York: The Dunlap Society, 1889-90), pp. 48-49.

[35]Parry, pp. 16-17.

[36]"Thoughts and Things," Sat. Press, February 11, 1860, p. 2.

[37]Sat. Press, June 2, 1860, p. 2.

[38]Quoted in Sat. Press, September 8, 1860, p. 3.

[39]Sat. Press, January 20, 1866, p. 40.

[40]The Leader, March 29, 1862.

[41]Sat. Press, February 3, 1866, p. 72.

[42]Sat. Press, February 3, 1866, p. 72.

[43]Sat. Press, September 2, 1865, p. 72.

[44]George Henry Lewes, On Actors and The Art of Acting, 2nd ed. (London: Smith, Elder & Co., 1875), p. 13.

[45]Sat. Press, September 9, 1865, p. 89.

[46]The Leader, October 11, 1862.

[47]The Leader, October 11, 1862.

[48]The Leader, October 4, 1862.

[49]Horace Traubel, With Walt Whitman in Camden, I, p. 456.

[50]Three Hundred Years of American Drama and Theatre (Englewood Cliffs, N.J.: Prentice-Hall, 1973), pp. 171-172.

[51]Sat. Press, May 26, 1866, p. 4.

[52]Sat. Press, February 24, 1866, p. 121.

[53]The Leader, October 10, 1863, p. 5.

[54]Barnard Hewitt, "Mrs. John Wood and the Lost Art of Burlesque Acting," Educational Theatre Journal (May 1961), pp. 82-85.

[55]Spirit of the Times, March 14, 1863, p. 32.

[56]Sat. Press, September 23, 1865, p. 121.

[57]William Winter, Brown Heath and Blue Bells: Being Sketches of Scotland with Other Papers (New York: Macmillan & Company, 1895), p. 194. Born June 24, 1834, in New York, George Arnold at age three moved with his family to Alton, Illinois. After twelve years, in 1849, they moved to Strawberry Farms, New Jersey, where a Fourierite Phalansterie had been established. After attempting to learn portrait painting, Arnold began a literary career in 1853. He wrote under several pen-names: Grahame Allen, George Garrilous, Pierrot, and the Undersigned.

[58]A copy of the New York Weekly Review is at the Music Collection, New York Public Library at Lincoln Center.

[59]Old Friends, p. 311.

[60]Henry Clapp, Jr., Letter to John Russell Lowell, October 10, 1865, by permission of the Houghton Library, Harvard University.

[61]Henry Clapp, Jr., Letter to William Winter, June 7, 1866, Humanities Research Center, University of Texas at Austin.

[62]Henry Clapp, Jr., Letter to Thomas Bailey Aldrich, October 1, 1867, Houghton Library.

[63]Clapp wrote Sydney Howard Gay, Managing Editor of the Tribune, from Redbank on May 14, 1872, asking him to send copies of the weekly and daily Tribune. Sydney Howard Gay Collection, Columbia Rare Book and Manuscript Library, Columbia University. Hereafter cited as Columbia.

[64]Quoted in Jefferson Winter, "As I Remember," Saturday Evening Post, July 31, 1920, p. 71.

[65]Parry, Garrets and Pretenders, p. 47.

[66]Henry Clapp, Jr., Letter to Edmund Clarence Stedman, May 14, 1874, Spec. Ms. Collection--Stedman, Columbia.

[67]Henry Clapp, Jr., Letter to Edmund Clarence Stedman, May 22, 1874, Spec. Ms. Collection--Stedman, Columbia.

[68]Henry Clapp, Jr., Letter to Edmund Clarence Stedman, May 31, 1874, Spec. Ms. Collection--Stedman, Columbia.

[69]Quoted in Parry, Garrets and Pretenders, p. 47.

[70]Old Friends, p. 65.

[71]Parry, p. 37.

[72]Howells, Literary Friends and Acquaintances, p. 66.

[73]Sat. Press, January 8, 1859, p. 1.

CHAPTER THREE

[1]Leader, May 11, 1861.

[2]Old Friends, p. 84-85; Spirit of the Times, January 17, 1863, p. 320.

[3]Information about the Wilkins family has been gleaned from: the

family monument at 142 Woodside Avenue, Woodlawn Ceme-
tery, Boston; obituaries of Edward G. P. Wilkins in Boston
Herald, May 8, 1861, and New York Herald of May 6, 1861;
Boston City Directories for 1850-1862.

[4]Noted in Boston Herald, May 8, 1861.

[5]See Francis Wolle, Fitz-James O'Brien: A Literary Bohemian of
the Eighteen-fifties, University of Colorado Studies, Series B,
Studies in the Humanities, Vol. II, No. 2 (Boulder: Univ.
of Colorado Press, 1944), p. 131.

[6]Correspondence with the Record Division, Columbia University
(March 1977) indicates that Edward G. P. Wilkins never enrolled at the University.

[7]Old Friends, p. 84-85.

[8]Leader, July 21, 1860, p. 5.

[9](New York: Dodd, Mead and Company, 1903), p. 22.

[10]"President Pierce at Castle Garden," New York Herald, July 15,
1853.

[11]Old Friends, p. 84.

[12]See Francis Wolle, Fitz-James O'Brien: A Literary Bohemian of
the Eighteen-fifties.

[13]Theta Delta Chi in the Summer of 1856 formed a graduate chapter
known as Lambda Graduate Association. It was discontinued
in the summer of 1857. Wilkins was initiated in January,
1857. See Wolle, p. 131.

[14]The New York Citizen, September 30, 1865, The Poems and
Stories of Fitz-James O'Brien, ed., William Winter (1881:
rpt. in American Short Story Series, Vol. 26, New York:
Garrett Press, 1968), p. xivi.

[15]Old Friends, p. 85.

[16]The New York Citizen, September 30, 1865, The Poems and
Stories of Fitz-James O'Brien, p. xlix.

[17]"Town Topics," n.d., Stephen Ryder Fiske Clipping File, Theatre
Collection, New York Public Library at Lincoln Center.
Cited hereafter as NYPL-LC.

[18]January 17, 1863.

[19]Leader, November 2, 1861.

[20]American Journalism, rev. ed., p. 232.

[21]Wilkes' Spirit of the Times, January 17, 1863, p. 320.

[22]Sat. Press, January 21, 1860, p. 3.

[23]Quoted in Willard Grosvenor Bleyer, Main Currents in the History
of American Journalism (Boston: Houghton Mifflin Company,
1927), p. 195.

[24]Bleyer, p. 195.

[25]Sat. Press, September 17, 1859, p. 2.

[26]Old Friends, p. 87.

[27]My Wife's Mirror (New York: French's American Drama no. 99,
1856), Folger Shakespeare Library.

[28]Young New York: Comedy in three acts as produced at Laura
Keene's Theatre, New York. Monday evening, November 24,
1856 (New York: John Perry, 1856), Library of Congress.

[29]New York Times, November 25, 1856.

[30]Anna Cora Mowatt (Ritchie), Preface to the London Edition of
Fashion, January 1850. American Culture Series II, Reel
305, University Microfilms.

[31]September 29, 1857.

[32]For a summary of Wilkins' adaption, see the New York Herald, March 28, 1861.

[33]Herald, March 28, 1861.

[34]Sat. Press, November 12, 1859, p. 2.

[35]New York Herald, December 10, 1857.

[36]Leader, July 14, 1860, p. 5.

[37]New York Herald, September 4, 1855.

[38]Herald, September 5, 1855.

[39]Herald, September 7, 1855.

[40]Herald, August 29, 1854.

[41]Herald, March 18, 1856, p. 4.

[42]Herald, January 23, 1857.

[43]Sat. Press, January 28, 1860, p. 3.

[44]Herald, April 6, 1858.

[45]The Hamlet of Edwin Booth (Urbana: U. of Illinois Press, 1969), p. 42.

[46]Leader, December 22, 1860.

[47]Herald, December 24, 1860.

[48]Herald, January 12, 1857.

[49]Leader, December 29, 1860.

[50]Herald, September 29, 1857.

[51]Harper's Weekly, November 7, 1857, p. 707.

[52]Leader, October 20, 1860, p. 5.

[53]Herald, December 27, 1856.

[54]Sat. Press, March 10, 1860, p. 3.

[55]Sat. Press, October 22, 1859, p. 2.

[56]Quoted in Leader, June 18, 1860.

[57]"Journalist and Poet," p. ii.

[58]Sat. Press, December 31, 1859, p. 3.

CHAPTER FOUR

[1]Old Friends, pp. 140-141.

[2]For biographical data on Winter's early life see: Old Friends; Jefferson Winter, "As I Remember," Saturday Evening Post, July 31, 1920, pp. 14-15ff; Richard M. Ludwig, "The Career of William Winter American Drama Critic," Diss. Harvard University, 1950; Robert Young, Jr., "Frosty but Kindly," unpublished biography of William Winter by his great-grandson; Daniel J. Watermeier, Between Actor and Critic: Selected Letters of Edwin Booth and William Winter (Princeton: University Press, 1971); family records and files in private files of Robert Young, Jr.

[3]William Winter, Letter to Henry Wadsworth Longfellow, January 26, 1855, Houghton Library, Harvard University.

[4]"William Winter entered the Law School on March 1, 1856 and received his LL. B. in 1857." William W. Whalen, Asst. Harvard University Archives, Letter to author, September 26, 1977.

[5]Mentioned in a letter from Winter to Longfellow, July 3, 1855, Houghton Library.

[6]Thomas Bailey Aldrich, Letter to William Winter, January 25,

1858. Quoted in The Library of the Late William Winter, Second Part, April 24, 1923, p. 7.

[7]Sat. Press, August 4, 1860, p. 2.

[8]Old Friends, p. 79.

[9]Correspondence between Winter and Longfellow relating to their first meeting is at Houghton Library.

[10]Letters at Houghton Library support this point. See Longfellow-Winter Correspondence, 1854-1862.

[11]Old Friends, p. 19.

[12]January 16, 1864.

[13]"Sketch of O'Brien," Introduction to The Poems and Stories of Fitz-James O'Brien, preface, xx.

[14]This information, written on a sheet of paper by William Winter, is in the files of Robert Young, Jr. Letters from Winter to Longfellow during the 1859-1860 winter provide information about his first year in New York (Houghton Library).

[15]The (New York) Albion, November 29, 1862. William Winter Scrapbooks in possession of Robert Young, Jr. (hereafter cited as WWS). The Albion was a weekly representative of British residents in the United States.

[16]"As I Remember," July 31, 1920, p. 15.

[17]William Winter, Letter to Henry Wadsworth Longfellow, October 26, 1859, Houghton Library.

[18]Longfellow, Letter to Winter, November 10, 1859, Folgar Shakespeare Library.

[19]Several historians have suggested that Winter wrote dramatic feuilletons under the name "Quelqu'un" (someone, somebody, anyone, or anybody). If he did, however, the pseudonym was shared with others. It first appeared on February 19, 1859, while Winter was living in Boston. Quelqu'un sometimes addressed his remarks to "General Reader," a technique Henry Clapp used in signed articles (January 1, 1859, for one). This strongly suggests Clapp as Quelqu'un but Winter learned from the old Bohemian and may have imitated his style. Given the definition of Quelqu'un, the column may have been assigned to anyone on the staff, although it seems logical that Clapp and Winter were the main contributors.

[20]Henry Clapp, Jr., Letter to William Winter, January 9, 1860, in files of Robert Young, Jr.

[21]Quoted by Jefferson Winter, "As I Remember," July 31, 1920, p. 78.

[22]Brougham contracted to pay Mrs. Winter $30.00 per week for the 1868-1869 season; Daly contracted her at $40.00 per week for the 1870-1871 season. Copy of contracts at Folger Shakespeare Library.

[23]Mrs. William Winter, Letter to Edwin Booth, June 2, 1869, Walter Hampden--Edwin Booth Theatre Collection and Library.

[24]"As I Remember," July 31, 1920, p. 71.

[25]Leader, February 13, 1864.

[26]Mrs. William Winter, "Memoranda for Billy," undated typewritten sheet (c. 1908) in files of Robert Young, Jr.

[27]William Winter, Letter to Henry Wadsworth Longfellow, April 9, 1861, mentions returning the $25.00 loaned in May. Houghton Library.

[28] From copy of letter dated 18--1861, in files of Robert Young, Jr.

[29] "Memoranda for Billy. "

[30] William Winter, Letter to Edmund Clarence Stedman, May 1, 1863, Spec. Ms. Collection--Stedman, Columbia University Library.

[31] William A. Seaver, a personal friend not connected to the theatre, assisted him on numerous occasions. But it was money borrowed from actors, managers, playwrights, that raised questions about his integrity.

[32] Albion, December 30, 1865, WWS. "It would be interesting, by the way, to know who wrote that editorial in the Herald on 'The Assassination of Caesar, '--an appreciative public would surely render a fitting tribute to the creature capable of writing such a monstrous and sickening libel upon a gentleman [Edwin Booth] whose private virtue and public triumphs and unsullied patriotism have endeared him to the American people, and made his name illustrious in the history of the American art. " Written in Winter's handwriting next to the article (in the scrapbook) is the following statement: "It was written by Stephen Fiske. " Fiske had defended Booth, however, in the Leader of April 22, 1865: "The stage and the public cannot afford to lose Edwin Booth, our greatest tragedian, and Junius Booth, one of our most careful actors, because John Wilkes Booth happens to be a villain. " No further evidence is available.

[33] Boucicault adopted a policy of hiring critics to assist him adapt plays. He sometimes included their names in copyrighting the script. This incident prompted harsh comments by all major critics; Stephen Fiske in the Leader was the most vocal.

[34] Private files of Robert Young, Jr.

[35] Albion, February 20, 1864, WWS.

[36] Albion, October 4, 1862, WWS.

[37] Albion, March 28, 1863, WWS.

[38] Albion, November 8, 1862; August 29, 1863, WWS.

[39] Albion, September 10, 1864, WWS.

[40] New York Tribune, March, 1871. Quoted in Ludwig, p. 137.

[41] New York Tribune, October 10, 1893, pp. 6-7.

[42] II (New York: Moffat, Yard and Company, 1913), p. 375.

[43] Ibid. , p. 507.

[44] New York Tribune, November 18, 1904, p. 7.

[45] The Wallet of Time II, p. 591-593.

[46] Quoted by Ludwig, p. 262.

[47] Albion, February 1, 1862, WWS.

[48] Albion, May 6, 1865, WWS.

[49] Winter describes Forrest in a number of his books. Much of the copy is identical. See Shadows of the Stage, III, 2, (New York: Macmillan and Company, 1893), 47-80; also The Wallet of Time, II, 101-132.

[50] This observation was made by Ludwig, pp. 94-95.

[51] Albion, October 18, 1862, WWS.

[52] Shadows of the Stage, III, 2, 68.

[53] Ibid. , p. 80.

[54] Watermeier, pp. 18-19 discusses the beginning of their friendship.

[55] Albion, October 4, 1862, WWS.

[56] The Hamlet of Edwin Booth, p. 94.

[57] Watermeier, pp. 40-41.

[58] Ludwig suggests that personal loyalties were a factor in shaping Winter's judgments, pp. 207-208. The critic's continued support of Booth, at times when the majority of his colleagues were criticizing the actor for uninspired performances, strongly supports this conclusion. See Shattuck, The Hamlet of Edwin Booth, p. 52.

[59] Brief Chronicles (New York: Dunlap Society, 1889), p. 213.

[60] Shadows of the Stage, II, 2 (New York: Macmillan and Company, 1893), 131.

[61] Ibid., I, 223.

[62] Vagrant Memories (New York: George H. Doran Company, 1914), p. 338.

[63] Brief Chronicles, p. 84.

[64] The Wallet of Time, I, 488.

[65] Robert Young, Jr. suggests this point: letter to author, September 8, 1978.

[66] See Jefferson Winter, "As I Remember," July 31, 1920, pp. 34-35; also Ludwig, p. 189; C.M.S. McLellan in his Le Chat Noir: A Review of the Players (May 1889) placed the following item under "Malicious Reports Denied": "William Winter has not gone on the road with the Daly Company."

[67] I, 354.

[68] p. 244.

[69] Boucicault had originally made these charges in the North American Review, September, 1877. In January, 1889, he debated the subject with William Winter at the Goethe Club.

[70] The Press and the Stage: an Oration (New York: Lockwood and Coombes, 1889), pp. 36-39.

[71] Quoted in Ludwig, p. 200. The original is at The Folger Shakespeare Library.

[72] Albion, July 1, 1865, WWS.

[73] Harrison Grey Fiske, Letter to William Winter, July 10, 1898. Folger Shakespeare Library.

[74] (New Brighton, Staten Island, 1918).

[75] "A Tribute to William Winter," December 15, 1909, privately printed, Folger Shakespeare Library.

[76] George P. Goodale, Letter to William Winter, March 20, 1911, Folger Shakespeare Library.

CHAPTER FIVE

[1] See New York Dramatic Mirror, June 13, 1891, for interview with Ali Baba (Arthur Hornblow); also Who's Who in the Theatre, 1912.

[2] Frederick Clifton Pierce, Fiske and Fisk Family (Boston: W. B. Conkey Company, 1896), p. 451.

[3] The Leader, September 16, 1865, p. 1. Fiske was writing under the pen-name of Ariel.

[4]Stephen R. Fiske, "Gentlemen of the Press," Harper's New Monthly Magazine, XXVL (February 1863), 361-367.

[5]April 18, 1863.

[6]April 8, 1863.

[7]Odell, Annals of the New York Stage, VII, p. 467.

[8]Correspondence of Augustin Daly and Joseph F. Daly and documents serving for memoirs, 1859-1899. Theatre Collection, NYPL--LC. Cited hereafter as Daly Correspondence.

[9]Evening Express, October 24, 1864, p. 2. See Albert A. Asermely, "Daly's Initial Decade in the American Theatre," Diss. CUNY, 1973.

[10]A letter from Augustin to Joseph on January 15, 1865, suggested this rivalry: "Do you feel, with me, like smashing 'Ariel' the new Leader man, who is possibly enough to be a dangerous rival to Le Pelerin [pen-name for Daly]. We must have a bold dash in The Courier on my return. Ariel is Fisky." Daly Correspondence.

[11]Stephen Fiske, Letter to William Winter, April 3, 1865, in private files of Robert Young, Jr.

[12]Quoted in The Hornet, July 5, 1873. British Museum.

[13]The Leader, September 16, 1865, p. 1.

[14]March 2, 1873.

[15]October 24, 1874.

[16]The St. James's Theatre: Its Strange and Complete History, 1835-1957 (London: Barrie and Rockliff, 1964), p. 171.

[17]Odell, IX, p. 534.

[18]Information from an undated Philadelphia newspaper clipping, Daly Theatre Scrapbooks, Theatre Collection, NYPL-LC.

[19]June 15, 1875, Daly Correspondence.

[20]January 15, 1876, Daly Correspondence.

[21]Undated clipping, St. Louis Times, Stephen Fiske Clipping Folder, Theatre Collection, NYPL-LC.

[22]Daly Correspondence.

[23]September 10, 1877, Daly Correspondence. Fiske had become indispensable to Augustin Daly, loaning him money, selecting and adapting plays, and serving as a personal agent. In a letter to Augustin, July 19, 1878, Joseph severely lectured him for borrowing money from his business manager: "Don't you think that in permitting him to pay your debts and advancing you money you surrendered your position to him. One of the very first principles in business is that the master should not borrow from the servant, for if the latter is creditor he is master."

[24]Daly Correspondence.

[25]Daly Correspondence.

[26]Spirit of the Times, April 28, 1888, p. 492.

[27]ST, October 27, 1894, p. 518.

[28]ST, September 13, 1879, p. 462.

[29]ST, December 13, 1890, p. 808.

[30]ST, October 26, 1895, p. 494.

[31]ST, April 8, 1882, p. 268.

[32]ST, November 15, 1890, p. 666.

[33]ST, September 23, 1893, p. 300.

[34]ST, January 15, 1887, p. 772.

[35]ST, October 1, 1887, p. 348.

[36]ST, December 24, 1892, p. 842.

[37]ST, May 9, 1891, p. 710.

[38]ST, May 23, 1891, p. 806.

[39]ST, August 26, 1893, p. 172.

[40]ST, January 28, 1888, p. 14.

[41]For a knowledgeable discussion about this controversy see Edwin Duerr, The Length and Depth of Acting (New York: Holt, Rinehart and Winston, 1963), pp. 356-403.

[42]ST, March 23, 1895, p. 334.

[43]ST, April 28, 1888, p. 492.

[44]ST, December 4, 1886, p. 584.

[45]ST, February 22, 1896, p. 162.

[46]Towse, Sixty Years of the Theater, p. 236.

[47]ST, May 14, 1895, p. 512.

[48]ST, October 18, 1884, p. 390.

[49]ST, November 10, 1888, p. 588.

[50]ST, March 9, 1889, p. 266.

[51]See Alfred L. Bernheim, The Business of the Theatre: An Economic History of the American Theatre, 1750-1932, p. 46.

[52]August 6, 1903, p. 109.

[53]Sports of the Times, December 20, 1902, p. 7.

[54]ST, December 11, 1897, p. 636.

[55]ST, October 7, 1893, p. 368.

[56]The New York Star, August 28, 1908, called Fiske "The New Dean of American Dramatic Critics."

[57]Quoted in Spirit of the Times, September 23, 1893, p. 300.

[58]ST, December 21, 1895, pp. 738-739.

CHAPTER SIX

[1]Quoted in Arnold T. Schwab, James Gibbons Huneker: Critic of the Seven Arts (Stanford: Stanford University Press, 1965), p. 72.

[2]I am indebted to Thomas Key Wright for his research on Wheeler. See Thomas Key Wright, "The Theatre Criticism of Andrew Carpenter Wheeler," Diss., University of Illinois, 1971. The Wheeler Collection (diaries, letters, scrapbooks) in the New York Historical Society was donated by Paul Wheeler through the efforts of Mr. Wright.

[3]There is no record of Wheeler's attendance at City College of New York. Between 1847-1853 the school was called the Free Academy and no records exist for this period. See Wright, p. 6.

[4]Mott, American Journalism, rev. ed., pp. 280-281.

[5]Dramatic Mirror, March 21, 1903.

[6]Nym Crinkle, The Iron Trail (New York: E. B. Patterson, Publisher, 1876), p. 14.

[7]New York Sunday World, August 30, 1874, p. 6.

[8]Quoted in the New York Journalist, n.d., Scrapbooks of A. C. Wheeler, courtesy of New York Historical Society (hereafter cited as NYHS).

[9]Diary of Andrew Carpenter Wheeler, March 1899 through October, 1902, NYHS.
[10]Dramatic Mirror, March 21, 1903, p. 14.
[11]Mott, American Journalism, rev. ed., p. 374.
[12]The Theatre of Augustin Daly, pp. 127-128.
[13]New York Dramatic News, May 19, 1877, p. 4.
[14]N. W. Ayer and Son's American Newspaper Annual (Philadelphia: N. W. Ayer and Son, Incorporated, 1887).
[15]Clipping in Miscellaneous Scrapbook, Wheeler Collection, NYHS.
[16]Dramatic Mirror, March 21, 1903, p. 14.
[17]Diary of Andrew Carpenter Wheeler. July 1873 to July 1878, pp. 35-36. NYHS.
[18]April 13, 1876, p. 5.
[19]April 22, 1876, p. 272.
[20]Dramatic Mirror, April 9, 1887, p. 2.
[21]Dramatic Mirror, April 9, 1887, p. 2.
[22]April 1, 1887, Wheeler Scrapbooks, NYHS.
[23]Promptbook of Jack Royal of the 92nd, NYHS. On the cover is noted "The Property of Harry Lacy."
[24]The Great Diamond Robbery & Other Recent Melodramas, Vol. VIII of America's Lost Plays. Barrett H. Clark, general editor. 20 volumes. Princeton, N.J.: Princeton University Press, 1940.
[25]Dramatic Mirror, September 14, 1895, p. 14.
[26]September 8, 1895, p. 5.
[27]September 7, 1895, p. 251.
[28]New York World, September 28, 1884, p. 13.
[29]The Theatre, VI (October 12, 1889), p. 521.
[30]Madame de Staël (1766-1817) novelist and woman-of-letters; Charles Augustin Sainte-Beuve (1804-1869) literary critic, known for his biographical approach to criticism; Hippolyte Taine (1828-1893) literary critic and author of History of English Literature (1863).
[31]Translated by H. Van Laun (New York: Leypoldt and Holt, Inc., 1883; rept: 1965, Frederick Ungar Publishing Co.)
[32]The Theatre, VI (October 12, 1889), 519.
[33]World, May 3, 1872, p. 6.
[34]Dramatic Mirror, February 25, 1888, p. 1.
[35]World, June 11, 1871, p. 2.
[36]Spirit of the Times, November 9, 1878, p. 374.
[37]Dramatic Mirror, January 14, 1888, p. 1.
[38]Dramatic Mirror, April 7, 1888, p. 1.
[39]Spirit of the Times, November 3, 1887, p. 377.
[40]The Hamlet of Edwin Booth, p. 93.
[41]The Theatre, VI (October 19, 1889), 528.
[42]Dramatic Mirror, January 19, 1889, p. 1.
[43]Dramatic Mirror, October 26, 1889, p. 1.
[44]"Edwin Booth's Richard," Scrapbook, Theatre Collection, NYPL-LC.
[45]Felheim, The Theater of Augustin Daly, p. 236.
[46]N. Y. World, January 11, 1874, p. 6.
[47]N. Y. World, May 14, 1871, p. 5.
[48]N. Y. World, October 23, 1870, p. 3.

176 / Bohemians and Critics

[49] N. Y. World, March 15, 1874, p. 6.
[50] World, February 19, 1888, p. 15.
[51] World, November 4, 1888, p. 13.
[52] World, September 15, 1889, p. 13.
[53] World, January 27, 1884, p. 5.
[54] Dramatic Mirror, December 15, 1888, p. 1.
[55] World, May 20, 1890, p. 5.
[56] Fitch to Wheeler, May 21, 1890, NYHS, folder 1886-1900.
[57] Dramatic Mirror, July 9, 1887, p. 1.
[58] Leader, February 25, 1871, p. 5.
[59] See Charles Shattuck, Shakespeare on the American Stage: From the Hallams to Edwin Booth (Washington, D. C.: The Folger Shakespeare Library, 1976), p. 127.
[60] Leader, September 23, 1871, p. 5.
[61] World, October 1, 1871, p. 2.
[62] March 17, 1877, p. 149.
[63] World, May 31, 1874.
[64] Ibid.
[65] Quoted in Percy MacKay's Epoch: The Life of Steele MacKaye, Genius of the Theatre, I (New York: Boni & Liveright, 1927), 270-271.
[66] World, June 9, 1893, Clipping in Theatre Collection, NYPL-LC.
[67] World, December 10, 1871, p. 6.
[68] Harper's Weekly, XLIV (April 14, 1900), 333.
[69] Ibid.
[70] World, January 20, 1893, p. 23.
[71] World, February 21, 1893, p. 5.
[72] January 8, 1970, St. Petersburg, Florida, with Thomas K. Wright.
[73] World, March 27, 1889, Clipping in Andrew C. Wheeler Newspaper file, NYHS.
[74] Andrew C. Wheeler Correspondence, 1902, NYHS.
[75] Diary of Andrew Carpenter Wheeler. Vol. 3, March 1896 to February 1899, p. 128. NYHS.
[76] Diary of Andrew Carpenter Wheeler, Vol. 4, March 1899 to October 1902, p. 189. NYHS.
[77] "The Decline of Joy," Typescript in Misc. file of theatrical essays, NYHS.
[78] "The Decline of Joy."

EPILOGUE

[1] Boucicault published his remarks "At the Goethe Society," in the North American Review, CXLVIII (March, 1889), 335-343. Winter's remarks appeared in the Atlantic Monthly, LXIV (September, 1889), 420-422.
[2] Mott, American Journalism, rev. ed., p. 411. The statistics in this paragraph are from Mott.
[3] (Vol. LIII, p. 4.).
[4] Julius Cahn's Official Theatrical Guide, (New York: Empire Theatre Bldg., Publishers, 1899).
[5] Bernheim, The Business of the Theatre: An Economic History of the American Theatre, 1750-1932, p. 30.

SELECTED BIBLIOGRAPHY

PUBLISHED

Bode, Carl. The Anatomy of American Popular Culture, 1840-1861. Berkeley: University of California Press, 1959.

Boller, Paul, Jr. American Transcendentalism, 1830-1860. New York: G. P. Putnam's Sons, 1974.

Brooks, Van Wyck. The Times of Melville and Whitman. New York: E. P. Dutton and Company, Inc., 1953.

Commager, Henry Steele. The American Mind: An Interpretation of American Thought and Character Since the 1880s. New Haven: Yale University Press, 1950.

Daly, Joseph Francis. The Life of Augustin Daly. New York: The Macmillan Company, 1917.

Duerr, Edwin. The Length and Depth of Acting. New York: Holt, Rinehart and Winston, 1963.

Felheim, Marvin. The Theater of Augustin Daly: An Account of the Late Nineteenth Century American Stage. Cambridge, Mass.: Harvard University Press, 1956.

Hartnoll, Phyllis. The Oxford Companion to the Theatre, 3rd ed. London: Oxford University Press, 1967.

Hewitt, Barnard. Theatre U. S. A.: 1665 to 1957. New York: McGraw-Hill Book Company, Inc., 1959.

Howells, W. D. Literary Friends and Acquaintance: A Personal Retrospect of American Authorship, eds. David F. Hiatt and Edwin H. Cady. Bloomington: Indiana University Press, 1968.

Hughes, Glenn. A History of the American Theatre, 1700-1950. New York: Samuel French, 1951.

Knepler, Henry. The Gilded Stage: The Years of the Great International Actresses. New York: William Morrow & Company, Inc., 1968.

177

Martin, Jay. Harvests of Change: American Literature, 1865-1914. Englewood Cliffs, N. J.: Prentice-Hall, Inc., 1967.

May, Henry F. The End of American Innocence: A Study of the First Years of Our Own Time, 1912-1917. Chicago: Quadrangle Books, 1964.

Meserve, Walter J. An Outline History of American Drama. Totowa, N. J.: Littlefield, Adams & Co., 1965.

Milne, Gordon. George William Curtis and the Genteel Tradition. Bloomington: Indiana University Press, 1956.

Moody, Richard. America Takes the Stage: Romanticism in American Drama and Theatre, 1750-1900. Bloomington: Indiana University Press, 1955.

_____. Edwin Forrest: First Star of the American Stage. New York: Alfred A. Knopf, 1960.

Morison, Samuel Eliot. The Oxford History of the American People. New York: Oxford University Press, 1965.

Morris, Lloyd. Curtain Time: The Story of the American Theater. New York: Random House, 1953.

Moses, Montrose J. The American Dramatist. Boston: Little, Brown, and Company, 1911.

_____, and Brown, John Mason, eds. The American Theatre as Seen by Its Critics, 1752-1934. New York: W. W. Norton & Company, 1934.

Mott, Frank Luther. American Journalism: A History of Newspapers in the United States through 260 Years: 1690 to 1950. Revised ed. New York: The Macmillan Company, 1950.

_____. A History of American Magazines. 5 vols. Cambridge, Mass.: Harvard University Press, 1930-1968.

O'Dell, George C. D. Annals of the New York Stage. 15 vols. New York, 1927-1949.

Parry, Albert. Garrets and Pretenders: A History of Bohemianism in America. New York: Covici Friede Publishers, 1933.

Pattee, Fred Lewis. The Feminine Fifties. New York: D. Appleton-Century Company, 1940.

Quinn, Arthur Hobson. A History of the American Drama: From the Beginning to the Civil War. 2nd ed. New York: F. S. Crofts & Co., 1944.

_____. A History of the American Drama: From the Civil War to the Present Day. Rev. ed. New York: Appleton-Century-Crofts, 1936.

Shattuck, Charles. The Hamlet of Edwin Booth. Urbana, Ill.: University of Illinois Press, 1969.

_____. Shakespeare on the American Stage: From the Hallams to Edwin Booth. Washington, D. C.: Folger Shakespeare Library, 1976.

Towse, John Ranken. Sixty Years of the Theater. New York: Funk & Wagnalls Co., 1916.

Watermeier, Daniel J. ed. Between Actor and Critic: Selected Letters of Edwin Booth and William Winter. Princeton, N. J.: Princeton University Press, 1971.

Westfall, Alfred Van Rensselaer. American Shakespearean Criticism, 1607-1865. New York: The H. W. Wilson Company, 1939.

Wilson, Garff B. A History of American Acting. Bloomington: Indiana University Press, 1966.

_____. Three Hundred Years of American Drama and Theatre: From Ye Bear and Ye Cubb to Hair. Englewood Cliffs, N. J.: Prentice-Hall, Inc., 1973.

Winter, William. Old Friends: Being Literary Recollections of Other Days. New York: Moffat, Yard and Company, 1914.

Wolle, Francis. Fitz-James O'Brien: A Literary Bohemian of the Eighteen-Fifties. Boulder, Colo.: University of Colorado Studies, Series B. Studies in the Humanities, Vol. 2, No. 2, 1944.

UNPUBLISHED

Angotti, Vincent L. "American Dramatic Criticism, 1800-1830." Diss., Univ. of Kansas, 1967.

Ludwig, Richard M. "The Career of William Winter, American Drama Critic: 1836-1917." Diss., Harvard University, 1950.

Miller, Tice L., "The Theatre Criticism of John Ranken Towse." Diss., Univ. of Illinois, 1968.

Morris, William Carl. "The Theatrical Writings of Henry Austin Clapp." Diss., Univ. of Illinois, 1973.

Wright, Thomas Key. "The Theatre Criticism of Andrew Carpenter
    Wheeler." Diss., Univ. of Illinois, 1971.

Young, Robert. "Frosty, But Kindly." An unpublished typescript
    biography of William Winter.

INDEX